MW00776649

Twenty-First Century Populism

Twenty-First Century Populism

The Spectre of Western European Democracy

Edited by

Daniele Albertazzi
Lecturer in European Media
University of Birmingham, UK

and

Duncan McDonnell
Dottorando di Ricerca
University of Turin, Italy

Andrew Kiam
The University of
Oklahoma
14. Jänner 2010

palgrave
macmillan

First published in 2008 by
PALGRAVE MACMILLAN
Houndmills, Basingstoke, Hampshire RG21 6XS and
175 Fifth Avenue, New York, N.Y. 10010
Companies and representatives throughout the world.

PALGRAVE MACMILLAN is the global academic imprint of the Palgrave
Macmillan division of St. Martin's Press, LLC and of Palgrave Macmillan Ltd.
Macmillan® is a registered trademark in the United States, United Kingdom
and other countries. Palgrave is a registered trademark in the European
Union and other countries.

ISBN-13: 978–0–230–01349–0 hardback
ISBN-10: 0–230–01349–X hardback

This book is printed on paper suitable for recycling and made from fully
managed and sustained forest sources. Logging, pulping and manufacturing
processes are expected to conform to the environmental regulations of
the country of origin.

A catalogue record for this book is available from the British Library.

A catalog record for this book is available from the Library of Congress.

Transferred to Digital Printing 2008

For Liz, Mara, Elena, May, Alice and Dylan

Contents

List of Tables

Acknowledgements

The original concept and approach of this book were devised by Duncan McDonnell in the summer of 2005, following which he and Daniele Albertazzi worked together on elaborating and developing the project. We are indebted to all those who have helped us in the intervening eighteen months. First of all, we must thank our contributors for agreeing to participate and for respecting often tight deadlines when submitting and revising their chapters. Second, a special word of gratitude is due to over twenty anonymous reviewers who were very generous with their time and whose comments on the various chapters were extremely useful. Third, we would like to thank Alison Howson and Gemma d'Arcy-Hughes at Palgrave Macmillan for guiding us through the publication process and for always being available to respond to our questions and queries. We are also grateful to Phyllis McDonnell for her essential help with proofreading during the final editing phase. Finally, Daniele Albertazzi would like to thank the School of Humanities of the University of Birmingham for agreeing to anticipate his study-leave as the manuscript was being finalized and Dr Joanne Sayner for taking over responsibility for the Culture, Society and Communication programmes in his absence.

Notes on Contributors

Daniele Albertazzi is Lecturer in European Media at the University of Birmingham. His research focuses on political communication, as well as Italian and Swiss politics. Daniele is currently co-editing (with Charlotte Ross and Clodagh Brook) *Resisting the Tide: Cultures of Opposition During the Berlusconi Years* (Continuum, forthcoming) and (with Paul Cobley) *The Media – An Introduction*, Third ed. (Longman, forthcoming).

Frank Decker is Professor of Political Science at the University of Bonn. His research interests focus on problems of institutional reform in western democracies, party systems and right-wing populism. Recent publications include *Der neue Rechtspopulismus* (Opladen, 2004) and the *Handbuch der deutschen Parteien* (Handbook of German Parties) (Wiesbaden, 2007), co-edited with Viola Neu.

Stefano Fella lectures politics at London Metropolitan University and previously co-ordinated EU research projects related to governance, civil society, immigration and anti-racism at the University of Trento. His publications include *New Labour and the European Union, Political Strategy, Policy Transition and the Amsterdam Treaty Negotiation* (Ashgate, 2002) and (with Carlo Ruzza) *Reinventing the Italian Right: Territorial Politics, Populism and Post-Fascism* (Routledge, forthcoming).

Reinhard Heinisch is Professor of Political Science and Director of International Studies at the University of Pittsburgh/Johnstown. His current research focuses on European Union Institutions as well as on identity-based populism in Europe and Latin America. His publications include *Populism, Proporz and Pariah – Austria Turns Right* (2002) and 'Adapting the American Political Process' (2007) in Branche, J., Cohn, E.R. and Mullennix, J.W. (eds.), *Diversity across the Curriculum: a Guide for Faculty in Higher Education.* Anker Publishing Company.

Paul Lucardie is Research Fellow at the Documentation Centre on Dutch Political Parties at the University of Groningen. His research focuses mainly on Dutch political parties as well as new parties and extremist movements in Canada and Germany. Recent publications include 'Prophets, Purifiers and Prolocutors: towards a theory on the emergence of new parties' (2000), *Party Politics*, (6) 2 and 'Populismus im Polder: von der Bauernpartei bis zur Liste Pim Fortuyn', in Nikolaus Werz (ed.) (2003) *Populismus. Populisten in übersee und Europa* (Opladen: Leske and Budrich).

Alfio Mastropaolo is Professor of Political Science and Head of the Department of Political Studies at the University of Turin. His latest publications are *La mucca pazza della democrazia. Nuove destre, populismo, antipolitica* (2005,

Bollati Boringhieri) and (with Luca Verzichelli) *Il parlamento. Le assemblee legislative nelle democrazie contemporanee* (2006, Laterza).

Gianpietro Mazzoleni is Professor of Political Communication in the Faculty of Political Sciences at the University of Milan. His current research interests focus on mass communication, media policy and political communication. His most recent publications include *La Comunicazione Politica* (2004) and *The Politics of Representation: Election Campaigning and Proportional Representation* (2004) (with Juliet Roper and Christian Holtz-Bacha).

Duncan McDonnell is a researcher at the Department of Political Studies, University of Turin where he is conducting research on the relationships between directly elected local leaders and political parties. He is also currently involved in projects examining the behaviour of new parties in government and populist leadership in Western Europe. He has published recently on the *Lega Nord*, subnational Italian politics and is the co-editor (with Daniele Albertazzi) of the special edition of *Modern Italy,* 10 (1) (2005) on 'Italy under Berlusconi'.

Gianfranco Pasquino is Professor of Political Science at the University of Bologna and also teaches at the Bologna Center of the Johns Hopkins University. His current research interests are political parties and political communication. His most recent publications are *Parlamenti democratici* (2006), the edited volume *Strumenti della democrazia* (2007), and *Le istituzioni di Arlecchino* (2007) (co-authored with Riccardo Pelizzo).

Jens Rydgren is Associate Professor of Sociology at Stockholm University. His research interests encompass the fields of political sociology and ethnic relations. He is the author of *The Populist Challenge: Political Protest and Ethno-Nationalist Moblization in France* (2004) and *From Tax Populism to Ethnic Nationalism: Radical Right-Wing Populism in Sweden* (2006).

Marco Tarchi is Professor of Political Science and Political Theory at the Faculty of Political Sciences, University of Florence. His current research interests focus on populism, the radical Right, and the political culture of Italian parties. His most recent publications include *Fascismo. Teorie, interpretazioni e giudizi* (2003), *L'Italia populista* (2003) and *Contro l'americanismo* (2004).

1
Introduction: The Sceptre and the Spectre

Daniele Albertazzi and Duncan McDonnell

Ghiţa Ionescu and Ernest Gellner (1969: 1) began their classic edited collection on populism by paraphrasing Marx and Engel's famous opening line: 'A Spectre is haunting the world – populism'. However, it was not quite the entire world that was being haunted in the late 1960s. Looking through the case studies in Ionescu and Gellner's book, we find chapters on North America, Latin America, Russia, Eastern Europe and Africa, but nothing on that part of the world in which most of the contributors lived and worked: Western Europe. By contrast, the present volume focuses exclusively on that area. This reflects the fact that while the likes of Ross Perot in the United States, Preston Manning in Canada and Pauline Hanson in Australia have all attracted sporadic attention as new populist leaders, the main area of sustained populist growth and success over the last fifteen years in established democracies has been Western Europe.

The rise of populism in Western Europe is, in large part, a reaction to the failure of traditional parties to respond adequately in the eyes of the electorate to a series of phenomena such as economic and cultural globalization, the speed and direction of European integration, immigration, the decline of ideologies and class politics, exposure of elite corruption, etc. It is also the product of a much-cited, but rarely defined, 'political malaise', manifested in steadily falling turnouts across Western Europe, declining party memberships, and ever-greater numbers of citizens in surveys citing a lack of interest and distrust in politics and politicians. Fostered by the media, an antipolitical climate is said to have grown throughout Western European societies in which people perceive politics to be more convoluted, distant and irrelevant to people's lives and politicians to be more incapable, impotent, self-serving and similar to one another than in the past. This perception has in turn affected electoral behaviour as increasing numbers of de-aligned and disillusioned voters either simply do not bother participating or become available and open to new, more radical, alternatives (Mastropaolo, 2005). In particular, these alternatives have emerged in the shape of populists who offer straightforward, 'common sense' solutions to society's complex

1

problems and adopt forceful 'man in the street' communication styles which are able to galvanize at least some of those who have lost faith in traditional politics and its representatives. They offer a 'politics of redemption' in contrast to the Establishment's 'politics of pragmatism' (Canovan, 1999). They claim that radical changes for the better are possible and that they can make them happen. In short, they promise to make democracy work. Indeed, while people may have less regard for politics and professional politicians, they continue to believe that democracy is the best form of government (Stoker, 2006) and populists vowing to reclaim the sceptre for its rightful owner – the sovereign 'people' – have been able to present themselves not as threats to Western European democracy, but as its saviours.

As a consequence of a combination of more favourable opportunity structures and astute agency, since the early 1990s in Western Europe, populist movements have achieved their best ever results in countries like France, Switzerland and Denmark and have entered national government for the first time in states such as Italy, Austria and the Netherlands. Moreover, as traditional parties increasingly seek out and promote telegenic figures who can communicate simple, all-embracing, crowd-pleasing messages directly to the public through the media rather than through Parliament, we can see evidence of a broad populist *Zeitgeist* in Western Europe in which not only have dyed-in-the-wool populists been successful, but where many other mainstream political leaders, such as Tony Blair and William Hague in Britain, for example, have regularly dipped into populism's box of tricks (Mudde, 2004). Nonetheless, despite the existence of broadly similar political and socio-economic landscapes and conditions across Western Europe, populism has clearly been far more successful in some countries than it has in others. The aim of this book is to provide explanations for this by showing how, why and in what forms contemporary populism has flourished (or failed) in Western European democracies. Before we go any further, however, we should make it clear what we understand by the term 'populism'.

Populism

Much like Dylan Thomas's definition of an alcoholic as 'someone you don't like who drinks as much as you', the epithet 'populist' is often used in public debate to denigrate statements and measures by parties and politicians which commentators or other politicians oppose. When an adversary promises to crack down on crime or lower taxes and yet increase spending on public services, it is 'populist'. When one's own side does so, it is dealing with the country's problems. 'To each his own definition of populism, according to the academic axe he grinds' wrote Peter Wiles (1969: 166) in Ionescu and Gellner's volume and among scholars the term is often employed in loose, inconsistent and undefined ways to denote appeals to 'the people', 'demagogy' and 'catch-all' politics or as a receptacle for new types of parties whose classification we are unsure of. Due to these inflationary, vague and partisan uses of 'populism', there are scholars who have discarded the term altogether in favour of other labels (for example, Collovald, 2004). Another factor held to diminish the value of 'populism' is that, as Margaret Canovan (1981: 5) notes, unlike labels such as 'socialist' or 'conservative', the meanings of which have been 'chiefly dictated by their adherents', contemporary populists rarely call themselves 'populists' and usually reject the term when it is applied to them by others. However, if this were a good enough reason to stop researchers from using a category they found useful, then the same treatment should be extended to 'far', 'radical' and 'extreme' – all labels that are rarely, if ever, willingly embraced by parties of the Right or Left. We believe, therefore, that if carefully defined, the term 'populism' can be used profitably to help us understand and explain a wide array of political actors.

We define populism as:

> an ideology which pits a virtuous and homogeneous people against a set of elites and dangerous 'others' who are together depicted as depriving (or attempting to deprive) the sovereign people of their rights, values, prosperity, identity and voice.[1]

Like those of Ernesto Laclau (2005) and Pierre-André Taguieff (2002), this view deliberately avoids conceiving of populism in terms of specific social bases, economic programmes, issues and electorates. Put simply, we believe that populism should not just be seen *against* such backgrounds, but *beyond* them. Consequently, our aim in this volume is to look at populism *per se* in contemporary Western European democracies, rather than exclusively as an appendage of other ideologies to which it may attach itself, for to do so is, as Yves Mény and Yves Surel (2002: 17) rightly argue, to miss out on populism's 'crucial specificity'.

In recent years, the dominant tendency in scholarly literature has been to identify and analyse the rise of populism in Western Europe as a phenomenon exclusively of the Right (for example, Betz, 1994). While this reflects the kind of issues, such as immigration and taxation, which populists have sought to capitalize on, we believe that the equivalence of populism with the Right can be misleading. In fact, the claim that the people (however defined) are the only legitimate sovereign and have been deprived of power can sit quite easily with leftist ideologies. Moreover, unlike Fascism, for example, populist propaganda insists on the values of equality (among the people) rather than hierarchy and it is the community rather than the state which is said to be paramount.

If they are not necessarily of the Right, then populists obviously cannot always be classified as 'extreme' or 'radical' Right either. According to Piero Ignazi (1994), in order for a party to be catalogued among the 'extreme right', its electorate must position itself at the extreme Right of the political spectrum (relative to other parties) and this must be combined with an ideology based or reliant on fascist values and ideas and/or one which positions itself as alternative and in opposition to the democratic system. Following this logic, labelling parties such as the Lega Nord as 'extreme right' is, at best, highly problematic, as Ignazi himself acknowledges (Ignazi, 2003). Moreover, in general terms, we find that:

(a) voters who support populist parties do not always position themselves on the extreme Right (quite the opposite in fact);
(b) a discernable link between certain parties and Fascism, while sometimes present – as in the cases of the *Front National* in France and the Freedom Party in Austria – is by no means the rule (Biorcio, 2003a: 7);
(c) in some instances, populists fight not for the demise of an existing liberal-democratic system, but for its preservation (see the example of the *Schweizerische Volkspartei/Union Démocratique du Centre* in Switzerland).

We believe, therefore, that this insistence on making 'populist' and 'extreme right' synonymous or lumping all populists under the 'radical Right populist' banner for ease of comparison (for example, Norris, 2005) is detrimental to our understanding both of specific mislabelled parties (the *Lega Nord* and the *Lega dei Ticinesi* to name but two) and populism itself. Like Taguieff (2002: 84), we also view populism as being highly compatible 'not only with any political ideology (Left or Right, reactionary or progressive, reformist or revolutionary) and any economic programme (from state-planned to neo-liberal), but also with diverse social bases and diverse types of regime'.

That said, as the reader will see, the populists discussed in this book do not generally seek legitimacy through the adoption of internationally recognized 'sacred texts'. Rather, while they merge their populism with more 'established' ideologies, notably liberalism, nationalism, conservatism, federalism and socialism, this occurs as part of a broader mission to restore democracy and government to the people. Ultimately, whatever their positioning on the Left/Right spectrum, the key feature of populists is their claim to be the 'true democrats', fighting to reclaim the people's sovereignty from the professional political and administrative classes (be they in regional or national capitals, or at supranational level in Brussels), as well as other elite 'enemies' who, through the sleight of hand of representative and deliberately arcane and complex politics, have stolen and perverted democracy.

Like all ideologies, populism proposes an analysis designed to respond to a number of essential questions: 'what went wrong; who is to blame; and what is to be done to reverse the situation'? (Betz and Johnson, 2004: 323). Put simply, the answers are:

(a) the government and democracy, which should reflect the will of the people, have been occupied, distorted and exploited by corrupt elites;

(b) the elites and 'others' (i.e. not of 'the people') are to blame for the current undesirable situation in which the people find themselves;
(c) the people must be given back their voice and power through the populist leader and party. This view is based on a fundamental conception of the people as both homogeneous and virtuous.

The people constitute a community, a place where, as Zygmunt Bauman (2001) says, we feel 'warm' and 'safe' and where there is mutual trust. Moreover, the community is a place where 'it is crystal-clear who is "one of us" and who is not, there is no muddle and no cause for confusion' (Bauman, 2001: 12). By contrast, the enemies of the people – the elites and 'others' – are neither homogeneous nor virtuous. Rather, they are accused of conspiring together against the people, who are depicted as being under siege from above by the elites and from below by a range of dangerous others. The strength of the people, and the reason that they will triumph over their enemies – if they make their voice count through the populist leader/party – is precisely their homogeneity and virtue. This view of the people as an exclusive community is linked to what Paul Taggart (2000: 95) refers to as the populist 'heartland' in which 'a virtuous and unified population resides'. This is not a Utopia, but a prosperous and harmonious place which is held to have actually existed in the past, but has been lost in the present era due to the enemies of the people. By vowing to return sovereignty to the people, the populist leader/party also commits to restoring this heartland and, with it, the 'natural order'. In this way, populists play on the idea of communities which have lost what they once had and will lose everything if they do not find their voice now and make it heard – rather than remaining as the silent, oppressed majority.

Populists therefore invoke a sense of crisis and the idea that 'soon it will be too late'. However, while they preach impending doom, they also offer salvation. Populism and its leaders offer the people, as Francisco Panizza (2005: 23) says, the 'promise of emancipation after a journey of sacrifice'. This journey is usually led by a charismatic leader who is portrayed as knowing instinctively what the people want. As Canovan says, 'populist politics is not ordinary, routine politics. It has the revivalist flavour of a movement' and 'associated with this mood is the tendency for heightened emotions to be framed on a charismatic leader' (Canovan, 1999: 6). The cornerstone of the relationship between charismatic populist leaders and the people is that while they remain one of the people (whether in terms of their vocabulary, attire, declared pastimes etc.), their unique qualities and vision mean that only they can be the saviour of the people.

Of course, the greatest sacrifice is made by the populist leaders themselves who are forced to put to one side their normal (and preferred) profession and instead enter the dirty arcane world of politics in order to save democracy. Seeing the normal procedures of parliamentary politics as frustrating the popular will (Crick, 2005), the populist advocates a direct relationship between 'the people' and their government. This can be reflected in calls for more ways for the people to express their opinions and for directly-elected leaders and reductions in the powers of parliament and other bodies. Most of all, however, as Cas Mudde says, populist voters want leaders they can trust and who give them hope: 'they want politicians who know (rather than "listen to" the people), and who make their wishes come true' (Mudde, 2004: 558).

On the basis of the definition of populism provided above, we see four intertwined principles at the core of this ideology:

(1) *The people are one and are inherently 'good'.*

They are a homogeneous and virtuous community. Divisions within them are false, created and nurtured by the intellectual and political elites, and can be overcome as they are of less consequence than the people's common 'nature' and identity. Who constitutes the people (and, by extension, 'the others') can be decided on the basis of race, class, local/national identities etc. or a mixture of various categories; however, what is common to all populist discourses is this juxtaposition of the 'good', besieged people with the 'bad' elites and dangerous 'others'. While the latter category may include groups sharing regional/national identity with the people, the main 'others' in contemporary Western Europe tend to be immigrants, due to the threat they are said to pose to native cultures and the social and economic problems they allegedly cause.

(2) *The people are sovereign.*

Those who govern are morally obliged to do so in the interests of the people who must once more become 'masters in their own homes', in the widest sense of the term. If the people unite and make their voice heard through the populist leader and party, then they can make democracy work as it should: as a pure reflection of the will of the people. As Gerry Stoker puts it, populism 'posits that the people are one, and their voice, if properly understood, has a unified and unifying message' (Stoker, 2006: 139).

(3) *The people's culture and way of life are of paramount value.*

This is (alleged to be) rooted in history and tradition and is thus solid, 'right' and conducive to the public good – hence the need to 'love', 'save', 'protect', 'treasure' and 'rediscover' *our* culture. Populism's ideological flexibility also originates from this principle. When populism meets exclusionary forms of nationalism and regionalism, loving one's culture translates into rejecting 'others' – those who are not of the community.

(4) *The leader and party/movement are one with the people.*

Populism celebrates 'the ordinariness of its constituents and the extraordinariness of their leaders' (Taggart, 2000: 102). As Max Weber says, whether or not charismatic leaders really possess the qualities claimed is not so relevant, the important point is that their followers are convinced that they are their man (or, occasionally, woman) 'of destiny' (Weber, 1978). They 'incarnate' the people's culture, articulate the will of the people, 'say what people are thinking', can see through the machinations of the elites and have the vision to provide simple, understandable solutions to the problems portrayed by the elites as complex and intractable. However, while blessed with qualities which are far beyond the norm, these leaders have remained in all other ways 'one of the people' and, hence, one 'with the people'. Two consequences of this principle are that the charismatic bond between leader and follower is absolutely central to populist parties and that populist leaders, since they need to be seen to be still ordinary men and women untainted by their association with the murky world of politics, tend to break the conventional linguistic registers and codes employed by the political class, adopting instead a 'direct' and at times even offensive language and style of communication. Finally, loyalty to the leader equals loyalty to the people. As a result, those within the party who disagree with the leader tend to be swiftly branded as traitors and added to the list of the 'enemies of the people'.

The book

As mentioned earlier, while almost all Western European democracies have seen populist actors emerge, not all of these have enjoyed the same levels of success or have been able to insert themselves as fixed points in the political lives of their countries. This is despite the fact that many of the same economic and social conditions apply across Western European states, most of which are members of the European Union. One of the reasons we embarked on this project therefore was to explore the question of why populism is not present in every Western European country in the same way and with the same degree of success and/or durability. Hence, unlike the overwhelming majority of work on contemporary populism, this study focuses firmly on countries, rather than parties. We are not concerned with providing descriptions of specific parties *per se* so much as understanding what kind of populism (if any) is present in a country and investigate why that is, or is not, the case. In particular, we are interested in the structural conditions which facilitate, or hinder, the rise of populism and the successful (or flawed) agency of those populists who try to exploit these conditions.

Studies of populism have tended, understandably, to focus on those cases where populist movements have been significant political forces, rather than question those in which they have not. Given the logic of this book, however, alongside countries in which populists have enjoyed unprecedented levels of success and even participated in government such as Italy, Holland and Switzerland, we felt it necessary also to consider those like Britain, Sweden and Germany where the new wave of populist parties has apparently affected politics to a far lesser degree. After all, fears about the effects of globalization and feelings of disenchantment towards political institutions can be found in both Britain and Sweden and yet no populist party has managed to establish a significant and lasting parliamentary presence in these countries. To what extent is this due to an electoral system that heavily penalizes new political formations (structure) rather than simply the lack of a charismatic and capable populist leader (agency)? Or is it the case that populist key words and strategies have permeated the political discourse of the main parties to such an extent in Britain that the space for a more obviously populist challenger has been greatly reduced? Or is it that the political culture of the country makes it more impregnable to populism, as Gianfranco Pasquino argues in this volume? As for Sweden, the first question that springs to mind is: why has no populist party akin to those which have been so successful in Norway and Denmark taken root? Is this because the major Swedish parties have managed to isolate populist challengers with a *cordon sanitaire* to such a extent that anyone attempting to go down the populist route can instantly be successfully branded and dismissed as 'extremist'? Finally, and moving on to another country apparently immune from populism, can strong populist leaders emerge at all when the political environment is so 'historically encumbered', as Frank Decker notes in his chapter on Germany?

As these brief examples show, more work is needed on the structural conditions which provide fertile ground for populism, how they interact with or even negate each other in different national contexts and how they have (or have not) been exploited by political entrepreneurs. It is only by studying how political actors, armed with specific and varied resources, are at the same time both constrained and enabled by a variety of structural factors, in ways peculiar to specific national contexts, that we can explain why populism has spread swiftly and relatively easily in some places, while making apparently few inroads in others.

The aims of this book therefore are:

(1) To assess the degree of 'openness' of Western European democracies to the new populist *Zeitgeist*;
(2) To examine the general Western European and country-specific structural factors which have created increasingly favourable conditions for the growth of populism or which, by contrast, have impeded its emergence and success;
(3) To identify the role of agency in the fortunes of populist movements. How have they exploited favourable structural conditions? How have they turned unfavourable conditions to their advantage?
(4) To discuss the degree to which populist themes and methods have been adopted by mainstream political actors, whether as a reaction to populist challengers or not.

With these aims in mind, contributors in part I were invited to set the stage for the country case studies of part II, by dealing with a number of key general topics that we have already touched on here: the relationship between populism and democracy (Chapter 2); the extent to which the rise of populism has been facilitated by the metamorphosis of traditional parties (Chapter 3); and, finally, the role of increasingly tabloidized media in facilitating the emergence of populism (Chapter 4).

Contributors to part II were asked to look at the interplay between structure and agency in promoting (or hindering) the appearance and growth of populist movements in specific countries. Among the structural factors to be considered (where relevant) were political culture; issues of religion and identity; immigration; the economy; the electoral system; disenchantment with politics and institutions; the party system; the role of the media; European integration; corruption. To be clear, we have followed Herbert Kitschelt's definition of opportunity structures as 'specific configurations of resources, institutional arrangements and historical precedents for social mobilization, which facilitate the development of protest movements in some instances and constrain them in others' (Kitschelt, 1986: 58). While structures constrain however, they also make possible and enable by defining 'the potential range of options and strategies' (Hay, 1995: 200). 'As their name implies', adds Sidney Tarrow, they 'emphasize the exogenous conditions for party success and, in so doing, contrast to actor-centred theories of success' (1998: 18). However, as Giovanni Sartori (2005) has famously argued in relation to parties, we believe that actors both influence and are influenced by structures so it is therefore important to understand the relationship and interaction between structure and agency rather than arbitrarily favouring the explanatory value of one over the other.

The usefulness of this approach can be tested by considering two of the countries discussed in this volume where populists have performed particularly well over the last decade: Switzerland and Austria. In Switzerland, the 'agent' Christoph Blocher, a prominent leader of the SVP/UDC who has led the radicalization of the party, successfully reorganized its Zurich branch, arguing that more professionalism was needed (also, importantly, in communicating with prospective voters). A consequence of the electoral success of the SVP/UDC in Zurich was that the example soon spread to other cantonal branches of the party, which also set out to reorganize themselves along the same lines. Blocher's work, therefore, has now left a lasting legacy that goes beyond his electoral success at the local and national levels. In a political environment that is still characterized by some degree of voluntarism, the SVP/UDC is now a much more professional election-fighting machine at the national (and not only cantonal) level. This is an excellent example of how agency, in its turn, affects structure. The Freedom Party (FPÖ) in Austria provides us with an example of the opposite development, i.e. how structural developments may be essential in order to trigger changes at the level of agency. As Reinhard Heinisch notes in this volume, it was in fact the structural reforms of the FPÖ which, by exacerbating the party orientation towards its leader, effectively enabled Jörg Haider's leadership to 'flourish'. Once free to take control of the party and unencumbered by internal opposition, Haider led the FPÖ to considerable electoral success.

Discussion of structural factors in the country case studies has therefore served as a platform for the analysis of populist agency in this book, by which we mean how populists have taken advantage of the opportunity structures present along with factors such as leadership, party cohesion, use of media, relations with other parties, etc. Furthermore, we asked authors to reflect on, where relevant, the degree to which populism has influenced and permeated mainstream politics in specific countries and, in particular, the question: 'who borrows from populism and how?' Where applicable, contributors were also encouraged to examine what happens to more moderate and traditional forces when they participate in government with populists for, as Meny and Surel (2002: 19) note, populist parties 'can also contaminate the other parties by influencing the style of leadership, the type of political discourse and the relationship between leader and followers' and this remains, in our view, an under-explored area of study.

The Spectre of Western European Democracy?

While Canovan (1999: 3) argues that 'populism is a shadow cast by democracy itself', Benjamn Arditi objects that 'we might want to refer to populism as a spectre rather than a shadow of democracy' as the reference to a spectre 'addresses the undecidability that is inbuilt into populism, for it can be something that both accompanies democracy and haunts it' (Arditi, 2004: 141). Using the same metaphor, Sir Bernard Crick recently wrote that 'populism is indeed a spectre haunting democracy from which it is hard, perhaps impossible, to escape entirely in modern conditions of a consumption-driven society and a populist free press' (Crick, 2005: 631). Irrespective of their different interpretations, what is clear from the above is that populism and democracy are inextricably linked. Moreover, like Crick, we too believe that Western European democracy's spectre will be around for some time. Indeed, the evidence so far in the twenty-first century is that, while Taggart's (2004: 270) observation that 'populist politicians, movements or parties emerge and grow quickly and gain attention but find it difficult to sustain that momentum and therefore will usually fade fast' may apply to cases such as that of the *Lijst Pim Fortuyn* in Holland, it is also true that populists like the *Lega Nord* in Italy, the Freedom Party in Austria and the Front National in France have all been significant members of their national party systems for decades now.

Moreover, not only have populists in Western Europe been more successful in the twenty-first century than ever before, but they have also entered government. Yves Mény and Yves Surel asserted in their 2002 volume that 'populist parties are by nature neither durable nor sustainable parties of government. Their fate is to be integrated into the mainstream, to disappear, or to remain permanently in opposition' (Mény and Surel, 2002: 18). Yet, events in recent years suggest that this may no longer be the case. Against all expectations, in 2005 Silvio Berlusconi became the longest continuous serving Prime Minister in the history of the Italian Republic, supported by a centre-right coalition which also included the Lega Nord. Moreover, neither Berlusconi nor Umberto Bossi (leader of the Lega Nord) did anything to shed their populist identities and become more like mainstream, traditional politicians. Furthermore, although it has long been believed that charismatic leaders are almost impossible to replace (Weber, 2005), the 2006 general election result of the post-Haider Freedom Party in Austria suggests that, while charismatic populist leadership is difficult to pass on, in the right circumstances, it can be seized and the party can go on to further successes (see Reinhard Heinisch in this volume). Populism has thus proved far more dynamic, resilient, flexible and successful than many commentators imagined. As we will see in this volume, in twenty-first century Europe, in the name of the people, the spectre continues to pursue the sceptre.

Note

1. To be clear, we understand ideology as a system of beliefs, values and ideas characteristic of a particular group (adapted from Williams, 1977: 55). Used in this way, the term refers to belief systems whose function is to explain why things are as they are by providing an interpretative framework through which individuals and/or organizations make sense of their own experiences, relate to the external world and plan the future.

.

Part I

2
Populism and Democracy

Gianfranco Pasquino

'Government of the people, by the people, for the people'. This famous phrase, pronounced by President Abraham Lincoln in his 1863 Gettysburg Address, could easily be accepted by democrats and populists alike. After all, Lincoln's formula is grand, but vague, composed of important words to be filled with equally important, but unspecified, contents. Moreover, as most authors (e.g. Canovan, 1981 and 1999; Mény and Surel, 2000 and 2002; Mudde, 2004) are fond of saying, there is an intimate connection between democracy and populism. However, there is also an inherent tension between them, which has rarely been fully analysed. The strong connection between democracy and populism is easily established since (a) both have firm and solid roots in the people and (b) both indicate the paramount importance of the people. While, of course, the definition of democracy can and must be made richer than a simple etymological reference to the 'power of the people', or to the even less clear 'sovereignty of the people', analysts and citizens alike know that where the people have no power whatsoever, there is no democracy. Lincoln's famous phrase can thus be interpreted in a populist way, i.e. by insisting that any increase, no matter how small, in the power of the people constitutes an increase in the quality of democracy. This comes close to being true if the power of the people is defined with reference to the most important constitutive elements of a democratic situation: the degree of information and participation of the citizens/voters, the intensity and significance of political competition, the likelihood of alternation in office and, finally, the transparency and flexibility of the mechanisms and structures of accountability characterizing the political sphere. However, not only do populists generally reject all structures of political intermediation between the people and the leader, but it is their very definition of the people that creates analytical and political problems.

As has been frequently noted, there are several plausible definitions of 'the people'. The first, contained in many constitutions, starting with the preamble to the US Constitution ('We the people of the United States...'), indicates that the people are the citizens, endowed with rights and duties, but above all with the power of sovereignty that – and this is an extremely significant aspect – *must* be exercised within the limits and forms codified in the constitution itself. This definition, I surmise, is the only one compatible with democracy. Hence, the 'people' are not, as often conceived by populists, an undifferentiated mass of individuals (see the introduction to this volume). Rather, they are citizens, workers, associations, parties, etc. The second definition of people concerns the nation. People are not only citizens who have the same rights and duties. They are, above all, those who share the same blood and inhabit the same territory (*Blut und Boden*). They belong to the same tradition and share the same history. The people are thus more than *demos*: they are *ethnos*. This definition is exclusionary and, when taken to extremes by populists, becomes incompatible with a democratic perspective.

Finally, there is a third definition of people which is based on a class view of society. Only the less affluent sectors of a society are considered to constitute the people: those left behind, who labour and strive to survive, those who are exploited by the elites, the Establishment, and even by organizations such as the parties and 'official' trade unions. It is in this definition that right-wing populists (e.g. those mobilizing the *descamisados* of Argentina) meet their left-wing counterparts (e.g. the French revolutionists who mobilized the *sans culottes*). These three definitions share a perspective and have something in common. For this very reason, the relationship between the people and populism has always been, and continues to be, highly ambiguous. It also, as a result, makes the relationship between populism and democracy similarly ambiguous, complex and, potentially, detrimental to democracy.

Among the many definitions that have been offered of populism (for an extensive list see Taguieff, 2002. Previous efforts can be found in Ionescu and Gellner, 1969; Canovan, 1981; Taggart, 2000), it would be difficult to find one which does not stress the power, role, importance and absolute decisiveness of the people. Thus, the real issue becomes the identification and specification of the ways and means by which the people can and do succeed in exercising their power. Though the dominant view (as synthesized by Tarchi, 2003) is that the populists are not necessarily anti-democratic, I believe that the opposite is in fact the case: populist perspectives are almost unavoidably incompatible with democracy, or with liberal democracy.

Leaving aside the fact that, in practice, populism has generally flourished in the absence of democracy or that it has challenged existing, though weak, democratic regimes, there are also populists who challenge not just 'real' democratic regimes, but the very essence of democracy. They entertain anti-democratic ideas such as the claim that elections may not just be manipulated, but useless. Or, even worse: elections may never reveal the 'true' will of the people. Such populists would like to bring an end to existing democracy, depicted as deteriorated and corrupted, with the aim, of course, of constructing a superior (i.e. 'populist') democracy. Nonetheless, only an empirical in-depth investigation of the reality and ideology of a series of comparable populist movements can offer a satisfactory answer to the questions of whether the populists are really willing to accept democracy, especially when they acquire political power, and whether, once in power, they have effectively done so. Most Latin American experiences, for example, would suggest that we reject the view that (a) populists do not challenge whatever democratic framework they find and (b) they are not willing to empty and destroy that democratic framework.

This chapter will firstly offer two working definitions of democracy and populism. Then, it will identify the situations in which the populist challenge to liberal democracies arises. Finally, it will focus on the consequences of the emergence and existence of populist challenges and movements for contemporary democracies. Individual populist leaders will not be dealt with specifically, primarily because our focus is on structural factors, but also because I consider populist leaders to be important almost solely if and when those structural factors already exist. Although those leaders may be instrumental in the appearance and functioning of a populist movement, they themselves are the products of structural factors.

Definitions and clarifications

According to many authors, democracy is a very elusive concept. Indeed, some years ago, David Collier and Steven Levitsky attempted to identify all the adjectives used to accompany and to specify the term 'democracy', although many specifications manipulate the concept and, more or less deliberately, end up distorting it (Collier and Levitsky, 1997). Incidentally, it is interesting to note that 'populist democracy' does not appear in Collier and Levitsky's list. While the concept of democracy may well stand on its own, given its long and revered history, the adjective most frequently used to accompany democracy is, without doubt, 'liberal' (subordinately: 'constitutional'). Above all for its elegance and parsimony, here we will use Joseph Schumpeter's definition of democracy, complemented by Giovanni Sartori's (1987) fundamental additions. Therefore, a regime will be considered democratic when there are periodical electoral competitions among teams of political elites and when these competitions are decided by the voters. As Schumpeter (1962: 269) puts it: 'The democratic method is that institutional arrangement for arriving at political decisions in which individuals acquire the power to decide by means of a competitive struggle for the people's vote'.

Taking into account Carl Friedrich's rule of anticipated reactions, Sartori added that

> elected officials seeking re-election (in a competitive setting) are conditioned, in their deciding, by the anticipation (expectation) of how

electorates will react to what they decide. The rule of *anticipated reactions* [my emphasis] thus provides the linkage between input and output, between the procedure (as stated by Schumpeter) and its consequences. (Sartori, 1987: 152)

It must be added that, in these democratic competitions, it is in the interest of leaders, both in government and in opposition, to acquire and distribute all the necessary information for voters to make up their minds. Incidentally, Sartori's important consideration opens up the territory of 'accountability' (Przeworski *et al.*, 1999), a relationship between voters and office holders that must be largely grounded in the possibility of voters having enough reliable information. Needless to say, accountability is a quality not especially looked after nor provided for in the relationship that populist leaders establish with their followers since those leaders lack or, rather, reject any institutionalization of the mechanisms and procedures connecting them with the people.

Schumpeter's definition above was also accepted by William H. Riker when working within the very different theoretical framework of social choice. Indeed, Riker was even less demanding than Sartori. His definition of democracy relies fully on an admittedly limited conception of liberalism which he places in sharp contrast, as we will see, with populism. Riker (1982: 248) writes that: 'Liberalism ... simply requires regular elections that sometimes lead to the rejection of rulers'. However, he appropriately adds that the preservation of democracy is grounded on the existence of constitutional limitations. Indeed, we should not forget that, in the past twenty years or so, a practical and significant distinction has emerged between electoral democracies and liberal democracies. It is this combination of 'regular elections plus constitutional limitations' that produces the kind of democracy James Madison had in mind and that has been embedded into the US Constitution (Dahl, 1956). Thus, while there may be many 'electoral' democracies in the world today, there are far fewer 'liberal democracies' (Diamond and Plattner, 2001). While liberal democracies offer an, admittedly not insurmountable, obstacle to the insurgence of populism, electoral democracies often become easy prey for populist challengers because they lack a solid and legitimate network of political and institutional mechanisms and structures. Also, newly created electoral democracies may lack structured parties and a stable party system. Perhaps, as argued by Alfio Mastropaolo in his chapter in this book, the decline of parties and the breakdown of party systems (e.g. the Italian one) are responsible for opening enough political space for populist phenomena. Successful contemporary democracies combine a precise definition of the rights of citizens, including the right of association, which is usually translated into the formation of political parties able and willing to compete according to precise political and electoral rules, alongside representative and governmental institutions. It is important to underline that, in liberal democracies, even the will of the people is subject to constitutional limitations.

Our discussion of democracy could certainly be expanded and made more robust by taking into account all the objections raised, especially by the 'participationists', to the modified Schumpeterian definition cited above, but it is now time to turn to populism. Here too, we encounter a significant amount of participationists, that is scholars who define a regime as democratic only when, and if, all citizens actively participate in the decision-making processes. We also encounter various definitional problems and so, for the sake of parsimony and elegance, here we will adopt the definition by Riker (1982: 238) which affirms: 'The essence of populism is this pair of propositions: 1. What the people, as a corporate entity, want ought to be social policy. 2. The people are free when their wishes are law'. Most importantly, Riker hastens to add that 'populist institutions depend on the elimination of constitutional restraints' and that 'the populist interpretation of voting justifies this elimination' (ibid.: 249). It is essential to note that Riker's definition of populism is focused on processes and outcomes, rather than on leaders. Populism is an aspect of the political culture or is, if you like, a specific type of political culture connected with the way a political system ought to work.

As is well known, Madison's major preoccupation was to avoid the tyranny of the majority (this is also Robert Dahl's famous 1956 interpretation). The solution was found not only in a system, as defined by Richard E. Neustadt (1991), of 'separate institutions sharing powers', but also in the differential allocation of political powers to the federal and State governments, that is, in the very structure of federalism. To a large extent, although not without conflicts (a civil war, or war among the States, between 1861 and 1865) and adjustments (from Woodrow Wilson's 'congressional government' to Arthur Schlesinger's 'imperial presidency'), this solution, encompassing a combination of a horizontal *division* of powers and a vertical *limitation* of powers, has proved successful. However, threads, elements and even experiments of populism, both past and present and at local and national levels, have not been lacking in the US. Therefore, the search for the conditions that give rise to the emergence of populism must continue. Some of these can be found in what one could call the American ideology or creed, as exemplified most prominently in Lincoln's Gettysburg Address. However, much depends on the ways in which government *of* the people is organized (again: participatory democracy, perhaps?); the ways by which government *by* the people is exercised (through representational institutions or through popular initiatives and referendums?); and the ways in which government *for* the people is realized/achieved (by the creation of a generous welfare State?). The debate regarding which institutional arrangements (presidential vs. parliamentary; centralized vs. federal States) are more conducive or opposed to the rise of populism must continue, but it seems appropriate to conclude this preliminary discussion of the differences between liberal and populist democracy with a long quote from an unjustifiably neglected scholar, William Kornhauser (1959: 131):

> Populist democracy involves *direct action* of large numbers of people, which often results in the circumvention of institutional channels and *ad hoc* invasion of individual privacy. Liberal democracy involves political action mediated by institutional rules, and therefore limitations on the use of power by majorities as well as minorities. The difference between liberal democracy and populist democracy, then, does not concern *who* shall have access to power (in both cases, there is representative rule); rather, it concerns how power shall be sought, the mode of access. In liberal democracy, the mode of access tends to be controlled by institutional procedures and intermediate associations, whereas in populist democracy the mode of access tends to be more direct and unrestrained.

The next section will deal with the 'ideological' conditions which indicate the possibility and acceptability of one or the other mode of access to political power, and the social conditions that shape an environment conducive to populism.

Ideological conditions

To suggest that there exists a precise, widely shared, cogent populist ideology would be an exaggeration. In any case, it seems advisable to use the term in the plural: 'ideologies'. Since the discrepancies among the different ideologies are many and wide and the 'structure' of the various ideologies not especially cogent, but shaky and fluid, it is preferable in the case of populism to speak of 'mentalities' (states of mind) instead of ideologies, much the same way as Juan Linz (2000: Ch. 4) suggested when defining authoritarian regimes. Our task, therefore, is to identify more precisely the components of these mentalities in order to see which of them, if any, are common to all populist experiences. One component is always present: the idea that the people are always far better than their rulers and that rulers often betray the interests and preferences of the people. As argued in the introduction to this volume, a clear antagonistic line is drawn between, on the one hand, the elites/ Establishment and, on the other, the (common) people. No matter who succeeds in 'awakening' and mobilizing the people and, *pour cause*, becomes the populist leader, the enemies are those in power, and, in some cases, other selected groups: financial tycoons, intellectuals, journalists – in a sense all those who are definitely not part of the common people, who simply do not belong to them. On the contrary, almost by definition, populist leaders embrace the ideas and mentalities of the people and identify with them. Populist leaders do not represent the people, rather they consider themselves – and succeed in being considered – an integral part of the people. They are of the people. For their part, the people acclaim the populist leader as one of them, but, at the same time, consider him/her better than them and recognize that s/he is endowed with the (often allegedly charismatic) qualities to lead them.

Which elements of the political culture are most conducive to the shaping of populist mentalities? There are two main elements which create the opportunity/space for the appearance of populist mentalities. The first one is a relatively common theme based on the rejection of politics, and, as a logical consequence, of politicians. There is no contradiction, however, between the rejection of politics and the political activism of populist politicians. Some political activities are always justified by populist leaders (and their followers) as temporarily indispensable in order to put an end to politics. This rejection of politics is more than a simple rejection just of 'representative politics', as Paul Taggart (2002) argues. Populist leaders promise that they will get rid of traditional politics as soon as possible, although they do not explain which kind of new politics they will construct, other than to say that the leader will be fully accessible to the people. The existence of an anti-political mentality among the people constitutes an excellent breeding ground for populist inclinations and attitudes. It is the preliminary condition for the unconditional delegation of authority to the populist leader. The most important difference within societies concerns the role and prestige of politics, as defined and assessed by the respective political cultures. Societies where the dominant political culture attaches no prestige to politics, but where, nonetheless, politics plays an important role in the allocation of resources, will in all likelihood develop strong and widespread anti-political sentiments (Crosti, 2004).

The second, more recent, element which is obviously closely linked to anti-political mentality is anti-party sentiment. In the populist mentality, there is no appreciation at all for the idea that we need groups of individuals who can acquire political and institutional knowledge and apply it to the running of public affairs. Party politicians are always considered an obstacle to the expression of the 'true' will of the people. Professional politicians are never seen as part of the solution. On the contrary, they are exclusively part of the problem because it is their competition as much as their collusion that is responsible for the appearance, on the one hand, of tensions, conflicts and divisions among the people, and, on the other, of stalemate, waste and corruption in the decision-making process. Only after the suppression of the existing politics – which is also held responsible for allowing particular social groups, tycoons and monopolists to become unjustifiably prosperous – will the people have a common purpose and be able to live in harmony. Left to itself, society would be free from conflicts, for it is politics which makes societies conflict-ridden. Though vague and ill-defined, the populist utopia depicts an undifferentiated society of individuals who work and produce and in which everyone knows his/her place. In this ideal world, only the populist leader knows more than anybody else and, hence, merits a higher status.

Let us return now to the argument that populists are not just against politics as such, but against 'representative politics' (Taggart, 2002: 71–79). In their desire to abolish all intermediate actors, associations and institutions, there is no doubt that representative politics is the main target for populists. However, if the goal is a closer and exclusionary connection between the people and the leader, then politics – with its conflicts, collaborations and compromises – will have to be abolished, leaving space only for the direct relationship between the people and the leader who, unshackled, will personally enjoy all decision-making (and representative) powers.

Classical democratic political culture constitutes no automatic barrier against populism. If democratic political culture emphasizes the decisive importance of the support given by popular majorities (majority rule) to all legitimate governments, then it easily becomes vulnerable to populist criticisms and propaganda. For example, it has often been said that there exists a 'silent majority', whose views are not taken into account by the 'official' parliamentary majority. This silent majority represents a potential recruitment and mobilization pool for populists. Can one find a political culture capable of offering a powerful barrier against populist challenges grounded both in a criticism of all elites and in a rejection of their role, especially their political role? To some extent, it is possible to argue that a political culture based on and characterized by deference (Kavanagh, 1980) does represent a major obstacle to the penetration of populist ideas. Deference means the recognition that all those who have achieved positions of leadership – political or any other kind – deserve respect. From this perspective, elites perform activities and duties otherwise not easily attributed or transferred to other, less trained, individuals. Traditionally, the defining traits of this culture of deference have been found in a number of Anglo-Saxon societies, in particular Britain. The people, as citizens, can exercise political power according to the traditions, conventions and rules of the game. Consequently, there are spheres of activity whose boundaries are rarely trespassed; there are areas of specialization and there are limits to the power of all groups. The recognition that (a) politics is a dignified activity requiring knowledge and hard work and (b) that parties represent aggregations of popular opinions and preferences are two decisive components of the liberal ideology of what legitimately constitutes competitive democratic politics.

There seems to be less room for populism in societies where deference and liberalism have impregnated and shaped the sphere of politics. Nonetheless, not even Anglo-Saxon democracies outside the UK (by which I refer to Australia, Canada and New Zealand, in addition to the USA) have totally escaped significant populist challenges. However, none of these challenges has been translated into outright victory at national level. The case of the

USA requires closer attention not only because, in the past, there was a major and dramatic insurgence of (agrarian) populism, but also because other less important, though still significant, instances of populism such as those embodied by Governor and Senator Huey Long, Senator Joseph McCarthy, Governor George Wallace and presidential candidate Ross Perot, have punctuated various historical periods and particular geographical areas (Ware, 2002). Indeed, the US case seems to suggest that the connection between populism and democracy remains real, strong and inevitable and that the line separating them is, and continues to be, thin. This line is bound to be especially thin in mass democracies, which should be carefully and clearly distinguished from mass societies.

A number of American scholars have long been critical of the trends within their society which give rise to a depoliticized mass society (Riesman, 1989), and rightly so, because all mass democracies are dangerously close to mass societies. Moreover, liberal mass democracies are bound to open up spaces of alienation for isolated individuals whose only escape will often be found in what they consider an emotional and direct relationship with a political leader. In order to clarify this argument, however, we must look at the social conditions underpinning the opportunities both for the insurgence of populism and for the survival of liberal democracy.

Social conditions

There are two different, although closely related, ways to define the social conditions most conducive to the likely rise of populism. The first focuses on individuals and their psycho-sociological characteristics. The second concerns the overall circumstances of a specific society. The individuals most likely to be attracted by a populist leader or to be involved in a populist insurgence share many common features. They are people who become open to a populist experience because they suffer from political isolation and alienation and are in serious need of emotional attachments, of both the vertical and horizontal type. Social isolation means that they are not connected with other individuals except through their own personal and material living and working conditions. Second, and most important, they are usually not members of any kind of associations/organizations, be they cultural, religious, or professional. And, if they are, they tend to be passive members. This may be due to the fact that these individuals have moved from an area in which traditional ties were sufficient to bind them to other members of that community into one in which new ties are difficult to create. Alternatively, they may have dropped out of a situation in which they had ties (e.g. through unemployment) and thus find themselves, willingly or unwillingly, unable to retain any social tie. At this point, these individuals not only find themselves socially dislocated, but, more specifically, have become 'available'. This is the condition, for example, experienced by many unemployed industrial workers who were attracted by the Nazis. Third, they may be too much pre-occupied with making a living to join any organization, and the few existing organizations might either seem unappealing and/or reluctant to take in new members. In this scenario, individuals therefore find themselves socially iso-lated and more exposed to populist leaders offering an experience of (albeit subordinate) involvement and participation.

In the absence of horizontal ties among their peers, individuals are left to rely on vertical ties with a leader and long for a sense of, otherwise impos-sible, belonging to a community. The overall situation described here is strongly influenced by the theory of mass society formulated by William Kornhauser. More precisely, he suggests that those in a mass society 'lack attachments to independent groups' (Kornhauser, 1959: 40) and that 'the population is available in that its members lack all those independent social formations that could serve as a basis of resistance to the elite' (ibid.: 41). Most importantly, 'populism is cause as well as effect in the operation of mass society' (ibid.: 103). As a note of caution, given that too few studies exist on the psycho-sociological conditions of those individuals involved in popu-list mobilizations, we could add that, perhaps, it is the very success of popu-list propaganda that breaks old associational ties and opens the way for the direct relationship between newly detached individuals and the populist leader. In the past, the radio was the very important instrument through which political propaganda and populist messages could be broadcast. Today, as indicated by Mazzoleni in his contribution to this book, television has become paramount in providing resources to populist politicians and in pos-sibly broadening the audience exposed to their messages and vulnerable.

As regards the conditions making a society especially exposed to popu-lism, that is, more susceptible to populist incursions, the most important one is certainly an overall sense of collective malaise. In some extreme cases, this malaise may turn into a widely shared situation of anxiety, which helps provide an environment in which any kind of populist/authoritarian experi-ment has the opportunity to appear and flourish. The level of authoritarian-ism will depend on the degree of existing social and political differentiation, as well as on the quality of the available technology. In static societies, such as nineteenth-century Russia, for example, populism is either an intellec-tual fantasy or a colossal failure. Only a society in transition may harbour a more or less modest dose of viable populism. At any point in time in a trans-itional society, masses of dislocated individuals represent an obvious target group for the populist solutions of ambitious political leaders. Today, we know that, in transitional societies, it is the theocracies in particular that stand to offer a plausible alternative to populism. And theocracies will try either to destroy most existing associations or to infiltrate them.

In the past, the most important transitions (Lerner, 1958; Deutsch, 1961) were those taking place from rural to urban areas, from agricultural to non-agricultural occupations, from traditional ties to some modern form of solitude, from a rather sheltered, perhaps oppressive, community life to the many challenging and risky opportunities of urban societies. In Latin America, transitions of this kind produced large masses of available individuals who contributed to the birth of – or provided support for – a variety of populist experiments. The best known and most studied of these experiments has been Peronism (1943–1955). It was the Italian sociologist Gino Germani (1975) who first highlighted the explosive combination of the mobilization of urban masses of *descamisados*, who had no previous organizational ties with the state of overall collective malaise in a society, Argentina, which was caught in a period of unsatisfactory transformation and painful difficulties. Widespread malaise bordering on collective anxiety is often the consequence of fears concerning unemployment, unforeseen political changes, waves of immigration and identity challenges. Of course, these fears not only relate to the miserable situation of the present, but are also projected into the foreseeable future.

The populist leader promises solutions, but, above all, clearly identifies the enemies (the scapegoats), attributes responsibilities and offers reassurance. However, the promised land is rarely the institutionalization of the populist movement and the satisfaction of all popular demands. In fact, the populist leader needs to prolong the transitional situation and, consequently, requires yet more enemies. As long as the transition continues, he/she will be needed. Hence, populist leaders do not attempt to institutionalize their power, draft new rules, abide by legal procedures, or construct permanent institutions. They rely instead on the periodical, though not necessarily too frequent, mobilization of their supporters. An alternative view, suggested to me by Marco Tarchi, is that populism bridges the gap between a stable society dominated by its elites and a modern society following a phase of modernization and that the populist leader plays the role of socio-political linchpin in this complex and difficult operation. However, too many Latin American cases run contrary to Tarchi's claim for it to be plausible.

Although Latin America has proved to be a fertile ground for all kinds of populist experiences (Pasquino, 1979), it is Peronism – with and without Peron – which remains the paramount example of 'successful' populism. Even when *el hombre* was no longer in the country or in power, for many years *los humildes* could still be mobilized in his name. Peronism offers another controversial lesson. Its overall trajectory suggests that populism is inimical, if not to the survival, then certainly to the full institutionalization and decent functioning of a democratic regime. It is difficult to argue that Peronism has been positively responsible for bridging socio-economic gaps in Argentinian society. On the contrary, the permanent streak of Peronist populism constitutes the most resilient factor rendering Argentinian democracy particularly difficult to construct and stabilize.

Those who are interested in the social conditions which create opportunities for the rise of populism can find a variety of puzzling cases in Latin

America, the most recent and significant of which is Venezuela (Tagle Salas, 2004). The ascent to power of the populist leader Hugo Chávez constitutes, in fact, the product of a series of not entirely unpredictable developments. The two major parties, COPEI and *Acción Democratica*, though competing at the polls and even alternating in office, were never fully committed to sustained attempts at mobilizing Venezuelan society and were unable to stimulate meaningful participation. Prescient scholars such as David Eugene Blank detected the problem a long time ago. In 1973, Blank asserted that 'the uncertain future of Venezuelan democracy is due not only to the continuing strength of traditional, authoritarian values, but also to the failure of populist political parties to penetrate the various mass subcultures sufficiently to instil in them a commitment to democratic values' (Blank, 1973: 282). Instead of acting as democratic educators, Venezuelan parties and their leaders relied on the prosperity created by oil and on the relative satisfaction of most Venezuelan voters who, we now know, were the source of specific, but not systemic, support. When oil prosperity, which had not been put to good use to encourage the diversification of economic activities, came to an end, the parties proved unable to formulate solutions for the incoming crisis and revealed themselves to be little more than empty shells. A situation of widespread malaise gripped the country and the situation thus became ripe for the emergence of an anti-party, anti-establishment populist leader. Venezuelan democracy simply collapsed. Not surprisingly, the populist leader Hugo Chávez, although enjoying significant popular support, has so far been both unable and unwilling to institutionalize his rule.

Political conditions

Ideological and social factors may be defined as conditions that facilitate the emergence of populism. However, the most significant conditions for the success of populism are political. Mény and Surel (2000: Ch. 2) indicate three political conditions as being decisive for the emergence of contemporary populism:

(1) the crisis of the structures of political intermediation;
(2) the personalization of political power;
(3) the increasing role of the media in political life.

What is important is not so much that these conditions appear to be, to a large extent, the irreversible product of contemporary societies. Rather, the problematic aspect requiring explanation is the fact that they work in different ways in different countries. It is the combination in diverse quantities of these political conditions with varying social conditions that opens the space for populism. While political parties as structures of political intermediation have declined in strength in almost all political systems, populism has not made its appearance in all political systems. Likewise, politics has become personalized in all contemporary democracies, but populist leaders have not emerged in all contemporary democracies. In order to assess the varying importance of the three above-mentioned political conditions, we need to analyse whole social systems and elaborate some indicators as to:

(1) how serious the crisis of the structures of political intermediation actually is;
(2) how significant is the personalization of politics;
(3) how pervasive is the role of the media (which media? owned by whom?) in political life.

Moreover, we need to provide a global view of these three processes and their interrelations.

Though one should never explain a complex phenomenon by relying on a single variable, this kind of temptation is very difficult to resist. Here, we will yield to it, but with a note of caution. Populism is a phenomenon bound to appear in almost all democracies. However, in order for populism to emerge and have a significant impact on the political system and society, there is one element above all others which must exist, i.e. the presence of a leader willing and able to exploit existing social conditions of *anxiety* and *availability*. If those social conditions do not exist, no populist force can emerge. On the other hand, the social conditions may exist, but in the absence of a political leader capable of exploiting them, no populist experiment will ensue. Only rarely will a political leader succeed in both tasks: first, creating and, second, exploiting the social conditions that will allow him/her to launch a populist challenge at an existing, though weakened, democratic regime. There are good reasons to believe that most political systems undergoing an institutional transition will be exposed to populist challenges. Leaving the subject aside here, although Mastropaolo deals with it in his chapter, this has certainly been the case of Italy since 1994. Indeed, the existence of a never-ending institutional transition goes a long way towards explaining the successful populism of Silvio Berlusconi. It may also be true that Berlusconi has taken advantage of his ownership of half the Italian television system and has fully exploited the opportunities deriving from his mastery of this medium. To be sure, television has most certainly contributed, as Giampietro Mazzoleni convincingly argues in this book, to the appearance of a kind of media populism in many European as well non-European democracies. However, what remains to be explained is the dominance exercised by Berlusconi over Italian politics for more than ten years. Since no other media populist-politician has been so successful, the explanation lies, as I suggested, in the institutional and political conditions of Italian democracy and in the inability to restructure a viable party system.

Conclusion

The possibility of populism is inherent, though not to the same degree, in practically all contemporary mass democracies. The very 'ideology' of democracy, its normative content that contemplates 'the power of the people' and suggests that political power must be exercised 'for the people' may lead, under some circumstances and through a distorted manipulated implementation, to populist recipes, claims, outcomes. More often, the concrete appearance of populist leaders, movements and demands must be considered an indication that a specific democratic regime is not working properly and so creates enough discontent to open up the space for a populist entrepreneur. The variety of political expressions that deserve to be labelled populist are, at the same time, the consequence of the poor functioning of a democratic regime and the harbinger of additional problems and challenges to come. After all, populism has never strengthened a democracy. On the contrary – leaving aside the issue of the quality of democracy – populism makes the democratic framework inexorably unstable. It has eroded existing democracies from within and from without. Indeed, in some cases, as many Latin American political systems (especially Argentina) have clearly shown, this erosion will not be easily mended for several political generations.

There are several reasons why populism exerts a negative impact on the democratic framework. The followers of populist leaders put an exaggerated amount of faith in them and will often continue to believe that any and all improvements of their plight may only come from the action of a leader endowed with extraordinary qualities. Second, the cohesion of the populist movement is essentially granted, and consolidated, by the identification, opposition and, in most cases, hostility directed against particular enemies: the Establishment, the politicians, the financiers of globalization, the technocrats, the immigrants, i.e. 'those who are not like us'. This overwhelming attitude of hostility is inimical to the acquisition of the fundamental democratic quality that allows the recognition of adversaries or competitors, but not of mortal enemies. Hostility prevents collaboration and accommodation and maintains a situation of conflict which is not conducive to an accepted democratic outcome. Third, given that it is based on a direct and immediate relationship between followers and leaders, populism rejects all forms of political and institutional intermediation as instruments which will inevitably distort and betray the true will of the people. Hence, not only does populism prevent the consolidation of democratic regimes, it also challenges existing democratic regimes, their parties and their institutions by offering the highly volatile direct relationship of 'followers-leader' as an alternative. Finally, weighed down by excessive expectations, populism cannot deliver. Either it becomes more radical, with some of its followers resorting to violence and terrorist activities, or, when burdened with frustrations, its followers end up in a state of social and political alienation. In both cases, society and the political system will find themselves in a worse situation than the one prevailing at the birth of populism. The absorption of all kinds of populism in a satisfactory democratic framework requires time, patience, changes in political culture and a lot of institutional wisdom. To my knowledge, there exists no case of successful institutionalization of a populist movement/experiment.

3
Politics against Democracy: Party Withdrawal and Populist Breakthrough

Alfio Mastropaolo

Two questions

Strange things have been happening in Western Europe. In fact, they have been happening to such an extent that to term them 'strange' is perhaps inaccurate. They have even been happening in the continent's oldest democracy where, as the local elections of May 2006 reminded us, there exists a party, the British National Party (BNP), which promotes racial hatred, demands draconian punishments for crime and loudly condemns the misdeeds of the political class. Of course, as Stefano Fella's chapter in this volume explains, the British electoral system makes it extremely difficult for the BNP to win seats in parliament. However, this does not mean that sooner or later a more conventional party in search of extra votes is not going to borrow from the rhetoric and themes which have clearly helped the BNP. In fact, if we look at the 2005 general election campaigns of both Labour and the Conservatives, we can see that this has already happened to some degree as regards issues like immigration and security. Moreover, at the 2004 European Parliament elections, the fiercely anti-European, welfare chauvinist and anti-Establishment UK Independence Party (UKIP) obtained a stunning result, gaining 16.1 per cent and 12 seats.

No less surprising is what has been happening in Italy over the last fifteen years, where three highly unconventional parties account for approximately half of the vote. There can be little room for doubt about classifying a racist, ethno-regionalist and openly anti-political party such as the *Lega Nord* in this manner. Nor should we underestimate the credentials of *Alleanza Nazionale* (AN). Notwithstanding its public declarations of respect for the rules and standards of liberal democracy, the party remains the legitimate political descendant of the post-Fascist *Movimento Sociale Italiano* (MSI) whose old symbol – the tricolour flame burning on Mussolini's coffin – sits proudly at the centre of the AN logo. Furthermore, on sensitive topics like immigration and security, the new party proposes measures which are incongruent with democratic norms. More complex is the case of *Forza Italia* (FI) which is a member of the European People's Party and which, in a careful division of labour, tends to leave racist rhetoric to its two above-mentioned junior partners. Nonetheless, in addition to its ambiguous position on Europe and marked anti-Islamic stance, FI also viscerally opposes what it condemns as old, professional politics and is highly intolerant of liberal democratic principles and rules.

To what species do parties like these belong? And to what species do the Norwegian Progress Party, the Danish People's Party, the Belgian *Vlaams Blok* (now *Vlaams Belang*), and the *Lijst Pim Fortuyn* in Holland belong? How should we view those heirs of Fascism which have emerged from complex recycling processes such as the *Front National* in France, the *Republikaner* in Germany, and the BNP in Britain? And what should we make of those movements such as the Austrian Freedom Party (FPÖ) or the Swiss People's Party (SVP/UDC) which at earlier points in their histories were far more moderate? It is particularly difficult to catalogue these parties within a single political family and, consequently, there has been much disagreement on which label should be used to describe them. In particular, what we have lacked is a convincing theory explaining their success. This chapter will seek to tackle these two questions. In doing so, it will put forward two theses. First, it will argue that what these parties have in common is that they embody the divorce of democracy from politics. Second, it will show that what stand out among the reasons behind their success are the profound changes which have occurred in democratic theory and practice.

In the next two sections, we will discuss the terms currently used to catalogue these parties. Labels are not neutral and each reflects a theory on the actors to which it is applied. The remainder of the chapter will examine the factors which have allowed populist parties to take root and will call into question the explanations most frequently offered. As we will see, while these tend to focus on social, economic and cultural transformations, they overlook the transformations in political theory and practice which have affected advanced democracies.

Labels

There are three main labels used to classify these parties. The first is that of 'extreme Right' which has been adopted by various scholars (Ignazi, 2003; Eatwell and Mudde, 2004; Carter, 2005). The use of 'extreme Right' in these cases, however, seems to be straining a category invented to designate parties which embraced violence, a hierarchical conception of society and the idea that all spheres of collective and individual life should be subordinate to the state. A less coloured label is that of 'radical right' (Kitschelt and McGann, 1995), which is often combined with others to create cocktails such as 'radical right-wing populist' (Betz, 1994). This brings us to the third label, which is that of 'populist' (Mény and Surel, 2000; Taggart, 2000; Panizza, 2005), a label which seeks to capture the ambiguous nature of these actors. This relates first of all to their political discourses which are often racist, intolerant, anti-political and delivered in violent and vulgar tones. Second, it highlights the exaltation in these discourses of the people as a single, united entity, with any internal divisions characterized as artificial and false. Third, although it acknowledges the adaptation of these actors to democratic rules, 'populism' also underlines the paradoxical use they make of democracy and their clear aversion to official politics – demonstrated by their self-promotion as champions of the people against the Establishment.

While, as the editors of this volume explain in the introduction, 'populism' has often been used, and misused, in vague ways (see also Collovald, 2004) and as a receptacle for new phenomena which are difficult to classify, the inflationary spiral affecting the term does not exclude a more sober use (for example, Canovan, 1981). Aside from its application to cases in Russia and the United States in the nineteenth century, until recently when we spoke of populism, we tended to think first of all of South America and the vast range of movements there which disdained class warfare, but acted in the name of the people and advocated the social and political integration of the poorest members of society (Germani, 1978). Still today, populism reappears in South America from time to time, most recently in Venezuela with Hugo Chávez and in Bolivia with Evo Morales. Characterized by the Pentagon as 'radical' populists, dangerous for democracy and comparable to Fidel Castro, these leaders have relaunched some of the themes and aspects of the political styles which were the hallmarks of Juan Perón and Getúlio Vargas such as personalized leadership, the absence of ideology, plebiscitary ceremonies, visceral opposition to elites (also at international level), redistributive paternalism and so on.

However, what do these manifestations of populism have in common with those such as the *Front National,* the *Lega Nord* and the Danish People's Party which have appeared in recent decades in established Western European democracies? If we leave to one side the rhetoric about 'the people', what else does the label 'populism' indicate? In fact, if we look at the trajectory of populist parties in Western Europe, we find few similarities with their purported South American relatives. They have different histories and different types of public. Even if both speak of 'the people', they do not do so in the same manner. Indeed, when the new populist vanguard appeared in Scandinavia at the end of the 1960s, the main issue it raised – in the name of the people – was that of welfare waste in order to attract the attention of the middle classes. It was a type of protest in many ways symmetrical with that of the movements of the New Left in the late 1960s which, rather than focusing on 'the people', preferred to juxtapose the authoritarian and oppressive paternalism of institutions – the state, parties, trade unions, the family, the Church and so on – with the virtuous and democratic spontaneity of civil society.

The symmetry between the two phenomena, however distant they may seem, should not be discounted. Both fiercely attacked the post-war consensus which linked parties of Left and Right and both helped thicken the atmosphere of mistrust surrounding politics which continues to afflict Western democracies. As far as populist parties are concerned, the *petite bourgeoisie* would remain their target audience until the 1980s and the advent of two important newcomers of neo-Fascist extraction: the *Front National* and the *Vlaams Blok*. What is evident is that the common denominator of these parties is not integration – as was the case, albeit in quite idiosyncratic ways, of South American populism – but exclusion. Moreover, since they do not express protest through the use of physical violence as Fascist-inspired movements traditionally did, but through verbal violence (occasionally tempered in electoral programmes), they are thus able to claim that they formally respect democratic procedures.

Antipolitics and identitarian democracy

It is perhaps this aspect of the relationship to democracy which, more than any other, the label 'populist' seeks to capture. Rather than elements which are not shared by all populists such as racism, nationalist fervour, or zero tolerance crime policies – albeit common to those of the radical Right – what links these actors is their paradoxical relationship with democracy. Populist parties are, in fact, not at all 'anti-system' in the sense of the term intended by Giovanni Sartori (1976: 132–133). They do not promote values which are extraneous to the system (and, as a result, they are sometimes suspected of paying mere lip service to the rules). What populists propose to establish is not a new political or economic order. On the contrary, they present themselves as parties which will restore an order that, in their discourse at least, existed in the past and which the errors and misdeeds of the political class, trade unions, public bureaucrats, big business and high finance have disrupted. To this end, they respect democratic rules and principles while, at the same time, reinterpreting and distorting them. There are three elements of democracy which they find particularly intolerable:

(1) basic individual rights;
(2) minority rights;
(3) politics in general, which in Western culture is synonymous with the defence of pluralism.

In opposition to these elements, populists put forward an all-absorbing and organic idea of the people which renders the principle of majority rule sacrosanct and absolute.

We can see the scant regard of populists for the rules of democracy first of all in their anti-political discourses. Although it boasts ancient ancestors, anti-politics is one of the most peculiar phenomena of contemporary politics, along with being an inexhaustible source of confusion both in public discourse and academic studies. If we try to disentangle its various strands, we can distinguish at least two principal variants: anti-politics 'from below' and 'from above' (Mete, 2005). We can ascribe to the first group the vast and differentiated range of belief and actions which are indifferent to, critical of, or protesting against politics. These extend from the lack of public confidence highlighted by numerous surveys, electoral abstentionism and volatility, to the rise in the vote for non-conventional parties and support for various types of movements such as those grouped together under the umbrella headings of no-global, pacifist and environmentalist.

Within the second group of anti-politics 'from above', we can place actors from a wide array of backgrounds including those outside the political system, those eager to enter it and even those who are inside the system, but who wish to rejuvenate grey public images and/or denigrate their rivals. There are many variants of anti-political discourse, but in recent years three have been most prominent. The first is the animatedly and deliberately contentious one of populist parties, which only superficially resembles that employed by collective movements. While both conceive of official politics as ill, for populists it is intrinsically so. Hence they claim that it produces useless divisions and should therefore be taken away from its traditional protagonists – the parties – and given back to the sovereign people and their leader. For the movements, free from the type of anti-pluralist outlook common to populists, politics only needs to be renewed by removing it from the grip of its self-referential official leaders and by stimulating activism by citizens and civil society. There is also a third, very frequent, variant which is close to neoliberal orthodoxy and which holds that it is the partisan aspect to politics that is overblown and inefficient and needs therefore to be scaled down in favour of a greater role for markets, independent agencies and experts (Schedler, 1997).

While there are many anti-political discourses in circulation, some of which are shared by conventional political actors, the specificity of populist parties lies in their paradoxical democratic fundamentalism. They scorn not only official politics and its institutions – parties, parliament, trade unions and public bureaucracies – but also social and political pluralism itself. Populism aims to foster and exploit anti-political feelings and actions. Indeed, having rejected the notion of politics as an encounter and contest between ideas, interests and parties and instead imagined a national community, unified around its leader, populism thus rediscovers and stretches two essential dimensions of politics (Schmitt, 1976): the opposition between friend and foe (whether internal or external) and the leader's sovereignty to decide – whether in charge of the party or the country.

Born in general as protest parties, populist parties are culturally rather crude and often display fierce anti-intellectualism. Nonetheless, this does not mean that we cannot find works of political theory in harmony with populist discourses and their democratic and anti-pluralist fundamentalism. I refer here to the reinterpretation of democracy during the Weimar era in Germany by the prestigious right-wing intellectual Carl Schmitt.

The starting point for Schmitt (1985) was the crisis of liberal parliamentarianism at the beginning of the twentieth century. He attributed this to the emergence of mass-based parties, whose fault it was that parliament had ceased to be a place where deputies took decisions based on arguments aimed at encouraging reciprocal persuasion and which had equal chances of being accepted. In Schimtt's view, deputies had become little more than delegates for parties, which imposed their wishes upon them according to the particular economic and class interests they were obliged to protect. Parliamentary decision-making thus became little more than the fruit of negotiations between opposing powers and this invalidated not only the process of discussion, but the very sovereignty of the state.

Of course, whether liberal parliamentarianism ever really functioned according to the mythologized principles of Schmitt is highly dubious. What is more important is that the remedy he prescribed contained a strongly anti-pluralist bias and cultivated the idea of an 'identitarian' democracy (Schmitt, 1928). This was founded on the establishment of an organic link between the people and a directly elected Head of State who, acclaimed by the public and holder of its trust, would be able to act without having to consider partisan concerns (Schmitt, 1931). The collegial authority of parliament would be substituted by a monocratic one, which would also designate supreme authority to the supposed will of the people (understood as a whole that was far more than the sum of its parts), as expressed by the electoral majority. This would occur at the expense of, amongst others, all other arms of the state and minority groups.

The liberal democratic tradition is entirely different, of course. In order to prevent undemocratic uses of democracy, the principle of the rule of the majority is accompanied by those concerning individual and civil rights and social and political pluralism. These are bolstered by robust measures designed to defend the rights of minorities, along with the co-existence of, and equilibrium between, elected and non-elected institutions.

It would be an exaggeration to say that new populist parties are proposing the exact model of identitarian democracy as imagined by Schmitt. However, their programmes, policies and actions do resonate with many of his ideas. They evoke a democracy which is in the firm grip of the people, nourished by elections and referendums, and thus no longer adulterated by the machinations, pedantry, corruption, clientilism and pluralism typical of official politics. Similarly, they promote personalized leadership and community-based actions – designed to restrain social pluralism, as to seek to eliminate it entirely would be unrealistic. Moreover, they tend to label as enemies all those who are different from the party and the people such as political opponents, dissenting voices, immigrants, homosexuals, Muslims, unmarried mothers, drug addicts, the long-term unemployed and so on.

Why is populism successful?

When discussing populism, the most difficult issue, however, is not the appropriateness of the term, but explaining the phenomenon which it denotes. How can we account for the fact that, almost everywhere in Western Europe, populists have been able to challenge and gain ground on conventional parties, which are not only armed with long-standing traditions, considerable political know-how, and massive financial resources, but which are often also protected by norms discouraging new entries into the political system? What changes in the political landscape have facilitated the emergence and success of new populist parties? The usual starting point when answering such questions is to look at the electoral following of these parties. It is believed that if we know which voters are attracted to populists, then it should not be too difficult to identify the conditions which have favoured populist growth. Unfortunately, as we might expect, given that votes for populists are often cast in protest, the evidence offered by electoral analyses is far from conclusive. What we do know is that males, the older generation, the unemployed, young people in search of work, manual labourers, artisans, small businessmen and farm workers are over-represented among voters for populist parties. We also know that the best indicator for populist support seems to be that of educational level. It is more likely that the less well-educated sectors of the population will vote for populist parties, although recently Kai Arzheimer and Elisabeth Carter (2006) have found that, in the case of extreme Right parties (some of which are among the parties discussed as 'populist' in this volume), it is those with intermediate levels of education who appear most favourably-inclined.

While the idea that the working classes have abandoned the parties of the Left to vote in large numbers for populists, generally of the Right, may be politically attractive for some, the fact that some manual labourers support populists does not allow us to draw any definitive conclusions. First of all, parties of the Right have always had a significant foothold within the working class. Second, in many areas, those from the working class and *petite bourgeoisie* live and vote side-by-side. Third, the category of 'working-class' has become extremely nebulous. After all, how comparable are post-Fordist workers – subject to conditions of high flexibility and perhaps working both for others and for themselves – with Fordist workers who were in stable long-term employment with the same company and usually highly unionized? Finally, while populist parties do attract votes from the working classes, it is certainly debatable whether we can infer loyalty to these parties from voting behaviour which is perhaps unstable and simply reflective of a form of 'exit' from a system that precludes 'voice' and in which the conventional parties have become much more distant from these sections of the population.

A more credible conclusion is that the electoral following of non-conventional parties reflects an overall condition of unease within western electorates, as a series of studies looking at developments in recent decades has revealed (Norris, 1999; Pharr and Putnam, 2000). This can also be seen both in the frequency with which voters support different parties (albeit generally within the same broad political area) from one election to the next and in the continuing decline in turnouts witnessed in almost all established democracies (see Lehingue, 2003). What is of interest to us here, however, is not just the fact that there is discontent with how democracies are governed and function, but the link between this phenomenon and populism. The thesis that the success of populism is simply due to the presence of (inevitable) crises is not particularly convincing. First of all, there was the crisis of capitalism. Now the capitalism of yesteryear and modernity are said to be in crisis. Above all, globalization and the end of the Fordist model, along with the decline of major public and private enterprises in the services sector, are held to have created an extremely difficult employment climate, characterized by low job security and increased flows of migrants in search of work. This, in turn, is pinpointed as the source of widespread anxieties and fears, which are exacerbated by:

(a) immigration which is alleged to threaten cultural identities;
(b) crime that is said to be growing everywhere; and
(c) the considerable deterioration of western democracies which have not only proved impotent when it comes to regulating the economy – which has escaped national borders and controls – but which have also been discredited by an endless series of corruption scandals.

(see Betz, 1994)

There is something a little bit too obvious about this account for it to be convincing, however. The 'crisis' is said to have unearthed a new, electorally significant cleavage between the winners and losers of globalization and shattered previous party loyalties. It is not clear, though, whether those who support populists are the losers – in need of reassurance and eager to punish those who are even lower down the social scale than them – or the winners, whose success has rendered them more traditionalist and belligerent (Kitschelt and McGann, 1995). In any case, it is argued that the extraneousness of populist parties to official politics, whose vices they have long condemned, gives credibility to their promises to restore the people's sovereignty and dignity by defending threatened national cultures, fighting crime, protecting the national economy, reducing taxation, halting the decline in public services and virtuously managing the state.

While this vision of populism reduces it to an inevitable side-effect of a supposed crisis, there is another hypothesis which merits consideration. Put simply: given that the world is constantly changing, is it possible that the problem lies rather in the way in which Western European democracies, their leaderships and their intellectuals have reacted to change? There are three particularly visible changes which have occurred over the last half century in these democracies and are relevant here:

(1) the decline in electoral turnouts;
(2) the evolution in the technology of the mass party;
(3) the reduced role of the state in providing services.

If, during the thirty years after the end of the Second World War, western societies benefited from politics and the state protected them from the market (and perhaps also protected the market from itself), it is also true that the parties and trade unions protected them. In that case, should we not then also count the withdrawal of the protection which democracy promised society amongst the factors that have favoured the emergence and success of populist parties?

The transformation of the parties

Once upon a time there was 'organized' capitalism (Lash and Urry, 1998), in the sense that it was regulated by the state and by social partnership involving confederations of employers and trade unions. But, no less important, once upon a time there was also 'organized' democracy, based on parties which not only took on the responsibility of governing, but which were also committed to bringing citizens into (and guiding them through) the labyrinth of universal suffrage and representative democracy. Moreover, they endeavoured to regulate pluralism and conflict, both within society and political life.

It was probably Max Weber (1980) who first underlined this capacity of the parties to regulate and organize democracy, warding off the much-feared plebiscitary democracy. The most polished theorist of the role of the parties, however, was Hans Kelsen. While Schmitt blamed parties for the end of the liberal regime, Kelsen (1929) viewed them not only as essential in enabling citizens to make their voices heard by linking them together, but as the *sine qua non* of democracy. Put simply, thanks to the compromise between parties, democracy could organize and recompose social and political pluralism.

In the years between the two World Wars, Kelsen's views went largely ignored. The tragedy of Fascism, which suffocated pluralism in the name of the state and its sole party, would be decisive, however, in rehabilitating the parties. As a result, in post-war Germany and Italy, their role was constitutionally enshrined and, with it, the legitimacy of pluralism. Everywhere in

Western Europe, parties of mass integration (Neumann, 1956) were recognized as the protagonists of democratic life, whose calling it was to select and train new political leaders and a new body of representatives. In these conditions, parties were not only encouraged to grow and organize, reaching mass dimensions, but were moved to aim to become one with society which, rather than suffocating, they vowed to promote politically. Of course, the society with which conservative parties were in dialogue was different from that of the confessional and socialist parties. Nonetheless, in representations of democracy, society was depicted as legitimately organized by the parties which (albeit with different levels of intensity) co-ordinated nearly every other form of association such as trade unions, co-operatives, sporting clubs, women's organizations, youth associations, etc. Indeed, this reached the point where, in many countries, the only forms of group activity which remained beyond the parties were the churches and religious associations (although these, of course, often maintained solid links with the confessional parties) and confederations of employers, whose links to the parties were usually more intermittent and weaker (Duverger, 1954).

This golden era of the parties came to an end when they performed a radical transformation, as best described by Otto Kircheimer (1966). Having established that economic growth and the Welfare State were smoothing out old cleavages and dissolving class identities by scaling down the redistributive claims of the working classes, Kircheimer argued that electoral competition had undergone a decisive change. With the entry of socialist parties into government, the goal of social integration had become secondary for parties which now set winning elections as their primary objective. As a result, they focused less on protecting their core constituencies and more on widening their potential basin of votes by reformulating more 'catch-all' programmes and thus abandoning issues which would divide the electorate in favour of those which would allow them to attract wider support.

Having downgraded ideology and collective mobilization, 'catch-all' parties freed themselves from the shackles of their wider organizations of activists and members. Citizens willing to involve themselves in political life increasingly became those who were simply interested in a political career. At the same time, the importance of candidates and party members serving in parliament and in government increased and these were the actors who would determine the fundamental positions of the party. Moreover, they would be answerable for their success or failure not to the party so much as to the electorate as a whole, which would be ultimately responsible for judging their ability to govern. This, of course, does not mean that parties came to resemble each other indistinguishably, as their constituencies and policy orientations did remain different. However, it is the case that their styles began to converge and that relations between competing parties became more relaxed. Parties sought to broaden their constituencies, but most of all they tried to avoid taking on heavy commitments which would tie them down if in government. They also increasingly began to promote, and rely on, the images of their respective leaders.

As we know, the 'catch-all' party is not the political party's final and definitive incarnation. Since the 1970s, in fact, another mutation has occurred with the rise of what Richard Katz and Peter Mair (1994; 1995) term the 'cartel party', denoting the oligopolistic transformation of inter-party competition through which parties have established links of co-operation/collusion. Emboldened by their positions of strength *vis-à-vis* the state, they worked together to discourage new entrants into the political market and to ensure their own comfortable survival, independent of elect-oral competition. In short, the parties found safe haven within the state, on whose resources they largely depend and of which they can almost be viewed as expressions (Van Biezen, 2004). There are understandable reasons behind this development. With the assumption of power by actors such as the Social Democrats in Germany and the Socialists (and Communists) in France, nearly all traditional parties became potential candidates for gov-ernment and, once their ideological idiosyncrasies had abated, it made sense for them to seek ways to regulate relations with their competitors.

This phenomenon has a paradoxical aspect to it: in an era of high-sounding rhetoric rehabilitating the 'invisible hand', the parties transformed the state into a structure at their service. The parties have also transformed: they have largely cast aside the newspapers and other propaganda channels pre-viously used to speak to the voters and have discouraged membership (Katz and Mair, 1992; Dalton and Wattenberg, 2000; Scarrow, 2000; Mair and Van Biezen, 2001). They have also reduced their self-financing capabilities and the voluntary work which derived from the membership body. In this way, they have suppressed their associational components and their potential for mass mobilization in order to transform themselves into streamlined agen-cies which can maximize vote shares by exploiting the financial resources available from the public purse and by using publicly funded television sta-tions over which, in many countries, parties effectively have control or at least exert considerable influence.

Parties of course still employ full-time functionaries, but their key activities of managing electoral campaigns, drawing up programmes and promoting them along with the images of their leaders – who have become the brand icons making one party distinguishable from another – are now delegated to public relations experts and political marketing gurus, whose relationships with parties are of a strictly professional nature. This has radi-cally changed the image of the party. Previously, they promised to change the world and to promote a more just and better society. In so doing, they recognized the capacity of politics to achieve such goals. Now, however, par-ties operate in a climate of permanent fire-fighting and the key expectation of them is that they remedy situations of immediate crisis such as inflation, excessive public deficits, lack of economic competitiveness, rising unemployment and so on. In this context, the capacity of politics for action and innovation appears modest and offers of political leadership respond essentially to three main criteria: novelty, firmness and morality. The leader must seem able to devise new responses, but within an extremely limited spectrum. He/she must appear 'new' and extraneous to traditional political circles. He/she must project an authoritative and resolute image and must be able to offer guarantees of morality, while also usually disparaging such qualities in his/her competitors. Naturally, appearance takes precedence over substance as the supposed 'new men and women' are frequently consummate professionals whose image has been carefully restyled by marketing experts and supporters in the media.

In reality, however, the relationship between parties and their membership is more complex than it might appear at first sight from the discussion above. While it is true that for a period the membership was effectively ignored, at other times successful recruitment campaigns have taken place. For various reasons, particularly symbolic ones, parties have an interest in maintaining a certain number of members. Nonetheless, many branches and committees, both at grassroots and other levels, through which members were able to interact with one another and the wider electorate, have fallen by the wayside. The old parties were founded on the practices of representative democracy and delegation. Members in local branches elected representatives to district and constituency organizations. These, in turn, sent delegates to party conferences which discussed and voted on policy positions and elected a broad national committee which could be convened between conferences. This committee would nominate a party executive and a leader who, together, would run the party.

In more recent times, to compensate for their more hierarchical and oligarchic natures, parties have often embraced the system of the grassroots directly electing leaders, with the pretence of thus giving greater voice to the membership. The leader of the party is chosen by the members, in some cases by primaries, in others by party conferences, thus nullifying all intermediate structures. It is highly dubious, however, that this has achieved the declared goal of making parties more transparent and democratic. By contrast, what is certain is that pluralism within parties has been compressed. In the presence of a leader who controls all the levers of the party and influences candidate selection, internal factions and groups have far less voice than before and the room for discussion is severely reduced. Party divisions were often quite artificial and corresponded to different ambitions within the leadership, but they also often reflected important political, cultural and territorial differences.

Finally, if the above reflects what has happened in terms of input, the changes regarding output have been no less significant. Parties produce leadership rather than ideas and control over policies has been expropriated.

Among the beneficiaries of this has been the ever-growing number of policy analysts as politics has been transferred to more protected and selective sites. In any case, we should point out that while parties may share a similar *modus operandi* and may all have become vote-maximizing, office-seeking agencies, dependent on the state, it remains true that they continue to appeal more to some segments of the electorate than others and have different agendas. Similarly, while party identification among the public may have waned, it has not altogether disappeared. Finally, while party programmes may well be nearly all inspired by neoliberal orthodoxy, their interpretations of it vary – much in the same way as catch-all parties subscribed to the post-war consensus, but deduced different meanings from it.

Why have parties changed?

Let us summarize for a moment. The evolution of the parties followed a parallel route to that taken by organized production. Mass-based parties attracted support by integrating the electorate and organizing it according to the same type of hierarchical model also adopted both by the state and the Fordist factory. If the latter was labour-intensive, the parties were membership-intensive. In similarly parallel fashion, the parties of today have dismantled their old organizational structures and assigned crucial segments of their productive cycles to specialized agencies, while superficially enhancing the role of members and activists through primaries and direct elections. It is clear, however, that while their 'shareholders' may be present at assemblies, they do not threaten the monopoly of the management, which often controls the composition of the body of shareholders. The parties have not become less important. Indeed, they continue to post impressive gains in terms of public offices secured. However, they have become something else, something which has diminished their democratic nature. What we need to look at now, therefore, is the question: why have parties changed so radically?

First of all, we should note that transformation does not mean crisis, but rather adaptation to new circumstances. The parties may have given space, in the intermediation between state and society, to interest groups, lobbies, movements and the media, but they still continue to dominate the scene by structuring political competition (Offerlé, 2002). In response to the question of why they have changed, there are two answers most frequently cited. The first is that the parties have also suffered from social change. According to this view, the disintegration of old class cleavages and shifts in values and cultural models (with the end of ideologies) have overwhelmed the great collective identities and redefined the associational inclinations and political and electoral behaviour of citizens. The technology of the mass-based party has been rendered obsolete by post-materialistic values and the emergence of new and more articulated forms of participation (Inglehart, 1977).

The second answer points the finger at the media – accused of having made parties superfluous both for citizens and for the elites. Citizens no longer acquire information from parties, but from the media which have distorted the logic of political competition. Since the media focus on the spectacular, in addition to assuming an instinctively polemical stance towards official politics, they tend to give pride of place to demands (superficially character- ized as more genuine) from so-called civil society, with the effect of exag- gerating these demands out of all proportion. Finally, not only have the media dispossessed the parties of their agenda-setting role, but the leader- ships of parties no longer have sufficient incentives to organize society. 'Parties as associations' required a lot of effort from party leaderships in terms of cultivating and involving the citizenry. However, this meant main- taining a burdensome apparatus which was rarely slow to assert itself and to seek to influence the leadership. Once politicians realized that collective action had become superfluous and that television allowed them to reach millions of voters at far less cost and more effectively (and that they could secure huge financial resources from the state with much less effort), they did not think twice about dispensing with both the 'party as association' and the apparatus which supported it.

There is more than a grain of truth in these answers, which have often been overlooked by those studying populism. Nonetheless, the transformation/ adaptation of the parties is also due to other factors which run even deeper. For one thing, it is highly doubtful that class cleavages have disappeared. A more likely possibility is that politicians and intellectuals have stopped examining and describing society through that lens, with considerable social consequences. In fact, the question of why parties have changed mer- its another, less obvious, response based on the changes – which have con- stituted a genuine cultural revolution – endured by the democratic para- digm. The starting point for this view is the contention that the transform- ation of western societies, economies, customs and cultures – along with the oil crises of the 1970s – opened up a window of opportunity for those in political, intellectual and business circles who were sceptical about democ- racy and who therefore conducted a ruthless and key revision of it, calling into question its success.

A first obligatory reference here is to the report for the Trilateral Commission by Michel Crozier, Samuel Huntington and Joji Watanuki (1975), although it is also worth mentioning the work of Niklas Luhmann (1990). The Trilateral Commission constitutes an extraordinary example of a multinational, political lobby (enjoying strong links with the economic- ally and financially powerful) which, like all political enterprises, invested in the political market in order to maximize its power. It did so at global level, putting forward a proposal that redefined what citizens were believed to want from democracy. According to the Trilateral Commission, democ- racy had involved citizens too much. It had made them too active. It had overprotected them, but to their own detriment, since it had pushed them towards making excessive and particularistic demands which damaged the effectiveness of democracy. The remedy, therefore, for the good of democracy, lay in driving redundant pluralism back towards society and out of the political sphere. This solution did not profess to wish to suppress social pluralism or fundamental rights such as the freedom of thought or association. Rather, it claimed to desire to put things back in their proper place by restraining a political pluralism which had become counterproductive and by revising the mechanisms of representation. After all, it was argued, democracies were now mature, predicated on solid agreements regarding their foundations, while what citizens really needed most of all was good government and good policies, carried out by authoritative and competent leaders, so that they, the citizens, could devote themselves to their own affairs in peace and tranquillity.

To this end, the Trilateral specifically called for an about-turn in how parties functioned: from being selective carriers of social pluralism, they should become selective filters of political pluralism. This opened the floodgates for a series of prescriptions and remedies from the literature on 'overload', which urged a revision of constitutional architectures in order to enshrine the pre-eminence of the executive and non-elected authorities, and to depoliticize crucial sectors of policy-making. In this way, from the idea that democracy should function thanks to hospitable and welcoming parties, the prevailing logic – above all that of the Establishment – moved towards an idea that, since the defeat of Fascism, only the most obtuse and isolated conservatives had dared to profess: that democracy, democratic participation and politics itself are harmful, particularly when administered in large doses. A qualitative conception of democracy was thus juxtaposed with the previous quantitative one. This new conception promised to make democracy more benign, more transparent and to restore directly to the citizens the sovereignty of which they are the holders.

To achieve the above, it is not always necessary of course to make constitutional modifications, but simply to reinterpret them. This can be done, for example, by compelling political competition to take place along binary lines with two leadership alternatives and thus depressing effects on political pluralism (Poguntke and Webb, 2005). Whether of course voters really can reward those who have governed well – or promise to do so better – and sanction those who have governed badly may sound nice in theory, but is doubtful in practice. First of all, there are the distortions as regards information and evaluation created by the media, politicians and other actors. Second, rather than carefully weighing up the merits of competing forces, voters mainly identify with one side or the other of the political spectrum and generally tend only to switch to the parties nearest their previous choice. When the party they prefer has little chance of victory, they may resort to tactical voting and reluctantly select the least unpalatable candidate, or abstain, or cast a protest vote. These considerations, however, have done little to damage the rhetoric surrounding the new democratic model which, in addition to ennobling the role of political entrepreneurs and strategic behaviour, expects that the competitive interaction of parties on the markets, or around the negotiation tables of 'governance', can resolve collective problems in a far more fruitful and democratic way.

Evidence that this model has been less successful than originally envisaged is implicit in the efforts made to bolster it with new forms of citizen involvement in politics such as surveys, referendums and changes to local democracy. This new 'post-democratic' model not only marks a radical break with the past, but legitimizes the surmounting of old institutions such as the parties 'as associations' and their role in bringing citizens into the political process. Of course, it is a selective model as it does not remove the parties, but reforms them profoundly. Moreover, if parties were founded on the idea of mobilizing large swathes of voters and therefore had an incentive to meet the needs of the weakest sections of society, by removing much of the possibility for representation which these sections had, then that incentive for the parties is also removed – a situation which considerably redefines the very idea of representation.

Indeed, representation has by now become a link, just like the consensus required for political authority, which those who govern weave downwards, by promising as compensation for those who are governed the latest successful political buzzword 'accountability' (Manin, Prezeworski and Stokes, 1999), or what we might call *ex post* auditing (Andeweg, 2003). In principle, it is sacrosanct that those who govern democratically should account for their actions and that elections should function as the fundamental auditing tool. However, the emphasis placed on 'accountability' in recent times raises the suspicion that it is merely an alibi that authorizes governments to disregard the wishes and interests of voters (while satisfying those of the most powerful and financially influential actors), by exerting their powers in whatever way they see fit or as most benefits their chances of re-election. In this scenario, democracy is only respected insofar as someone – perhaps working in a political rating agency – verifies the legality, morality and effectiveness of (real or presumed) government action and informs the citizens, who then must judge accordingly at election time.

The rhetoric surrounding the new democratic model is powerful and is clearly in tune with neoliberal orthodoxy. Authorized to abandon citizens to their destinies and to dismantle that costly and redundant linkage between rulers and ruled that was the old-style party, western political elites have enthusiastically embraced the new model. This is not least because it is consistent with the precepts of neoliberalism which demand less state involvement and that the partisan element of politics be reduced to a minimum. In conclusion, therefore, should we really be so surprised not only that public scepticism about politics has grown, but that large sections of the electorate (often the most vulnerable), bereft of the integration, protection and guiding influence provided by the parties, have fallen under the spell of populists, even if only to show their displeasure and disquiet?

The fact that phenomena such as the redefinition of the democratic paradigm, the transformation of the parties, the slow retreat from welfare provision and the success of populism have all occurred contemporaneously leaves little room for doubt that they are interlinked. Democracy nowadays treats citizens with indifference, as mere consumers of its offers of leadership. Meanwhile, the influence of economic and financial powers and organized corporations has grown, particularly when they have autonomous access to the media, or even possess their own media channels.

It is well known that, on both quantitative and qualitative levels, turnout is conditioned by the degree of political competence and the specific contexts voters find themselves in. In previous times, the functions of socialization and education carried out by parties were complementary to, or even in place of, those of formal schooling. Moreover, since party identities and electoral behaviour are influenced by reference points in the circles which voters come into contact with, the parties were thus able to act as decisive reference points (Gaxie, 1978: 240–253). The function of socialization has, however, largely been delegated now to the media, which subordinates it to its own logics and need for spectacle. It is also well known that the least culturally equipped voters are those most easily swayed by crude and simplified propaganda, of which populist parties are the incontrovertible masters.

It should not surprise us at all, therefore, that populists have been able to offer a significant section of lower class voters an attractive opportunity (other than simply abstaining) to express their sense of detachment and dissatisfaction with conventional politics. Nor should it surprise us that populists have been able to garner support from parts of the middle classes, particularly the self-employed who receive little protection from the state and who fear losing the prosperity and status which they have accumulated. In the past, this section of society tended to look towards traditional conservative parties, which in turn protected them, albeit using different methods than those employed by socialist parties. However, now that the self-employed have also been abandoned to the influence of the media, should it really strike us as strange that they too have often turned to populist parties?

The ubiquity of populism

According to Sir Thomas Gresham's law, bad money drives good money out of circulation and, in much the same way, populist and anti-political styles and discourses have spread through the political arena, to the detriment of the worthy elements that were there before. Before concluding this chapter, however, there is a final hypothesis that we would like to put forward. This can be summed up in the question: is it the case, in addition to having renounced their mission to protect citizens and having dismantled the old mass parties, that political leaderships have also facilitated the rise of populist challengers not only through the anti-political and anti-pluralist stances inherent in various organizational and institutional innovations, but also in their use of the discourses and attitudes encapsulated in Margaret Canovan's term 'politicians' populism' (Canovan, 1981)?

Populists have developed their ambiguous democratic fundamentalism by exploiting the failures of democracy. Likewise, for its part, the post-democratic model has been developed and applied by using the supposed failures of democracy as a motivating factor. There would thus appear to be a mutually reinforcing effect at work. If populists disdain the rights of the individual and those of minorities, it is also the case that more conventional actors also now, albeit in less dramatic ways, share the same intolerance of political pluralism and of the concept of politics as encounter, debate and discussion – and all the intricacies and slowness that this concept entails. Moreover, these actors do not shirk, again albeit in less bellicose terms, from resorting to the rhetoric of 'the people' and from using anti-political gestures aimed at replacing more genuine forms of citizen involvement (Mair, 2002: 81–98).

Three elements stand out above all others in this discussion. The first is the propensity to deny, or dilute, all political divisions. Official politics has discovered a non-partisan vocation which delegitimizes political pluralism and nourishes itself with appeals to the *rassemblement*, thus devaluing even the basic distinction between Right and Left. The second element consists of the repeated condemnations of the useless intrigues and disputes of politics, of its poor morality, and of its distance from citizens – both in a democratic sense (i.e. the charge that the people are no longer sovereign) and in terms of the deep and resolute negligence of the struggles faced by the common man. Obviously, those levelling such criticisms aim first and foremost to attract the attention of the media, only then to accuse them of aggravating political problems through spectacularization. The third and final element is that of the dramatization by politicians of their public presence, which begins with their private lives (to demonstrate that they too are 'of the people' and not of the Establishment) and extends to their often flaunted scorn of the official practices of politics, manifested in awkward attempts to fraternize with citizens and their emphasis of the non-professional nature of their political activity.

There are numerous potential examples of this, but one can suffice: that of Tony Blair who, having renamed his party 'New' Labour, was struck by an irrepressible intoxication with popular sovereignty. Thus, having broken the old link with the trade unions, the party adopted primaries. Moreover, Blair promotes an image of himself as a non-conventional politician, intent on making politics noble once more by restoring its morality and by placing the people at the centre of a political discourse full of references to the community, but also with non-partisan policy preferences and goals. Of course, we should note that, in Blair's view, moral principles take precedence over the views of the people expressed in surveys or through public protests, as his reaction to the weight of feeling against British involvement in Iraq demonstrates (Mair, 2000).

It seems appropriate therefore to ask, in conclusion, whether it is not the case that conventional leaderships have in fact fomented the anti-political scepticism of citizens and played a crucial role in discrediting politics? This being so, might it also therefore be the case then that the spectacular and disingenuous manner in which conventional leaderships have portrayed both themselves and democracy has provoked that poisoning of the public view of democracy which, more than anything else, new populists take advantage of?

4
Populism and the Media

Gianpietro Mazzoleni

Populist landscapes

The European political landscape of the last decade has been home to numerous political figures that have stood out by virtue of their personality and their voicing of popular discontent. These include the likes of Jean-Marie Le Pen, Jörg Haider, Christoph Blocher, Pim Fortuyn and Silvio Berlusconi, all of whom are among the more recent manifestations of the populist political climate affecting much of contemporary Europe, as discussed in the introduction to this volume.

Independent of their ideology, the leaders of populist movements and parties often have features in common that clearly contribute to their popularity and political appeal: in most cases, they are charismatic figures and possess a great deal of media savvy. Furthermore, as Gianfranco Pasquino notes in his chapter, 'Populist leaders do not represent the people, rather they consider themselves – and succeed in being considered – an integral part of the people. They are of the people'.

These features usually combine to assure a lasting public notoriety and intense media visibility that leaders use as political capital in the pursuit of their goals in their domestic arenas. This has certainly been the case with Le Pen, who has succeeded in attracting (and deploying to his advantage) the criticism of the press, while Austria's Jörg Haider's personal glamour and controversial stances have brought him public attention both at home and abroad. A somewhat similar communications strategy was employed by Pim Fortuyn in striking sensitive chords of popular concern (for example, in relation to Muslim immigration) and exhibiting a glitzy outspokenness that assured him constant media interest. In fact, we can say that almost all populist leaders display flamboyant personalities and pursue highly contentious agendas that attract media scrutiny.

Personal charisma and media savvy have thus played a significant part in the origins and subsequent construction of populist movements. Surprisingly, most recent political science research has largely disregarded them both on the grounds that charisma is not measurable, while media scholarship implements analytical categories that do not easily marry with the systemic approach of most political science work. An examination of the existing literature on populism confirms that 'little has been written on how the media work as the initiators or catalysts of public sentiments, how media content may voice sectional populist claims' and on how the media can be turned into powerful, if unwitting, allies of populist leaders (Mazzoleni, 2003: 2).

Do the media contribute to the rise of populism?

Looking at the most well-known cases of populist phenomena in Europe, we can see that leaders and movements often seem to rely on some sort of 'media complicity'. In many instances, the European media appear to have contributed to a legitimization of the issues, key-words and communication styles typical of populist leaders. 'Underdog' leaders who strive to gain public attention have regularly proved able to exploit the media's proclivity towards anything that 'breaks the routine' in political arenas, by resorting to communication strategies that ensure media coverage. The result of this 'supply and demand' relationship is an increased visibility and significant reverberation of the populist message among a wide audience. In other words, the media, intentionally or not, may serve as powerful mobilization tools for populist causes.

Clearly, no assumption is made here of causal links between the media and the spread of populism. Nonetheless, if we examine the processes of media-driven representation and the symbolic construction of favourable opinion climates – and of populist leadership, credo and action – we find that the media provide a significant degree of support for the rise of populist phenomena. The media factor, of course, is by no means the only independent variable here. That is to say, media action cannot be separated from the other structural factors considered in this volume, such as the nature of the political system and the specific features of the social and cultural political climates.

The example of social and political malaise – a common precondition for the growth of anti-political sentiments – shows that both political and media factors form a unique alliance, whose catalyst may be found in the country's political culture at a given time. This malaise is certainly not provoked by the media, but the media do play a role in disseminating it, either by simply keeping it on a country's public agenda, or by spreading political mistrust and a mood of fatalistic disengagement – all elements that can be easily and promptly exploited by populist politicians.

Furthermore, systemic phenomena such as the decline of a mass party interact to a very significant extent with media-driven processes, yielding new realities such as 'media parties' and, in our case, populist movements that rely heavily on the mass media, and are led by politicians who, with few exceptions, are themselves astute 'news makers'.

The question of whether the media accord an invaluable and extraordinary public status to the upsurge of populist ideas, populist leadership and populist forces stands out as the key question to be addressed. In other words, do the media contribute to the political legitimization of these movements, by assuring them first of media-based legitimization, i.e. a visible place in the national polity? Is this result unintended and inescapable? What are the implications for the health of democratic life? This chapter will discuss these and other related questions from a political communication perspective and by drawing on mass communication theory.

The media factor

When speaking of 'media', we refer to a very complex whole that includes senders, channels, contents, audiences, print and electronic outlets, journalism, the entertainment industry and others. There is, however, a risk of failing to distinguish between the diverse weightings of each of these components on societal phenomena. This is also the case with the study of the relationship between 'media' and populism. For our present analysis, the focus will be on the news media. This means looking at how print and electronic journalism has dealt with populism, how journalistic routines and narratives have affected the coverage and presentation of events and leaders, and how populist leaders themselves have interacted with the news institutions.

The classical distinction between mainstream and tabloid news media is of great value in this analysis, as it has been argued that these two types of news outlets adopt different approaches in their treatment of populism (Mazzoleni, 2003: 15–16). In most countries, the established news media are the mouthpieces of the ruling classes. In terms of their degree of integration with the elites, 'they tend to adopt a law-and-order attitude and to use their journalistic weapons for the defense of the *status quo* when it comes under attack from anti-establishment forces, such as protest groups and populist movements' (Mazzoleni, 2003: 16). Political communication scholarship (Blumler and Gurevitch, 1987) has labelled this attitude 'sacerdotal', arguing that the mainstream media in particular tap primarily into the interests of the ruling political, economic and cultural classes, even when they engage in criticism or conflict (Bennett, 1988). These media tend overtly to combat or downplay protest/populist threats, contributing to their containment. However, there is evidence that the public cynicism of particular media outlets and certain campaigns against political corruption, government misdeeds and controversial policies, may be held responsible for the diffusion of political discontent and even anti-political attitudes among the citizenry. This is fertile ground for populist sentiments, even when media abide by the rules of balanced and pluralistic presentation of political events (as in the case of public service media) (Ociepka, 2005).

A quite different picture is offered by the tabloid or popular news media. These print and television outlets are by no means mouthpieces of the Establishment. Their 'vision of the world' has a commercial character and responds primarily to 'market imperatives'. Hence, ratings and competition for advertising resources seem to be the paramount elements of these businesses. The commercial approach produces a journalism which craves the sensationalistic coverage of events, exhibits a strong preference for personalized story-telling and searches for news that stirs the emotions or provides for a kind of political voyeurism. In brief, popular journalism implements to the highest degree the classical laws of the news-making profession, focusing to a greater extent than the quality-mainstream press on the eccentric aspects of social reality. It is not surprising, therefore, that these media give passionate attention to what happens in the usually animated precincts of populist movements.

Media populism

Political arenas around the globe have long been affected by a general process of 'mediatisation' of political leadership and action (Mazzoleni and Schulz, 1999). The media – and especially television – have become increasingly central to the political process, to the point that political communicators now have to come to terms with the constraints of news production within the media industry. There is an ongoing adaptation of political public performances, language and at times even policy-making, to the demands of an increasingly commercialized mass media. Thus, the mediatization of political communication is often identified with the marketization of the public representation of politics. The implications of such changes in the realm of politics are diverse and all relate, to varying extents, to the dynamics of populism as they serve as the 'necessary background for populist messages' (Ociepka, 2005: 209).

The transformation of political language into spectacle is the most evident effect. In contemporary society, where image is paramount, political leaders must be good 'actors' and master the tools of drama in order to address effectively a domestic audience that has become increasingly distracted from politics. Pierre-André Taguieff (1997) emphasizes the mastering of television – the spectacle-medium by definition – by populist leaders, observing that 'populism has already turned into telepopulism. The successful demagogue of postmodernity is the telegenic tribune' (cited in Mény and Surel, 2000: 125). In Switzerland, for example, the success of Christoph Blocher's SVP/UDC party is to be found in the 'extraordinary media aura of its leader' (Tourret, 2000: 52). Blocher's case is an interesting one, because in a country where the mediatization of politics is hardly practised, the SVP leader's talent as a communicator has prompted the rise of an unprecedented 'spectacle-politics'. In particular, German language television made Blocher a true star of the popular programme *Arena*, thus offering him a nationwide audience (ibid.).

The personalization of political leadership is a further implication of the mediatization of politics and is closely connected to that of dramatization. The media have a far greater preference for stories about real people than for boring speeches or abstract issues presented in a bureaucratic style. Populist leaders, as noted earlier, are all strong personalities that perfectly fit the news media's demand for the spectacular and emotional treatment of social reality, including political life. In the 2002 general election campaign in the Netherlands, 'television news coverage of the parties was highly personalised, and the LPF coverage focused heavily on the leader' (Cherribi, 2003: 160). In Italy, Silvio Berlusconi has run his 'personal party' *Forza Italia* since 1994 with a strong personalized leadership. Parties such as the French *Front National* (FN) or Belgium's *Vlaams Blok* (now *Vlaams Belang*) have always been strongly identified with their leaders. Indeed, we could say that their destinies, like those of nearly all populist movements, are tied to the life cycle of their leaders.

The mediatization/marketization of political communication is intertwined with a broader shift in the media industry worldwide towards forms of content that respond primarily to audience demands and tastes by providing a larger supply of entertainment and sensationalism, especially in the information domains, and thus creating what Douglas Kellner (2003) has called the 'infotainment society'. Once again, television stands out as the medium that best epitomizes this trend in the news industry. Interestingly, in France, television is often nicknamed '*la machine à populisme*'. In 1990s Europe, the classical model of public (and socially responsible) broadcasting fell into deep crisis in the face of fierce competition from commercial channels in both the domestic and continental media marketplaces. This is seen by some analysts as one of the reasons behind the rise of a 'soft-videocracy' in certain political contexts. As the Italian philosopher, Remo Bodei (2003: 41), observed:

> millions of adult and active citizens, men and women, are all equally captured by 'domesticated' politics, in the double sense of a politics introduced [by television] into the home and of a politics tailored to the style and modalities of domestic behaviour, expectations, fears and disputes. Accordingly, the protagonists of political competition take on the same elements (of being likeable or not, of inspiring 'fans' to be for against them) that surround the other heroes of the small screen.

The Berlusconi phenomenon is clearly a case of populism that combines a political communication style with popularized television language and contents. Similarly, part of the success of Jörg Haider in Austria is attributed to his 'skilful use of [communication] strategies, which correspond with contemporary media logics. [...] His performances are exemplary for the personalisation and popularisation of politics' (Hipfl, 2005: 60, 70). In short, political populism nests perfectly in an environment where media populism thrives. It is no surprise, therefore, that recent research has presented convincing evidence that there exists a close link between the two forms of populism. As Cas Mudde (2004: 554) notes, when the media 'struggle for readers and viewers, and consequently, [...] focus on more extreme and scandalous aspects of politics', all this provides a 'perfect stage' for populist figures who find 'not just a receptive audience, but also a highly receptive medium'.

By 'populist media' or 'media populism', we mean highly commercialized media production and/or news coverage that yield to general popular tastes, as in the case of tabloid media. It comprises both the concepts of commercial treatment of collective imagery (and of public affairs) and of the sweeping 'popularization' of media practices and content. Jay Blumler and Dennis Kavanagh (1999: 220) note that:

> the voiced opinions of men and women in the street are being tapped more often in a veritable explosion of populist formats and approaches: talk shows; phone ins (with both even-handed and aggressively opinionated hosts); solicitation of calls, faxes, and e-mails for response by interviewed politicians; studio panels confronting party representatives; larger studio audiences putting questions to politicians through a moderator; and town meetings of the air, deliberative polling and televised people's Parliaments. The identities and styles of these efforts are extraordinarily diverse, ranging from the combative to the reflective and from glossy voyeuristic to the ultra-Athenian.

The influence of such populist/popularized media apparatuses on the diffusion of populist ideas is evident if we consider that forceful politicians can count on the readiness of these communication channels and that these same channels can also serve as vehicles reflecting people's sentiments back to them. Clearly, the political messages that populist media disseminate are of the kind that can appeal to mass audiences, very much like what occurs in the realm of popular culture. As the *Le Monde* columnist Patrice de Beer observed after the 2003 French parliamentary elections:

> Lots of people here read no papers. They have television. Television also became focused on society and pop culture, *as is the news* (Italics mine). It mixes up pop culture and current affairs. It sets a particular agenda. Look at the last election when television highlighted crime, immigration, the 'inner city'. It gives people the idea that society is dangerous, totally corrupt. It turns them away from public life. It helps the extremists like Le Pen. (in Lloyd, 2005)

This convergence of goals between the populist media and populist political movements is normally unintentional. While there are cases in which media outlets openly back populist leaders, the most conventional pattern is that of a 'production bias' (Entman, 1989) – a synonym for the inevitable 'slant' built into all news production processes, especially those of the commercial media.

This convergence of goals sees the media pursuing their own corporate ends by striking emotional chords on issues such as security, unemployment, inflation, immigration and the like. At the same time, populist leaders and their movements gain status, visibility and popular approval by generating controversy, scuffling with incumbent political leaders and resorting to inflammatory rhetoric.

Populist strategies to secure media attention and support

As has already been mentioned, populist leaders tend to be consummate players with the media and clever newsmakers. It is interesting therefore to look at the most successful communication strategies implemented by populist movements in order both to tap into the public mood and capture the media's attention.

The personality traits of the leading figures have a strong bearing on the public image of their populist movements and parties. Charismatic or not, all share a 'populist' communication style. Their appearance and attire is one aspect of this. As Brigitte Hipfl notes: 'journalists liked to comment on Haider's various dress styles and labelled him a male model' (Hipfl, 2005: 64), while Umberto Bossi (of Italy's *Lega Nord*) deliberately went for casual clothing and brandished big cigars. In France, Jean-Marie Le Pen wore a red scarf over his mouth when speaking of leftist censorship. Another aspect is the language they use: Le Pen is an excellent orator who makes sharp puns about rivals while Bossi has used northern dialect and manipulated national (or regional) symbols (for example, the *Lega* holds rallies in Pontida, symbolic city of the northern Italian medieval insurgence against German emperors). Such personality features serve as strong poles of attraction for the popular media, as they often fit into the 'story-telling' frames of media industries (Kellner, 1990: 112).

However, to be effective, the leadership of a populist movement has to consider employing media management techniques that respond to the increasing professionalization of political action. Not all populist leaders use the sophisticated means that presidents, prime ministers and other major politicians employ in modern political warfare or make recourse to the 'scientific engineering and targeting of messages' (Bennett and Manheim, 2001: 282). Rather, in general, the communication strategies of populist leaders and movements include:

1. playing the role of the underdog;
2. use of professional expertise;

3. rallies;
4. free media publicity;
5. staging events; and
6. tactical attacks on the media.

(Stewart, Mazzoleni and Horsfield, 2003)

Playing on an underdog status is an uncertain strategy as it is not always successful. Le Pen and Bossi have paradoxically gained more support when targeted by unfriendly news coverage. In various elections, Silvio Berlusconi has cleverly exploited the aggressive hostility of the liberal Italian press and his supposed 'demonization' by the opposition. Like Berlusconi, Haider and Le Pen have also used professional media relations advisers and, in so doing, have succeeded in getting less hostile coverage. Similarly, in Belgium, the *Vlaams Blok* benefited from a professional leadership, strong and verbally skilled politicians and a pronounced communication strategy – perfectly suited to striking the anti-political chords of the population (Jagers and Walgrave, 2003).

However, the old 'pre-mediated' forms of political communication have been by far those most favoured by populist leaders. Bossi, Haider and Le Pen used their rallies to stand (and be seen to stand) amongst ordinary people and to address their constituencies directly, often using language they would not use in the media. The controversial and protest nature of populist leadership, as previously observed, assures them of constant media attention, especially in the early days of their movements. This free publicity accorded to the leaders and their ideas enables them to capitalize on their strong public visibility and explains why, for example, the *Lega Nord* decided not to invest much in campaign propaganda (Mazzoleni, 1992).

Another strategy widely implemented in the political arena is that of staging events both during and outside election campaigns. As Beata Ociepka observes:

> populists often inspire media events by introducing issues into the public discourse in order to launch the process of opinion building. [...] The importance of public opinion surveys in contemporary democracies between elections provokes populists to perform media events in order to support the notion of 'a permanent election campaign'. The aim of such permanent election campaigns is full mobilisation of the electorate, for the long term, and especially before elections. (Ociepka, 2005: 210, 211)

Populist leaders and their movements thus possess a special ability to make headlines and appear on breaking news, depending on the particular mood of the country. Amongst the ways they do this are via press conferences, theatrical events, photo-opportunities, or by making inflammatory statements. Being a political 'pop star' or 'media-icon' makes it easier for leaders like Haider to put on a show and adapt public presentations to the pop-culture-style presentations of media celebrities (Hipfl, 2005). One important side-effect of this courtship of the media, however, is that observed by Todd Gitlin (1980) with respect to the student protest movements of the 1970s in the USA, i.e. populist movements that 'professionally' use the media may pay the price of losing control over their self-definition.

Along with a careful strategy of courting the media to their benefit, populist politicians have at times also implemented the opposite strategy – that of bullying certain less-than-friendly media outlets – in an attempt to shore up support among followers who claim their voices are not represented by the (mostly) mainstream media. They also flout any negative public image (or definition) of the movement that may have been propagated by media perceived as representing the voice of the Establishment. This accounts for the setting up of party-controlled daily newspapers like the *Lega Nord's La Padania*. This type of media plays the dual role of supporting the movement's ideology, policies and battles in addition to reinforcing its identity among followers, and serving as a showcase of the movement to the 'outside world'.

Not all of these strategies to attain sympathetic coverage or support from the media meet with success. The elite media – those that reflect the political culture of the Establishment – can raise barriers against attempts by populists to secure their direct or indirect support. However, as Yves Mény and Yves Surel acutely observe, 'in the game of mutual exploitation/ manipulation between the media and politicians, populist leaders can always gain a comparative advantage, at least in the beginning. Having little to lose and everything to gain, they feed the media with provocative and fiery statements, and with violent attacks on their opponents' (2000: 126).

From 'hard' to 'soft' populist communication

As outlined earlier, the processes of marketization and tabloidization of the news industry have affected all political action, leaders and political discourse worldwide. Populist politics is thus only one part of a political environment that has been moulded by the changes in political communication since the end of the Second World War (Blumler and Kavanagh, 1999). In other words, established parties and mainstream politicians share with populists significant degrees of media-centred, spectacularized, personalized and audience-pleasing communication.

Within this commonality of communication patterns in the media environment, a specific trend (which is not confined to Europe) can be singled out – the 'populist contamination' of mainstream political discourse. While some mainstream political players (both leaders and their parties) have resisted at least the most conspicuous and controversial manifestations of the mediatization of politics (Mazzoleni and Schulz, 1999), it appears that populist language has become a sort of *koiné* for many others. This is a process that also concerns other important aspects of the evolution (and crises) of liberal democracies – both in the old western world and in the newer democracies – and has created anxiety about what might be the likely outcomes of a populist drift in contemporary political arenas. On the one hand, it seems that some mainstream politicians are diffusing a kind of 'soft populism' that recoils from the excesses of 'hard' populist communication (with all its possible boomerang effects on moderate electorates), while at the same time espousing the same, or similar, attitudes and stances on issues dear to populists such as immigration, crime, unemployment, and the effects of European Union enlargement. On the other hand, there is a 'soft populism' that ordinary political action shares with populists which appeals directly to the people and is often intolerant of the constraints of elitist, representative democracy. It is important to note, however, that the language used by these 'soft populists' – who mostly address moderate voters – is quite unlike the boisterous speech of the 'hard populists'.

In this sense, populism may be seen as a communication style which is adopted by political actors seeking to display their proximity to the people. Populism appears, therefore, as a 'master frame, a way to wrap up all kinds of issues' (Jagers and Walgrave, 2003). Many mainstream European political leaders and parties have been observed reverting at various times to either or both kinds of 'soft populism', in a clear attempt to ride the populist wave that continues to influence European economic, political and cultural climates, especially with regard to the challenges to European security and stability posed by globalization. The established parties thus use messages that are ultra-simplified and populist in tone, in an attempt to show their closeness to sensitive sectors of domestic public opinion and to capture transient emotions in disaffected voters (see also Alfio Mastropaolo's chapter).

In Italy, Berlusconi has often appealed to voters, for example, by rejecting policies as a response to supposedly widespread popular demand. In France, during the 2005 riots in the banlieues, Nicolas Sarkozy borrowed language from the *Front National* that targeted the heartland of moderate French voters worried about the problems of ethnic integration. In his 1995 presidential campaign, Jacques Chirac adopted a populist rhetoric in his condemnation of elites, hidden economic powers and Europe's democratic deficit (Mény and Surel, 2000:123). Tony Blair has also tactically adapted his communication style to the post-September 11 opinion climate. As Yves Mény observed:

> Blair has weakened the Labour party and instead stressed his communication with the people. In that sense, his leadership contains a populist element [...] In any case, populism in the UK goes through the tabloid press. Blair's decisions in relation to the Iraq conflict were criticised by the political elites, but supported by a large section of the popular press. (Mény, interviewed by Gnoli, 2003: 39)

In the Netherlands, Pim Fortuyn was credited with bringing to an end the 'political correctness' of political discourse which was held to be typical of traditional public debate. Dutch politicians (and the media themselves) are no longer afraid to speak out about issues such as immigration and the cultural integration of Muslims and to lay bare their deeper concerns. As Oussama Cherribi noted: 'a year after Fortuyn's tragic death [...] the main political parties on the Left and Right have adopted as their own the anti-Islam and assimilationist policies of the LPF [*Lijst Pim Fortuyn*], and positive images of the leader continue to be widespread in the press' (Cherribi, 2003:267).

The media-marked life-cycle of populist movements

Comparative analysis of populist phenomena has illustrated that the rise (and, in some instances, the fall) of populist leaders and movements is influenced to varying degrees and at different stages of their respective 'life-cycles' both by the way the media have covered events, figures and messages and by the success of their own media management strategies. Applying a frame of analysis from Julianne Stewart, Gianpietro Mazzoleni and Bruce Horsfield (2003) to the European populist phenomena, we can divide into four distinct phases the diverse impacts both of media factors on populist movements and of populist movements on the media.

The ground-laying phase

This is the phase of diffused malaise in domestic public opinion in which the media mostly play an indirect role in facilitating the rise of organized populist forces. Media coverage may spread a sense of malaise and can trigger anti-Establishment reactions and political disaffection. The ensuing climates of cynicism and disenchantment provide ideal ground for the dissemination of the views of political leaders such as Le Pen, Haider, Bossi, Blocher and Dewinter as they start to gather electoral support and thus enter the political arena. Apart from the dramatization of the country's ills by both elite and tabloid media, the populist media plays a role in spreading the populist message. In fact, in some countries, certain populist media buttress new populist movements by catering to the entertainment needs of their audiences and/or by highlighting negative stories that might stimulate public unrest. In other words, we can find a sort of 'convergence of goals' in what has been labelled 'newsroom populism'. This was the case, for example, in Austria when tabloid newspapers fuelled an opinion climate that favoured Jörg Haider (Plasser and Ulram, 2003). According to Brigitte Hipfl (2005: 58), popular television programmes, such as 'Big Brother', 'can function as "normalising contexts" for populist strategies and become part of the "space of opportunities" for populism'.

In Belgium, the success of the *Vlaams Blok* (VB) in 2003 was indirectly facilitated by the phasing out of the *cordon sanitaire* raised by the national press to keep in check the diffusion of xenophobic sentiments put forth by that party. Various news media began to cover some of the controversial issues that made the political fortune of Philip Dewinter in an attempt to defuse the VB's challenge to the country's political *status quo*. This meant opening the doors of mass communication to the extreme Right. In doing so, the Flemish media (with the significant exception of the mainstream paper *De Morgen*) opened a Pandora's Box (Arnauts, 2003). In fact, the heavy coverage of criminal stories comprised a large part of the daily news diet 'which in Belgium has been found to be linked to one particular item on the menu: crime news' (ibid., 53) and researchers have detected a correlation between this diet and support for the Far Right (Walgrave and De Swert, 2004).

The insurgent phase

Populist movements gradually gain popular support and build up their organization to the point where they can effectively challenge the other parties. From the perspective of media-populist relations, this phase is characterized by two main features:

1. populist leaders seek to secure the direct attention of the media by displaying a large array of communication tactics;
2. the mainstream media and tabloids respectively manifest very different attitudes towards the search for public visibility by these leaders.

During this phase, it is possible to observe the media savvy of leaders in action: they stage controversial events, engage in verbal extremism and fiercely attack government policies (for example, on immigration, taxes and social welfare). Bossi's neo-Celtic liturgies, Haider's remarks about the Nazis and the Jews, Fortuyn's outspoken statements on Islam are all 'newsworthy' realities that the media will automatically cover in their pursuit of corporate goals. In the case of Fortuyn, many within the Dutch media 'pro-actively contributed to establish Pim as a brand name in his ascent to political power, so that he already had a sympathetic audience among opinion leaders as well as the general public' (Cherribi, 2003: 149). Fortuyn 'brought the journalists exciting news... [and]... journalists through their own media logic have done nothing other than stimulate the hype' (ibid.: 161).

In contrast to the apparent willingness of commercial media to provide substantial and continuing access to controversial and politically destabilizing populist platforms, the elite media demonstrate considerable angst in attempting to conform to the statutes of good journalism while avoiding contributing inadvertently to the rise of anti-Establishment forces. Although they have no choice but to cover these events, there is some evidence that the elite media either underestimate the overall political significance of these parties, or else that they seek to undermine the populist upsurge by adopting tones of outrage and ridicule. This was the case in the relationship between the Italian mainstream media and Bossi at various stages in the *Lega Nord's* life and with regard to Berlusconi's flamboyance and self-interested policies. A similar tactic was also adopted by the French liberal media in its treatment of Le Pen on several occasions.

The established phase

This is a critical phase for populist movements. Once they have achieved public legitimization through their presence in parliament (and even in government), the media tend to become disenchanted with them. Populist leaders lose some of their original charismatic appeal and find it more difficult to retain the media spotlight than they did in previous phases. Moreover, the political agenda they must address in parliament or in government no longer has the sensational aura that it used to have. Any continued inflammatory rhetoric is overlooked by the media as being chiefly directed towards the movement/party's constituency. Both the established media and commercial outlets no longer experience the dilemmas they faced in phases one and two: their defence of the existing order is overtly displayed. Comparative analysis has shown two interesting patterns in the conduct of the media with regard to populist phenomena during this phase. First, there is the possibility of conflict between the previously supportive populist or tabloid media and the leadership of the populist parties. For example, when FPÖ politicians entered the governing coalition, the tabloid newspaper *Kronen Zeitung* became critical of Haider and his party's agenda.

Second, the mainstream media can display an unprecedented deference to populist parties that have gained power. This can be explained in terms of the 'sacerdotal' attitude common to most elite news outlets. In Italy, once the *Lega Nord* and its leader joined the Berlusconi-led government in 2001, it began to receive more serious attention, even though it had often been ridiculed in the insurgent phase (Biorcio, 2003b). The same occurred with Denmark's Pia Kjærsgaard, founder of the *Dansk Folkeparti*, after her electoral and personal success at the 2005 elections, and following her support of Anders Fogh Rasmussen's government coalition. In 2006, the party's popularity rose dramatically in the opinion polls following the *Jyllands-Posten* Prophet Muhammad cartoons controversy. To a certain extent, Le Pen and the FN also received compliant media treatment during the 2002 presidential campaign. Indeed, the major French television channel, TF1, was accused by the Socialists of having given such excessive coverage to Le Pen and his position on security questions that it was nicknamed TFN.

The decline phase

Clearly this is not a phase that is relevant to all European populist leaders and movements. On the contrary, most of the movements mentioned in this chapter are still fairly successful and continue to receive significant media attention. The conduct of the media in the decline phase varies from country to country: media attention may be prompted by the newsworthiness of a 'sensational' fall in popularity of a formerly controversial leader, or by the appearance of competitors in the national political marketplace, as was the case with the split in Le Pen's party a few years ago. The hypothesis by Fritz Plasser and Peter Ulram (2003) that, if the FPÖ were to lose its media popularity, it would surely fall into decline is a most interesting one. This is in fact occurring in Austria with the BZÖ, a party founded by Haider and his sister that joined the Schüssel cabinet, but then gradually lost popular support (cfr. Heinisch in this volume). Given the close interdependence of populist movements and the media as well as of charismatic leaders and their parties, this hypothesis might well apply to other cases. The murder of Pim Fortuyn attracted huge media coverage and mustered significant electoral support, but the movement that survived its leader lacked his charisma and media savvy, and therefore did not survive, among other factors, the consequent media disinterest (Cherribi, 2003; see also Lucardie in this book).

Populists, media and democracy

To answer the earlier question of whether the media are accomplices in the creation of populist climates and the rise of populist movements, there is some convincing evidence that there are close ties between media-centred processes and the political phenomenon of populism. All phases in the life-cycle of a populist movement are affected by some sort of media-driven influences, and populist leaders cannot disregard the seductive power of the media. If they do, they risk marginalization. This intrinsic interdependence can be seen in terms of 'media complicity' in building the destinies of populist leaders and their movements.

The existence of a 'media populism' that has its origins in the typical patterns and practices of commercial media outlets (such as the tabloid press, talk radio and infotainment TV shows) offers an undoubted, if largely unintentional, backdrop to the flowering of populist climates by disseminating sentiments ranging from popular discontent on particularly hot issues to vehemently anti-political attitudes. This is why researchers refer to a 'convergence of goals' between the media and populists. They need each other. The media must cover the sensational stories provided by contentious, often flamboyant (and in some cases 'media darling') figures while populist leaders must use the media to enhance the effectiveness of their messages and build the widest possible public support. Beata Ociepka (2005: 223) uncovers similar trends when assessing the role of the domestic media in the rise of Polish populism: 'The relationship between the media and populist politicians is reciprocal. Both sides in the relationship are conscious of possible manipulation, but at the same time are fated to cooperate'. This seems to be a rather common phenomenon in Europe (and elsewhere), no matter how different the political and cultural contexts in which populism emerges.

The evidence from comparative research shows that the media are far from being compliant, submissive 'accomplices' to populist politicians. In contrast to an apparent convergence of goals between populist movements and the populist media, there is a patently more adversarial attitude adopted by the mainstream media, albeit with some interesting exceptions. The different handling of populist issues and leaders by the Establishment media in the various phases of the populist party life-cycle reveals an 'evaluation bias' (Entman, 1989), exactly the opposite of the 'production bias' built into typical news-making processes. However, an important distinction should be made here, as the elite media in some cultural environments can display contradictory responses to populists in the sense that they may not be completely hostile to new movements, especially in their very early stages.

The adversarial type of 'evaluation bias' is the most common one in advanced democracies. This 'takes the form of committed defence of the *status quo* and the adoption of a "law and order" frame', that makes the media 'play the role of paladins of the established political order' (Stewart, Mazzoleni and Horsfield, 2003: 234). There may also be some (production) bias in a 'convergence of policies', especially when the established media back populist actions. For example, the media fostered the cultural claims of Fortuyn and the nationalist agenda of Haider, and have favoured movements considered essential to large-scale political manoeuvres – as in their occasional support for Bossi's bullying of the old political class in Italy on the eve of its demise following the 'Clean Hands' judicial investigations of the early 1990s.

A final reflection should be made on the implications for the health of western European democracies of the evidence of strong – even if not always intended – collusion between the goals of the media and the political strategies of populists. In other words, what contribution have the media made to the democratic process by interacting with populist phenomena and diffusing their messages within popular culture? In many cases, due to their preference for applying emotional codes in public information, the media have played a role that is anything but supportive of 'quality' public debate or the creation of an informed citizenship. This factor, together with the 'social and political conditions' (Cfr. Pasquino in this book) that precede the emergence of leaders capable of exploiting them, has contributed to the rise of many hard and soft populists and, through the simplification and personalization of crucial issues that merit more considered treatment, has helped legitimize personalized political and populist leaderships. There is also a serious risk that citizens and voters will identify themselves with these political 'stars' in a dangerous 'information short-cut' that translates swiftly into electoral support for the nationalistic, xenophobic and reactionary policies advocated by many populist leaders. The fact that populism presents itself as a 'democratic' phenomenon – claiming to cure established democracies of their ills – makes the picture of the enlarged Europe's democratic evolution even more indistinct, particularly in relation to the challenges posed by large-scale immigration and economic globalization.

It seems that what has been identified with 'media populism' is the irresistible global mass communication environment that facilitates the circulation of populist streams in the democratic body. However, while it might be obvious and convenient to blame the media for this trend in the European political environment, pursuing this interpretation equates to furnishing an alibi for phenomena that should really be looked for elsewhere. After all, the media act to some extent as mirrors of society. As stated in the introductory paragraphs of this chapter, the media are not 'independent variables', but rather are 'intervening variables' in cultural, social and political processes that have more 'structural' origins. Moreover, recent sociological work points to media populism as a positive resource for democracy and informed political citizenship, in that it 'may offer a way into politics for people otherwise excluded or bored' (Van Zoonen, 2005: 150). That is not to say, of course, that the media are 'neutral' players in the populist political game. What we can say is that the news media in particular bear the responsibility for exercising criticism and vigilance in their portrayal of political reality, be it populist or mainstream.

Part II

5
Austria: The Structure and Agency of Austrian Populism

Reinhard Heinisch

This chapter seeks to provide an analysis of populism in contemporary Austrian politics. Conceptually, it is divided into two segments: the first explores the structural factors which have facilitated the rise of populism; the second is devoted to examining populist agency. While any account of Austrian populism will inevitably focus on the Freedom Party (FPÖ), it needs to be emphasized that this political phenomenon is much broader and continues to evolve.

Populism is understood here as a form of political mobilization that makes constant reference to the 'common/little people' portrayed in opposition to malevolent elites and dangerous outsiders. The 'people' are thus portrayed as a unitary entity in the sense that divisions among them are not genuine conflicts of interest, but are simply caused by the machinations of self-serving factions (Canovan, 2002). Populists make primarily emotional appeals and mobilize voters through simplistic and dichotomist rhetoric, the use of scapegoats, outrageous claims as well as spectacular acts. Populism is also characterized by subordinating ideology to opportunism and political expediency. It is thus marked by contradictory positions as well as dramatic programmatic shifts in order to maximize popular appeal. In Austria, populism has also had a special affinity with the rich event culture typical of a tourist country in which art festivals, sports, folkloric festivities and their coverage in assorted lifestyle media provide an important platform from which to reach voters. The populist agenda is generally eclectic, advocating both anti-statist positions and authoritarian law-and-order ideas. Over time, Austrian populism has evolved from middle-class anti-system protest to the promotion of radical claims based on cultural and ethnic identity.

Opportunity structures

The rise of populism in Austria in the past two decades is first and foremost associated with a set of systemic features inherent in the Austrian political model, which, by 1980, had entered a crisis of legitimacy. In particular, the emergence of the FPÖ under Jörg Haider as a rightwing populist (middle-class) protest party was defined by its radical opposition to the characteristics intrinsic to Austrian consociationalism (see Table 5.1 below).

Political organization

In terms of political organization, the Austrian model was designed to internalize political, economic and social conflict by creating three intersecting institutional frameworks (Lehmbruch, 1967; Katzenstein, 1984):

1. the state institutions and administrative bureaucracy;
2. the institutions of Austro-corporatism, and, as the overarching bracket;
3. the two major political parties, Social Democrats (SPÖ) and the Conservative People's Party (ÖVP) along with their affiliated networks.

A systemic feature known as *Proporz* allocated shares of political influence proportionally between the major two parties, not only ensuring their control over the country's political institutions, the bureaucracy, labour market associations and public enterprises, but also extending to all areas of public life. What Gehrhard Lehmbruch (1967) dubbed *'Proporzdemokratie'* reinforced the hegemony of the two main parties to the almost complete exclusion of all other political actors. The power of the SPÖ and ÖVP rested also on their enormous membership and the elaborate patronage system associated with *Proporz*. Its various features became the prime target of sustained populist campaigns by the Freedom Party in the 1980s and 1990s. More than any other aspect of Austrian politics, it allowed the FPÖ to define itself as a

Table 5.1   The Freedom Party in Austrian parliamentary elections (selection)

Year	Vote %	Seats
1956	6.5	6
1966	5.4	6
1975	5.4	10
1983	5.0	12
1986	9.7	18
1990	16.6	33
1994	22.5	42
1995	22.0	41
1999	26.9	52
2002	10.0	18
2006	11.0	21

Source: Bundesministerium für Inneres.

protest party fighting for the 'common man' against the overbearing and unaccountable elites.

A related systemic feature of the Austrian model is that of the Grand Coalitions, referring to the formalized cooperation between the major parties which occurred between 1945 and 1966 (under ÖVP leadership), and between 1986 and 1999 (under SPÖ leadership). This involved the two parties engaging in behind the scenes negotiations and passing legislation in the form of so-called package deals. Such measures frequently resulted in lowest common denominator solutions of great complexity. The compromises required and the lack of transparency thus provided ample opportunities for populist attacks.

In the second Grand Coalition, the rise of the Freedom Party had an additional arresting effect on the two major parties. Analyses of election results after 1986 show a decrease in substantive competition between the Social Democrats and Conservatives (Schedler, 1995: 21). As the FPÖ weakened the Social Democrats and Conservatives asymmetrically, the SPÖ became locked in place as the dominant political force. While the ÖVP gradually shrank to middle-party status, its role as indispensable coalition partner for the Socialists increased because, without the Conservatives, the SPÖ could not form a government. Hence, the stronger the FPÖ became, the more the other two major parties needed one another and the less they competed with each other.

Economic organization and governance

Austrian economic organization and social policy were defined by what is generally regarded as the most highly centralized corporatist system among all advanced economies (Talos, 1985). This system of Social Partnership refers to an inter-organizational concertation process between five major associations – representing labour and business interests – and the government, as well as an intra-organizational aggregation of interests within each organization's domain. Internal decision-making was characterized by relative informality (often through gentleman's agreements) and extended to a broad range of policy issues, including the administration of the national social insurance and pension system. A mechanism called *Personalunion* ensured that these frameworks not only intersected institutionally, but also in terms of personalities, by permitting functionaries to hold multiple powerful positions in different political institutions. Moreover, Austrian law granted the Social Partners a privileged position in the parliamentary process, including the absolute right to be consulted on government bills. The extraordinarily high centralization and accumulation of political power thus created clear potential for abuse while lacking effective control mechanisms.

With Austria's transformation into a stable middle-class society, the consensus model and its extraordinary stability mechanisms became increasingly criticized as anachronistic and self-serving (Pelinka, 1981; Talos, 1985).

As a latecomer to the Austrian political scene in 1955, the FPÖ thus stood outside the consociational framework and was well-positioned to condemn its excesses and convincingly call for its dismantling.

Value shifts and demographic change

After the Second World War, Austria initially maintained the closed ideological camps that had existed in the First Republic (1918–38). Several decades later, in the late 1960s and early 1970s, the country entered a period of structural political dealignment encompassing increased electoral volatility and a gradual breakdown of the closed ideological milieus. Greater inter-party competition – the SPÖ was in opposition from 1966 to 1970 – and subsequent social and political reforms undertaken by the Social Democratic majority government under Chancellor Bruno Kreisky restabilized the political system until the late 1970s. However, the prosperity of that decade helped shift the political weight to the (new) middle-class, which embraced a new liberal renaissance, valuing individual choice and personal advancement. From the late 1970s to the mid-1980s, Austrian politics entered a period of 'affective dealignment' which saw growing alienation from traditional politics. The increase in scepticism *vis-à-vis* the state as an agent of progress was mirrored by emerging post-materialist value orientations and a corresponding desire for alternative political choices (Plasser *et al.*, 2000; Heinisch, 2002). This phase was followed by a third period in the late 1980s and early 1990s, characterized by an increasing protest-orientation. A string of political scandals and numerous cases of influence peddling that had surfaced in the 1980s deepened the disillusionment with the political elites (Pelinka, 1996). The emerging culture of protest was thus defined by strong alienation from (and hostility to) those in power (*Systemverdrossenheit*) (Plasser and Ulram, 1996: 394). Some 47 per cent of Austrians therefore preferred 'new parties in the political arena' whereas only 10 per cent had supported this idea a decade earlier (Ulram, 1994: 92).

The shift away from the traditional parties increased to the extent that they could no longer guarantee the economic benefits and social protection of previous times. Growing fiscal constraints and international competitive pressure reduced the economic policy space of the government. The perceived decline in social competence was a problem in particular for the Social Democrats, as we can clearly see from polls conducted during that period (cf. Ulram, 1994: 95). Moreover, the SPÖ was also perceived as increasingly technocratic, with the result that the percentage of people feeling that the Social Democrats represented 'ordinary people' dropped from 57 per cent to 42 per cent (Ulram, 1994, esp. Table 3.1).

Summing up, as a system of ultra stability, the Austrian model found it difficult to react to change. The ensuing crisis of legitimacy therefore presented considerable opportunities for new political parties outside the centres of power that were able to style themselves as (middle-class) protest movements.

Ideological cleavages

A different, but equally important, systemic feature is that of ideological cleavages. When the FPÖ appeared in 1955, it became the political successor to the League of Independents (VdU), a group founded six years earlier which had attracted former Nazi party members and others discontented with the existing party choices. The Freedom Party thus became the indirect heir to Austria's so-called 'third camp' (*Dritte Lager*). German-nationalist and libertarian in orientation, this political tendency stood historically in opposition to both the Catholic Church and clerical conservatism on one hand and Marxism on the other. The political division of the Austrian bourgeoisie into a clerical Austrian nationalist and German nationalist subculture explains the relative weakness of the ÖVP to this day in certain regions. Although a considerable political force in the First Republic, the German nationalists ended up the political losers of post-war Austria as they had no representation in the new institutions of power.

To ensure Austria's emergence as an independent Western democracy, the elites constructed a 'founding myth of post-war Austria as a nation of victims' and of 'Austrians as *non-Germans*' [sic] (Bischof and Pelinka, 1997: 3) although, as Max Riedlsperger (1998: 28) observes, 'at least half of the population' did not share this view. Even the idea that most Austrians were part of a 'non-political [German] *Kulturnation* based on a common language, history and ethnicity was equated [by the political elites] with Nazism, and the rejection of the concept of an Austrian nation was regarded as right-wing extremism' (Wischenbart, 1994: 77).

Standing outside the bipartisan project of creating an 'Austrian nation' had several important consequences for the Freedom Party and its role in Austrian politics. For one, it provided the FPÖ, despite its bourgeois character, with an identity and tradition distinct from that of the Conservatives. It also initially ensured a small but loyal following, particularly among academics and business circles, and allowed the Freedomites to maintain a strong foothold in regions of the country with significant anti-Catholic or German-nationalist orientations, such as the provinces of Upper Austria and Carinthia. It is no coincidence that Jörg Haider was socialized in the German-nationalist milieu of Upper Austria and then launched his political career in Carinthia, from where he entered the national political scene and served as governor for many years.

Perhaps most importantly, the FPÖ's ideological distinctness served it well when the ideas underlying the policies of its political competitors were increasingly called into question in the 1980s. Its libertarian tradition gave the FPÖ credibility when it demanded the liberalization of the economy. Its

German nationalist, and thus unapologetic, stance on the role of Germans and Austrians who served in the Second World War allowed the party to take political advantage when many Austrians were irritated by international criticism that the country had not come to terms with its culpability in the Second World War and the Holocaust – particularly during the 'Waldheim affair' in 1986 (Heinisch, 2002). Moreover, the FPÖ's rightwing nationalist credentials also made it, in the eyes of many voters, a reliable opponent of foreign immigration. Finally, the Freedom Party's distance from the Austrian post-war project enabled Haider to act as what the Austrian philosopher Rudolf Burger terms 'the personified antithesis to political correctness' (2000: 8). By violating the taboos and discourse conventions imposed by elites, the Freedom Party is said to engage in acts of 'symbolic liberation' (ibid.) and thus exposes the underlying lack of sincerity of the elites.

National identity and surrogates

An important structural factor in the rise of populism relates to the ambiguity of the Austrian national identity. The construction of modern Austria was part of a process, which William T. Bluhm (1973) aptly called 'building an Austrian nation'. As late as 1867, the people in the non-Hungarian half of the Habsburg monarchy still lacked an official name and, as Franz Mathis observes (1997: 21), 'a more general feeling of belonging together, of sharing a common spirit of citizenship, of being a national entity'. Instead, overbearing regional and local identities have persisted to this day. Moreover, the country's configuration today – essentially the result of defeats and disintegration – rendered modern Austria's history rather short and shameful. In response, the political elites looked at the nation's long imperial legacy to create a new national mythology (Bischof and Pelinka, 1997) and an identity separate from that of Germany so that 'all Austrian roots in German history became a taboo' (Bischof and Pelinka, 1997: 5). Consequently, when Haider referred to the idea of an Austrian nation as an 'ideological miscarriage', it was considered an outrageous provocation by the political elites, but met with approval by a part of the Freedomite clientele.

The uncertainty of what defines Austrians and their historical accountability entails a collective feeling of vulnerability *vis-à-vis* foreign influences, resulting in surrogate forms of identity (Wodak and Matouschek, 1993; Heinisch, 2002). The Austrian way of life or *Lebensart* – referring to an eclectic collection of customs, values, habits and social mores – has taken the place of a national identity founded on a shared historical experience. This cultural ambiguity has created space for populist mobilization aimed at exploiting latent fears and multi-layered meanings. The Freedom Party's use of the term 'over-foreignisation' and campaign slogans such as 'Vienna must not become Chicago' should be understood in this context, therefore, because 'foreignness' arguably constitutes a special threat to surrogate forms of identity.

Ethnic cleavages and national character

Ethnically rooted in both Germanic and Slavic heritages, Austrian society was shaped by Western, Italian and Eastern influences which are reflected today in the cultural and linguistic differences between the Western Alpine regions and the Eastern lowlands, in the tension between the rural traditionalism of the provinces and the urban progressivism of Vienna and in the clash between a deeply Catholic and profoundly secular subculture.

Of Austria's nine federal states, Carinthia merits separate consideration. The southernmost Austrian state was shaped politically by ethnic cleavages and competing cultural influences. Considered Austria's stronghold of pan-German nationalist thinking, it has been marked by persistent tensions between its German-speaking and Slovenian populations. For decades after the war, the latent conflict between the two sides continued to mobilize German nationalist and right-wing sentiments that had abated in the rest of the country. As the only political party whose past agenda included an explicit commitment to German (cultural) nationalism, the Freedom Party was better positioned than its competitors to take advantage of these cleavages. Haider's speeches to war veterans and (anti-Slovenian) 'resistance fighters' along with the nationalist celebrations of Carinthia's deliverance from annexation by its Slavic neighbour explain, in part, his popularity in that state.

The historical weakness of Conservatives is also related to the fact that the Catholic Church was seen as too closely aligned with Slovenian interests. When the SPÖ's hegemony in the region collapsed due to political scandals and internal conflict, the Freedom Party therefore emerged as the dominant force. In this, Carinthia is an anomaly in Austria and provided the centrally important powerbase from where Haider and his party launched their bid for national success. Taking advantage of Carinthia's authority under federal law, the state continues to pander to anti-Slovenian interests and has served as a test bed for populist national policy initiatives.

External influences

From the latter half of the 1980s, Austrian politics were increasingly influenced by external developments, in particular integration into the Single Market, the European Union (EU) and European Monetary Union (EMU). However, the transition of Eastern Europe, the Balkan wars and a massive influx of foreign immigrants presented the country with a staggering array of political challenges for which policymakers had to devise coping strategies. For instance, growing fiscal problems and the internationalization of the economy required the privatization of state-owned industrial assets, resulting in a net loss of 70,000 out of 102,000 jobs – previously filled by core SPÖ voters – in a state sector which had once been the pride and bastion of the Austrian Social Democracy. Because older workers were hit hardest, the government relied on early retirement schemes as a means of adjusting the labour supply. However, this pushed social expenditure to unsustainable levels (27.4 per cent of GDP in 1991). With nearly 70 per cent of all social spending absorbed by the pension system, painful austerity measures were politically costly, but unavoidable, if Austria was to meet the criteria for EMU entry. Populist actors like Haider, therefore, were able to play on and exploit the fears associated with these changes and appeal to those negatively affected.

Probably no external factor contributed more to the rise of rightwing populism in Austria than the issue of foreign workers and immigrants. Although Austria had relied on *Gastarbeiter* since the 1960s to help reduce labour market costs and keep consumer prices lower than forecast, the fall of the Iron Curtain presented new challenges. The availability of a pool of highly skilled but relatively cheap labour in their immediate vicinity allowed Austrian companies to move low-value added production across the border. Although this benefited the economy on the whole, its impact on the Austrian workforce was uneven, penalizing low-skilled labourers and depressing overall wage levels. This was compounded by a sharp increase in non-labour-related asylum seekers from the former Yugoslavia and other Eastern European countries as well as illegal day labourers (BfWuS, 1992). Consequently, the total share of foreigners was close to ten per cent of the population and 8.8 per cent of the total workforce (Wils and Fassmann, 1994: 342). The situation was especially difficult in Vienna, where immigrants were often channelled into urban ghettos, resulting in high concentrations in some areas. Although Vienna remained generally a safe city, there was a noticeable rise in crime, allowing the popular press and populist politicians to paint a dark picture and thus exacerbate anti-foreigner sentiments.

We can conclude therefore that the specific political arrangements of Austria's post-war model created a range of opportunities for populist agency. The latter was increasingly successful as structural opportunities were boosted by the political and economic changes that occurred from the 1980s onwards.

Populist agency

The quintessential historical model for Austrian populists remains the former mayor of Vienna, Karl Lueger (1844–1910). Acclaimed for his landmark communal and social reforms, Lueger was also notorious for his anti-Semitism and xenophobia as he campaigned in Vienna against the influx of other ethnic groups from the far-flung Habsburg Empire. Like populists later, Lueger employed hate speech and the use of scapegoats to mobilize support, but subordinated ideology to political opportunism.

In the highly fragmented political environment of Austria's First Republic, populism served as a means of mobilizing support. Mass rallies, radical oratory, personality cults and emotional appeals to a vaguely defined 'popular will' along with the summary denigration of political opponents were characteristics shared by all three political camps. The growing radicalization led to the establishment of the authoritarian *Ständestaat* in 1933, culminating subsequently in German annexation and the catastrophe of the Second World War. In response, post-war Austria emerged with a fundamentally different political culture.

In the consensual post-war climate, radical populism became something of a taboo in mainstream party discourse and occasional forays into populist politics were the exception and not the rule.

Populist actors in state and national politics

While largely absent at national level, a more innocuous variant of populism thrived in provincial politics, where it manifested itself in the form of powerful state governors. Called *Landesfürsten* (State Princes), political figures like Eduard Walnöfer of Tyrol and Josef Krainer of Styria were styled as father figures (*Landesvater*) who boasted an extraordinary concentration of political power and patronage. Backed by enormous personality cults, they were defined not only by their unconventional mannerisms, common touch and great oratorical skills, but by their keen sense of the codes that existed in their local societies. They were thus able to appeal successfully to the community which they governed and deepen people's special attachment to it.

Later, in response to the growing scepticism towards politicians, the established parties began recruiting a new type of 'anti-politician' in the form of political outsiders: the so-called '*Quereinsteiger.*' A first such example was the former television ombudsman Helmut Zilk, who was recruited by the Vienna Social Democrats. No longer posing as a traditional *Landesvater* of the Vienna city state, Zilk, as mayor (1984–94), styled himself rather as the outspoken champion of the little people among the powerful. Media-savvy and mindful of the value of celebrity, he was not afraid to take on his own party and defy political conventions.

Current successful state governors such as Erwin Pröll of Lower Austria and Gabi Burgstaller of Salzburg have learned to combine the image of *Landesvater/mutter* with the style and mannerisms of non-politicians in the sense that the 'personality is both brand and program'.[1] Aware of the value of entertainment, they successfully use the rich Austrian event culture ranging from sports to summer festivals as their political platform. During his early years as Governor of Carinthia, Jörg Haider in particular was a pioneer in the exploitation of sports, music and folklore for image-making purposes and made it a part of his political style.

At national level, populism re-emerged with the new political parties. The Austrian Green Party engaged in spectacular acts as well as using an unconventional political style to undermine existing political canons. Drawing on the repertoire of the counter-culture from which many party members came, their style and appearance was designed to appeal to the sensibilities of their clientele – made up of generally young and non-traditional voters.

The populism of the Freedom Party (see below) not only went much further in its efforts to dissolve the existing conventions, it also created a climate in which populist agitation became more common. The influence of the party on Austrian political discourse also affected other political parties. Thus, even the governing Social Democrats felt it necessary in 1996 to recruit Viktor Klima, a telegenic manager, from the oil industry as its candidate for the chancellorship. No stranger to populist rhetoric himself, Klima was thought to compete more effectively with Haider.

Whereas Zilk, Pröll or Klima blur the line between modern political marketing and populism, more typical populists have also emerged. Hans-Peter Martin and Gerhard Hirschmann (at state level in Styria) styled themselves as champions of the common people against overbearing elites and founded party lists bearing their names. The more successful of the two, Hans-Peter Martin (who gained 13.9 per cent in the 2004 European elections) served as a member of the European Parliament. He railed against wholesale corruption on the part of the politically powerful and mobilized his voters with shocking revelations and sweeping accusations regarding his fellow MEPs. However, with only 2.8 per cent of the vote in the 2006 national elections, his list failed to win any seats. Although figures like Martin and Pröll emerged because of a climate that has become more amenable to populist politics, such politicians may arguably represent a way to contain more radical forms of populism.

Fielding populist candidates was one of several strategies used by the mainstream parties to combat radical populism. Another was to refuse cooperation and alliances with them. Applied especially by the Social Democrats under Chancellor Franz Vranitzky (1985–96), this tactic was subverted by the gradual appropriation of Freedomite agenda items such as restricting immigration (Parnreiter, 1994; Heinisch, 2002), which undermined the government's long-term credibility. Eventually, the political exclusion of Haider began to break down when the Freedomites became capable of occupying positions of power due to their electoral strength. In response, the Conservatives in particular argued that the best way to 'defang' Haider was to expose the FPÖ to the burden of government.

Austrian media and populism

Arguably the most important populist actors in Austria aside from the Freedom Party are the tabloids. No periodical is more important in this respect than the *Neue Kronenzeitung* ('*Krone*'). With some two million readers (44 per cent of the reading public), it is by far the largest and most influential print medium in the country and thus no politician dares cross it. The paper's formula for success has been to create a permanent sense of insecurity against which it purports to fight. In terms of ideology, it is rather eclectic. It embraces a diffuse kind of rightwing Austro-patriotism, the flip side of which have been periodic bouts of anti-Semitism, extreme hostility towards immigrants and foreign workers and generally negative views on continued European integration and globalization.

In several campaigns, Haider could rely on the complicity of *Krone* when warning against foreign threats (for example, EU enlargement) or lashing out against those deemed by both the Freedomites and the newspaper as 'un-Austrian', such as controversial artists and immigrant support groups. Yet, the *Krone* is not a Freedom Party mouthpiece and generally panders to what is popular and sustains its readership. On important issues, it also opposed Haider and often caters to the politically successful irrespective of party affiliation. The success of the *Neue Kronenzeitung* makes it difficult for other tabloids and 'medium brow' papers to coexist. Those which do, such as the weekly *Die ganze Woche*, tend to rely on the familiar populist mix of outrage and sensationalism along with a similar thematic predilection.

The Austrian media also stand accused that their excessive, although often critical, coverage of the Freedom Party leader, especially on national television and in newsweeklies, helped create the 'Haider phenomenon'. His notoriety undoubtedly helped with circulation and viewing figures, while the added coverage gave him national exposure and allowed the FPÖ to portray itself as a victim of a leftist media bias. Creating an underdog mythology in the sense of being persecuted by powerful elites was an important part of Freedom Party image-making (see Mazzoleni in this volume re. similar strategies adopted by populists elsewhere). Nonetheless, Haider was very aware of the importance that visual media such as television and lifestyle magazines played in his own popularity and success given that, in his style and appearance, he differed markedly from typical politicians.

Structure and agency of the Freedom Party

Under Haider's leadership, the FPÖ underwent an extraordinary metamorphosis. For decades, it had languished as a small opposition party, receiving between 5.4 and 7.7 per cent of the vote. It catered mainly to anti-clerical libertarians, academics and entrepreneurs favouring greater flexibility and liberalization. The party also included a significant segment of pan-German nationalists, some with rightwing extremist and neo-Nazi sympathies. When two of its chairmen, Friedrich Peter and Norbert Steger, tried to push the party in a more liberal direction, the FPÖ also began co-operating with other parties. Under Steger, the Freedomites even entered coalition government with the Social Democrats in 1983. This, however, riled the Freedomite base to such an extent that it enabled Haider, then head of the Carinthian branch, to take over the party in 1986, with the help of the German nationalist wing.

Following Haider's installation as chairman, the FPÖ underwent three phases, in each of which it adapted to changes in the political context. These three stages can be labelled:

1. 'the political rebel phase' (1986–91);
2. 'the social populist phase' (1991–96);
3. 'the anti-internationalist phase' (1996–2000).

The spectacular growth in support, which saw the FPÖ rise from five per cent in 1983 to 26.9 per cent in 1999, solidified Haider's unassailable position at the head of the party. Its entry into a coalition government with the ÖVP in 2000 heralded the beginning of a distinct fourth period in Freedom Party evolution, marked by Haider's formal withdrawal from the national leadership after international criticism.

Structure of the FPÖ

The Freedom Party's success as a radical populist opposition party was greatly aided by its structure and organization. The emphasis on its 'movement' character was designed to complement its two operational principles: authoritarian leadership and permanent revolution. Frequent rotations of officials and periodic shake-ups of decision-making bodies created a dimension of 'permanent revolution' (Luther, 1997: 290). The party even transformed itself temporarily into a *Bürgerbewegung* (Citizen's Movement).

The most important structural feature was the party's exclusive orientation towards its leader and it adapted itself organizationally to maximize his power. Organizational reforms in 1992 and 1995 diminished the power of party institutions and strengthened the top leadership around Haider. Specifically, representation in the party's (formally) highest decision-making body was replaced by a system rewarding electoral success instead of regional party membership. This process diluted the power of the traditional party apparatus and shifted the priorities away from programmatic development and membership-building to shorter term strategies, popular campaigns and fighting elections. Since it was the most successful branch organization in electoral terms, Haider's Carinthian FPÖ benefited most from these changes, which allowed him to wield influence over the national party long after his resignation as chairman. Furthermore, by depending on Haider's tireless campaigning for their electoral success, regional FPÖ functionaries usually acquiesced whenever he pushed the party in particular directions.

Other organizational changes affected the FPÖ's 13-member Presidium, which was responsible for the day-to-day affairs and was *de facto* the most powerful party institution. Given that its members owed their careers to Haider, these loyalists formally implemented many of his decisions and silenced internal critics (Luther, 1997: 289). The authoritarian nature of Haider's leadership was underscored by sweeping 'purges' of party officials at all levels and of varying political philosophies (Heinisch, 2002). These measures ranged from more or less voluntary departures after people had been humiliated and demoted to outright expulsions following disciplinary action (Zöchling, 1999: 187). In 1992 alone, the Freedomites changed two federal deputy party leaders, one federal party executive, five regional party leaders and a number of candidates and elected functionaries at state and local levels (Bailer-Galanda and Neugebauer, 2000: 115). Many of these had fallen out of favour because they opposed policies or candidates supported by Haider (Bailer-Galanda and Neugebauer, 2000: 36–37). The leader also removed potential rivals and individuals occupying posts he coveted, along with silencing those obstructing the party's ideological repositioning (Zöchling, 1999: 192–194). In this way, he rid himself of the leading exponent of pan-Germanic nationalism (Krimhild Trattnig) and the main figure on the party's libertarian wing, Heide Schmid, who subsequently formed a new party, the Liberal Forum. Haider also flexed his muscles by indicating that displays of allegiance could result in forgiveness for officials who had fallen out of favour. The cult of obedience reached its peak in 1998 with the pledge of loyalty dubbed the 'Contract of Democracy', which he demanded all party officials sign (Riedlsberger, 1998: 31).

When Haider recruited party officials, therefore, he was interested in loyalty to him personally and in already well-known people such as athletes and entertainers. He especially sought those who appeared young and flamboyant like himself, several of whom he recruited on his legendary disco-tours. Subsequent *ad hoc* appointments and quick promotions created conflicts in local branches, but reinforced the image of permanent revolution. Summing up, the organizational changes thus paralleled the FPÖ's repositioning as an increasingly centralized populist party.

Agency of the FPÖ

Organizational modifications alone are not sufficient to explain the enormous power wielded by Jörg Haider both during and after his tenure as chairman. From the start, he took advantage of his access to the media and pursued a strategy of 'jumping the gun' by announcing policy positions and personnel promotions through the media and thus prejudicing decisions before they were internally debated (Luther, 1997: 290). The populist turn of the Freedom Party was reflected in the fact that programmatic objectives were decided according to Haider's personal ambitions and preferences rather than by internal discussions and consensus. Shorter-term objectives and strategies (for example *Aktionsprogramme* and *Wahlprogramme*: 'Action Programmes' and 'Election Programmes') increased in importance at the expense of overall party development and long-term programmatic planning (Horner, 1997).

In Haider's communications strategy with the media and the public, his image was his main asset. He routinely used sport-related and pop-cultural imagery in his political advertising, even changing his attire to match the message. Carnival-type events and highly stylized appearances signalled levity and an entertainment quality that broke with the conventions of Austrian political campaigning, attracting the young and less political voters in particular. Haider's use of imagery, exaggeration and simplification was disarmingly effective. The Freedom Party also engaged in corollary strategies such as employing parliamentary procedures to create difficulties for the government and making frequent use of citizen initiatives and petition drives to promote its agenda.

The FPÖ under Haider subordinated ideology and programmatic direction to political expediency. In its 'rebel phase', the party's goal was to convince the public that Austrians were sustaining a corrupt and wasteful system that catered exclusively to the special interests of political insiders. Thus, the typical protest voters who dominated the FPÖ's constituency until the early 1990s were much more often male than female, and tended to come from an urban middle-class background (see Plasser and Ulram, 2000: 232). Nonetheless, the Freedomites also succeeded in appearing in different guises in different political settings, thus maintaining a pan-German nationalist posture far longer in Carinthia than elsewhere.

The FPÖ's shift to social populism reflected the party's adaptation to the political conditions that emerged as a consequence of the post-1989 geopolitical changes. Economic liberalization challenged Austria's organized market economy, causing a fundamental (identity) crisis of the Austrian model and triggering a surge of new fears and anxieties. It was in Vienna, which was especially affected by the collapse of the Iron Curtain and where the Freedomites had been traditionally weak, that the FPÖ launched some of its most virulently xenophobic and racist campaigns. This tactic proved so successful that, in the 1991 elections to the Vienna state legislature, the Freedomites gained 162,000 votes, increasing their share from 9.7 per cent to 22.5 per cent. The party was particularly effective in attracting former SPÖ voters who had become disillusioned and, by the end of the 1990s, the Freedomites and Social Democrats enjoyed roughly equal levels of support among blue-collar workers (Hofinger *et al.*, 2000).

Beginning in the mid-1990s, the FPÖ increasingly advocated a new Austrian patriotism. Departing from its pan-Germanic tradition, the Freedom Party began championing Austria's specific cultural heritage (Plasser and Ulram, 2000: 227). In doing so, the FPÖ tapped into a traditionalist resurgence in which a desire to 'return to the roots' and 'back to nature' promised an escape from the accelerated process of modernization. Accordingly, immigrants were no longer seen mainly as potential criminals and economic competitors, but more broadly as a threat to the fabric of Austrian society (Betz, 2002). Freedom Party campaigns skilfully contrasted the concept of multiculturalism with that of '*Überfremdung*' (over-foreignization). In 1997, a new party programme explicitly endorsing '*Österreichpatriotismus*' (Austrian Patriotism) was unveiled, replacing its long-neglected liberal Salzburg Programme from 1985 (*Programm*/FPÖ, 1999: 108). The new programmatic approach focused on the Christian character of Europe and was thus clearly intended to mobilize demands based on identity (Betz, 2002). Summing up, the agency of the Freedom Party was above all designed to maintain political momentum and the sense of permanent campaigning.

The FPÖ's failure in government

The diplomatic sanctions imposed on the FPÖ-ÖVP government by (among others) 14 fellow EU member states greatly contributed, in fact, to the coalition's initial cohesion. Once these ended in September 2000, however, the Freedomites were increasingly beset by internal conflict. While, nationally, the party was trying to promote an image of respectability, its grassroots, along with Haider, demanded a return to the successful populist formula. Moreover, now that the FPÖ was no longer in a position to gain votes by attacking the government and was instead responsible for introducing cutbacks, the party began to lose ground in regional elections. The growing dispute within the FPÖ prompted Haider to mount a grassroots revolt against the national party leadership. In response, ÖVP Chancellor Schüssel called for new elections in November 2002, resulting in a landslide victory (42.2 per cent of the vote) for the Conservatives. Simultaneously, the Freedom Party was reduced to 10.1 per cent of the vote, less than half its previous share. Nonetheless, the party renewed its coalition with the ÖVP in 2003, albeit now with much less leverage over government policy.

After further losses in state and local elections, a rebel group around Heinz-Christian Strache of the FPÖ's Vienna branch threatened to force a change in the party's direction. Fearing an erosion of his power, Haider – with Schüssel's support – engineered a coup by the leadership against its own party's grassroots. On 4 April 2005, several prominent party members – including Haider, the national party leader, the vice-chancellor and most of its 18 representatives in parliament – left the FPÖ and founded a new party called 'Alliance (for the) future of Austria' (Bündnis Zukunft Österreich – BZÖ) (Luther, 2006). As a consequence, the old FPÖ was split at all levels, resulting in bitter infighting over party resources and identity. While the BZÖ under Haider continued the coalition with the ÖVP, thus retaining the resources of a party in government, it lacked a following, electoral legitimacy and clear programmatic direction. Only in Carinthia, where Haider pressured nearly the entire local Freedomite branch into joining the BZÖ, did the new party have a real organization and so was able to constitute a serious political force. In turn, Heinz-Christian Strache was elected chairman of the (rump) Freedom Party.

In the first election in which FPÖ and BZÖ competed against each other – in Styria – the former lost all its seats in the regional legislature, but still obtained a far larger share of the vote (4.6 per cent) than Haider's BZÖ (1.7 per cent). The real test for Strache came in the Vienna election on 23 October 2005. Following a virulently xenophobic and racist campaign, the FPÖ succeeded in defying low expectations and polled almost 15 per cent – far more than the BZÖ's 1.2 per cent. Using the same strategy for the federal elections on 1 October 2006, the party managed to increase its vote nationally, securing 11 per cent. No longer under Haider's leadership, the BZÖ, by contrast, barely crossed the four per cent threshold. Even this modest success was almost entirely due to Haider's strength in Carinthia from where the BZÖ drew nearly half its support.

Summing up, the FPÖ's problems as a government party can be largely attributed to its populist characteristics: weak institutions, excessive personalization and permanent mobilization. The party's recruitment of personalities with mainly popular appeal meant that it lacked competent policymakers. In less than two years, therefore, half of all FPÖ cabinet members had either resigned or needed to be replaced, often in embarrassing circumstances. In terms of style and appearance, the public clearly had quite different expectations of a party in government than in opposition (Fallend, 2004; Heinisch, 2003; Luther, 2006).The Freedom Party's inability to fill many positions, especially at the second and third tiers, was a boon for the Conservatives, who often controlled the policymaking process even in departments nominally under a Freedomite minister.

Devoid of a consistent ideological or programmatic framework, the FPÖ sent mixed and confusing messages by simultaneously advocating neoliberal and protectionist positions. Moreover, the focus on personalities and the absence of effective institutions meant that conflicts between political leaders in the party invariably caused irreconcilable rifts between factions loyal to one or other leading figure. The exclusive orientation toward the figurehead Haider meant that his self-aggrandizing antics, unpredictable turns and interference in national and international affairs had a negative effect on the public's perception of the party as a whole. Finally, as the coalition's junior partner (in the sense that the Conservatives controlled the chancellorship), the Freedom Party had only a limited opportunity to take credit for policy successes, whereas any attempt at populist mobilization was constrained by its coalition partner. In short, by being everybody's second choice – those content with the government reforms favoured the ÖVP while those opposed voted for the SPÖ and the Greens – the Freedom Party in government had no significant electorate to which it could appeal.

Generally speaking, the FPÖ's fate in government highlights a key problem for radical populist parties in public office: if they adapt too quickly to their new role, show moderation and compromise, they become just like any other centre-right party and lose their *raison d'être*. If, on the other hand, they maintain their radical posture, they are likely to be deemed unsuitable for high public office and to encounter the problems outlined above. Consequently, the reconstituted Freedom Party under Strache returned to the successful formula of radical identity-orientated populism and all-out opposition.

Conclusion

The proliferation of populist groups in Austria and the results of the 2006 general election suggest that a significant segment of the electorate remains susceptible to this political agenda. In fact, by relying on strongly xenophobic and anti-EU campaigns, the FPÖ and BZÖ together captured some 15 per cent of the vote in 2006. Populism is thus not wedded to the 'Haider phenomenon', as he has clearly been reduced to a regional political factor. However, the increased competition for the same reservoir of voters makes it seem unlikely that any single political figure will become as dominant as Jörg Haider was at the zenith of his power. Moreover, it is evident that the BZÖ faces an uphill struggle in that it shares the FPÖ's programmatic positions, but appears more compromising, whereas Strache's hard-line opposition is of far greater appeal to its target audience.

The strength of populist splinter parties continues to bedevil an Austrian political system which is not accustomed to minority governments and multiparty alliances. Yet, as the tortuous negotiations between the two major parties showed, the return to a centrist Grand Coalition was not a marriage of love. Only the prospect that new elections would strengthen the smaller parties at the expense of the Social Democrats and the Conservatives forced the two to the negotiating table. Moreover, Schüssel's hope of recreating a rightwing triple alliance of ÖVP-FPÖ-BZÖ was rejected by Freedomite leader Strache. This proved doubly ironic, for it made the return to a Grand Coalition inevitable, even though the Freedomites had always lamented this option. Moreover, it confirmed that Strache had recognized that opposition was politically a far more lucrative place for a populist party to be in than a junior role in government.

Generally speaking, the increased competition during the period from 2000 to 2006 between a centre-right government and a centre-left opposition narrowed the opportunities for populist actors. Nonetheless, issues of identity and culture along with personal safety continue to fuel what Hans-Georg Betz (1993) calls the 'new politics of resentment', providing Strache and others with ample room for populist agitation. The tactician Schüssel may have 'defanged' Haider at the price of pandering to far-right interests on immigration and minority rights, but he clearly did not succeed in neutralizing radical rightwing populism.

Note

1. Own interviews conducted in December 2004 and June 2005.

6
Italy: A Country of Many Populisms

Marco Tarchi

Italian style populism

According to some observers, populism found its 'richest testing ground', its 'paradise' in Italy in the late 1990s (Zanatta, 2002: 286). As Guy Hermet wrote, Italy 'has transformed itself into the site *par excellence* of populism's triumph over the classical parties' (Hermet, 2001: 396). During the five years of the centre-right Berlusconi administration (2001–2006), composed of *Forza Italia* (FI), *Alleanza Nazionale* (AN), the *Unione dei Democratici Cristiani e di Centro* (UDC) and the *Lega Nord* (LN), the press has often stressed the populist character of the government and its policies.

If we consider some of the fundamental characteristics of populism identified in the scholarly literature, there is no doubt that the actions of Berlusconi and his allies, both in opposition and in government, clearly match the description of this phenomenon:

(a) the tendency of its leaders to claim for themselves an extraordinary and instant capacity to interpret and articulate the needs of the people;
(b) the impatience with the formal rules of liberal democracy which get in the way of their 'mission' to promote the public good;
(c) the repeated references to the common sense of 'ordinary people' and the traditions shared by the majority of the community;
(d) the attacks on professional politicians and their long drawn-out procedures, and those on intellectuals and trade unionists, accused of wishing to divide the people along class lines.

(Canovan, 1981; Mény and Surel, 2000; Taggart, 2000)

And yet, if we look at the electoral results of the so-called 'Second Republic' (1993–2006), during which time there have been substantial changes in the Italian party system, we do not find any populist movement that has won success comparable to that obtained by the Freedom Party (FPÖ) in Austria, the People's Party in Denmark, the *Lijst Pim Fortuyn* in the Netherlands or the *Front National* in France. The most important of these, the *Lega Nord*, reached its peak with 10.2 percent of the vote in the 1996 general election, before declining to 3.9 percent in 2001, the year in which the party, allied with the centre-right House of Freedoms (*Casa delle Libertà* – CDL) coalition, took its place in government with three senior ministers (the party leader Umberto Bossi at Institutional Reform; Roberto Maroni at Welfare, and Roberto Castelli at Justice) and a number of junior posts. To understand this apparent contradiction of a 'populist' government without a strong movement backing it, we need to examine the specific nature that this phenomenon has assumed in Italy (Tarchi, 2002; 2003).

Whether, like Cas Mudde (2004), we consider populism as an ideology based on the conviction that society is divided between the 'pure' common people and the corrupt holders of power, or whether we consider it rather as a mentality, a *forma mentis*, connected to a vision of social order based upon a belief in the innate virtue and primacy of 'the people' as the legitimating source of all political and governmental action (Tarchi, 2004), it is clear that populism may take on highly different forms and levels of intensity depending on:

(a) the different meanings attached to the notion of 'the people';
(b) the structural circumstances in which it occurs;
(c) the characteristics of its agents.

In particular, populism can inspire structured and lasting mass mobilization, led by a political leadership with a highly coherent programme; or it can translate into a largely improvised style that 'tends to bring together different symbolic materials and to root itself in multiple ideological locations, taking on the political guise of that area which welcomes it', and which appears as a 'collection of rhetoric put into action through the symbolic exploitation of particular social representations' (Taguieff, 2002: 80). These two modes of expression of the populist mentality may present themselves together in a single subject or they may develop separately. The unique character of the Italian case lies in the simultaneous and vigorous development of both dimensions by two markedly distinct groups: the first by the *Lega Nord*, the second above all by Silvio Berlusconi, but also by other political actors. This latter group includes Marco Pannella's *Partito Radicale,* the left protest movement of the *Girotondi* [lit. 'ring-a-ring-o'-roses' groups], *La Rete* of former Palermo mayor Leoluca Orlando and *Italia dei Valori*, the party founded by ex-magistrate Antonio di Pietro, who became the face of the battle against political corruption in the First Republic.

However, whilst the *Lega* has based its appeal on a notion of the people as both *ethnos* and *demos*, and thus interlinked its denunciation of the political system with references to ethno-cultural and territorial identities (Schmidtke, 1996; Biorcio, 1997), the other political entrepreneurs of Italian populism

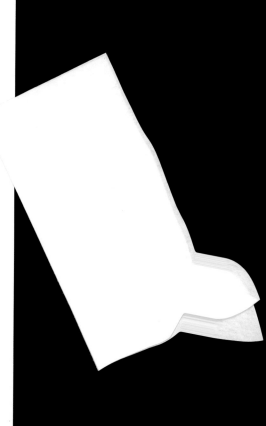

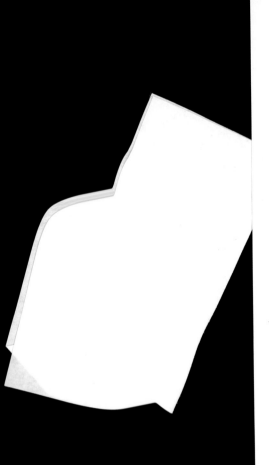

have sought to give exclusive voice to the mass of citizens, supposedly neglected by indifferent and selfish elites, by concentrating on an anti-political, anti-party message (Bardi, 1996; Diamanti, 2004; Mastropaolo, 2000 and 2005; Poguntke, 1996). Indeed, despite the fact that they tend to be considered together as populist parties, we can in fact distinguish clearly between the *Lega* and *Forza Italia*. Whilst the *Lega Nord*, whose actions are patently inspired by the populist mentality, merits the 'populist' label, the party created by Berlusconi is much more similar, in its organization and behaviour, to the other Italian parties as, within *Forza Italia*, the expression of this antipolitical populism is entirely delegated to the leader, who has made it a trademark of his political style, but not a source of ideological inspiration.

The factors behind the spread of Italian populism in the 1990s

To understand the underlying causes of the populist wave that inundated Italian politics in the 1990s, we need to take a long-term perspective in order to identify the contribution of (a) the particular structural factors facilitating this sudden growth, such as the widespread and deep distrust of the political class and (b) the actions of individuals who have deployed populist arguments and stereotypes, with the aim of building a new electoral space or extending an already-existing one.

Even if we leave aside the considerable legacy of over twenty years of fascism – a regime which, strictly speaking, we cannot term 'populist' because its ideology subordinated the people (and the nation) to the state, but whose propaganda contained various populist formulae – we should note that, even before the end of the Second World War, the profound lack of trust in the political class felt by many Italians was being openly expressed. Benefiting from this were those like the *Uomo Qualunque* (Everyman's Front) (Setta, 2005), a prototypical European populist movement and direct precursor of French *Poujadism*, which, in the South of Italy, competed with the Christian Democrats for the moderate-conservative vote in 1946–7. With the disappearance of *Uomo Qualunque* and the fleeting success of those, such as Neapolitan shipping magnate Achille Lauro's National Monarchy Party, who attempted to profit from its legacy, hostility towards the political class and parties, considered as parasites and enemies of the collective interest engaged solely in the defence of their own privileges, remained strong in Italian society for decades, generating chronic dissatisfaction with the functioning of democracy. As the regular Eurobarometer surveys testify, from 1972 to 1994 this discontent reached a percentage of the population almost double that of other European Community countries, never falling below 70 per cent and on some occasions approaching 90 per cent (Morlino and Tarchi, 1996). When, beginning in 1992, the investigations of Milanese magistrates revealed the extent and depth of corrupt networks in public bodies for which the parties – principally those in government, but also those in opposition – were responsible, the psychological gap between the citizens and political elites, which had lain smouldering beneath the surface of this clientelistic system, transformed into a shout of protest which found a willing audience amongst populist political entrepreneurs mainly of the Right, but also of the Left.

In addition to the antiparty reaction which followed the *Tangentopoli* scandals, various other factors contributed to the explosion of populist protest in Italy. First of all, even if surveys demonstrated that dissatisfaction with the political class and the party-politicization of institutions was present throughout the country, it encountered a populist response predominantly in the North, i.e. in those regions in which, according to Putnam and others (Putnam, 1993), the social capital of civic spirit was strongest. We are not, therefore, dealing with a simple explosion of anger deriving from cultural backwardness and/or an inability to adapt to modernization. Rather, it is important to put events within their broader political context. With the fall of the Berlin wall, the anti-communist glue that for almost forty years had ensured a solid relative majority for the Christian Democrats suddenly dissolved, and a part of the northern electorate which had always voted for it became available once more. Moreover, these voters were unhappy with welfare policies which were blamed for a high tax take, a marked increase in bureaucracy and what was perceived as an imbalance in favour of an inefficient and unproductive South (Huysseune, 2006). Casting central government and the despised 'politicians in Rome' as robbing the public purse – summed up in the slogan 'Thieving Rome' (*Roma ladrona*) – and proposing federalism as a panacea for the North's ills, the *Lega* reopened a centre-periphery cleavage which the formation of the unitary state had never completely sealed. By combining emphasis on the 'Northern Question' (Bull and Gilbert, 2001; Gold, 2003) with the classic populist strategy of blaming the political and economic elites, it thus demonstrated how Italian political culture was much more fragmented and contradictory than suggested by conventional accounts (Diamanti, 1996).

The rapid success of the *Lega* between 1989 and 1992 is partly due to these essential characteristics, but can be further explained in the light of other structural factors:

(a) the decline in the attraction of ideology following the end of the clash between the capitalist West and the socialist East, which diminished the capacity of the existing parties to mobilize, and so put millions of disillusioned voters onto the electoral market;
(b) the progressive secularization of society, as demonstrated by the crises of traditional Catholic associationalism, which weakened the links between church institutions and public opinion in areas like the Veneto

and part of Lombardy, opening up a gaping hole in the traditional bank of Christian Democratic votes;

(c) the economic crisis which followed the 'golden age' of the 1980s. This triggered a shift in the epicentre of the economy from the large industrial productive system (subject to painful restructuring and unemployment) to small and medium enterprises, which opposed the imposition of taxes to fund the Welfare State, and was intolerant of the hurdles posed by red tape and the trade unions (Cento Bull, 1993);

(d) the significant increase in immigration from poorer countries and, in particular, the clandestine arrivals on the Italian coast of large numbers of African and Asian immigrants (from 300,000 to 400,000 on average each year, although some of these move on to other European countries). Over the course of the last twenty years, this influx has increased the amount of foreigners officially resident in Italy – without counting those who are illegally in the country – to 4.2 per cent of the total and 10 per cent of the workforce in certain sectors of the economy. The multi-ethnic transformation of many local communities – especially in the regions of the North offering employment opportunities for immigrants – fuelled fears for public order and cultural identity. Consequently, the *Lega* targeted these communities with openly xenophobic propaganda (Cento Bull, 1996), designed to enlarge its electoral base, especially amongst the lower classes, who were concerned about competition from immigrants willing to work illegally for less money and with no union protection.

Populist praise for the virtues of the hard-working 'little man' – characterized as the guardian of traditional ways of life who is tired of the machinations of a political class which had broken its promises and is suspicious of 'progressive' intellectual sermonizing – gained a swift and positive welcome in various sectors of Northern society (the entrepreneurial and commercial *petite bourgeoisie* in particular, but also among manual labourers and farmers). Thanks to the proportional representation electoral system, which permitted it to run alone and therefore highlight the most radical elements of its programme, and the existence of a protest electorate, the *Lega* began to see increasing numbers of its candidates elected to municipal and provincial councils in the North, with the party often holding the balance of power. The spontaneous and aggressive language of its representatives, almost always new to politics and lacking education in good institutional manners, on occasion provoked indignant reactions from the other parties, who, in order to block the *Lega*'s progress, agreed various tactical alliances between themselves, notwithstanding the ideological distances that separated them. This was the case, for example, in the autumn 1993 mayoral election second rounds in some of the larger northern cities. The effect of this *cordon sanitaire*, however, was to emphasize the 'diversity' claimed by the *Lega* leadership, who continued to promote themselves as the genuine interpreters of the 'real country', at war against the arrogant 'legal country'. The anti-establishment message of the party, independently of the success obtained in the North, provoked attention and imitation in other parts of the country, contributing to the strong growth, in the 1990 local elections, in the number of protest lists from outside the main parties and to an increase in abstentionism – which jumped from 8.4 per cent in 1976 to a maximum of 19.1 per cent – above all in the South, where the *Lega* could not directly attract support for its anti-southern polemics and where home-grown movements had not yet emerged. The electoral potential of populism thus became a crucial element in the dynamics of the political system.

Proud isolation, however, ceased being of benefit to the *Lega* following its success in the 1992 general election (when it gained 8.7 per cent of the national vote, including more than 17 per cent in the North), due to the change from proportional representation to a predominantly majoritarian electoral system first at local level in 1993, and then at national level in 1994. This naturally favoured those parties, unlike the *Lega*, willing to form coalitions. Having rejected this option at the 1993 local elections, when it stood alone against candidates of the Left, the Centre and the Right, the party had to accept that, however solid its electoral base, this would generally not be enough to win against opponents grouped together in a coalition (the only exception among the big cities being Milan where, from 1993 to 1997, Marco Formentini served as mayor), especially those on the Left. The risk of being abandoned by a large part of the electorate which it had won over in the preceding years – who were attracted by the party's populist message, but eager to back winning alternatives to the Left in a climate of ever-more-acute polarization – led to the *Lega*'s decision in 1994 to form an alliance with Silvio Berlusconi, who presented himself not only as a potent fellow-traveller, but also as a potentially fierce competitor. As is well known, the meeting/clash between the two most important Italian populist actors produced opposing results: immediate success in the March 1994 general election (albeit with a reduction in the *Lega*'s overall vote-share to below the level reached two years previously, provoking fears of a vote drift towards their new ally), but within months a bitter and acrimonious end to the alliance and, hence, the government. This was followed by years of reciprocal insults and accusations, before a *rapprochement* in 2000 and a new agreement which ultimately led to general election success in 2001 and joint participation in government until 2006.

The *Lega Nord*, or identity populism

Berlusconi and the *Lega* have offered two distinct varieties of populism, sometimes conflicting, but more often complementary. In this lies both the reason for the success, from 2000 onwards, of their alliance, and the roots of the instability in this coalition relationship, in which Bossi's party seems beset by an inferiority complex from which it has rarely succeeded in freeing itself. The need to strike a balance between the different expectations and ambitions of the parties of the *Casa delle Libertà* has made the positions of the *Lega* appear extreme, with the result that the party has not been taken into account in many areas of government business. Only in the federal reform of the state, the *Lega*'s key issue, did it manage to obtain full agreement from its allies, but the party's blackmail potential, even if it has often been a source of tension in ministerial ranks (Albertazzi and McDonnell, 2005), has remained on the whole very limited, and a significant part of their electoral promises has remained on paper (Hopkin, 2004).

To maintain a significant role and not give the impression to its supporters of being completely subordinate to its partners, the *Lega* has continued to exhibit in government some of its most typical traits. In this, it contrasts strongly with *Alleanza Nazionale* which has continued doggedly along the path of complete institutionalization. Unlike most other parties originating in the extreme Right, AN has been very careful not to be swayed by the sirens of populism and has instead spent much effort in establishing an image as a responsible party. The message expressed in the manifestos, newspapers and documents of the *Lega* has thus remained to the point, Manichean and directed at the man in the street. Appeals are made to local identity as the basis for the reconstruction of a homogeneous community, solid and secure, where class discrimination does not exist and where the recognition of certain interests (and values) common to all is clear and not up for discussion. Even if in milder tones than those which characterized the secessionist period of 1996–99, the dream of creating an independent Padania remains a cornerstone of Bossi's speeches, which are designed to exorcize fears that his movement could finish up like the other parties.

The dedication towards the leader that legitimizes, in the eyes of the movement and its followers, any change or U-turn by the leadership (Tarchi, 1998: 151–153), has facilitated this strategy. The rejection of part of the symbolic apparatus built up over the years such as the mass rallies in Pontida, the virtual proclamations of the Republic of Padania, and the pseudo-pagan consecration rites was justified as an indispensable sacrifice at the altar of the party's new goal of federal devolution – one of the central elements of the constitutional reform bill passed by the Berlusconi government but overturned by voters in a June 2006 referendum.

Without forsaking the immediate, aggressive, crude and exaggerated language that has always characterized it, and continuing to recognize the charismatic authority of Bossi following his serious illness, the Lega has attempted to remain as faithful as possible to its programme over five years in government by tailoring its ideological messages to the circumstances. Hence, the party's exaltation of the virtuous, hard-working small entrepreneur and its defence of craftsmen and small tradesmen struggling against major supermarket chains and banks (that is, the powers-that-be who would strangle them), have served as platforms for *Lega* proposals to reduce taxes and reform the pension system to benefit such classes. Meanwhile, in public rallies and speeches, the *partitocrazia* (partyocracy) has continued to be a favourite target, with the power that parties still exercise over society condemned as a source of corruption which leads citizens not to respect the law, overturns natural meritocracy and distorts economic competition through clientelism. Attacks on the Italian state, for many years viewed from a regional and autonomist perspective, have been transformed into criticisms of inefficiency, oligarchic degeneracy and submissiveness to the powers-that-be: supra-national bureaucratic institutions like the European Union (EU), high finance and big business. The emphasis on cultural roots has been revitalized by September 11, which brought a brusque end to the party's criticisms of American imperialism (for instance, during the Kosovo conflict) and heralded a strident anti-Islamic campaign accompanied by calls to restore the primacy of 'Christian civilization'. This was accompanied in *Lega* discourse by a vociferous and sudden attachment to 'Western values', which had been previously repudiated and dismissed as a hypocritical mask for the hegemonic interests of the United States, cast as being in conflict with those of Europe.

The party did not, of course, limit itself during the five years between 2001 and 2006 to statements or acts of protest, but also tried to exploit its position in government. For example, *Lega* ministers attempted to attach their own names to significant pieces of legislation: Bossi took on the task of introducing a stricter law on immigration; Castelli promoted a controversial reform of the judicial system; Maroni was at the forefront of efforts to restructure the pension system. The struggle against the much-loathed globalization, for years a hobby-horse of the movement, continued under the guise of the frequent (and never granted) requests to pass protectionist measures in favour of goods 'made in Italy' – in particular the introduction of high tariffs against low-cost products from China and other Asian and African countries.

In order to take best advantage of the opportunities that the crisis of the First Republic offered it, the *Lega* has, since its inception, presented itself as a populist movement with protest and identitarian features. The party depicts itself as fighting to free its people both from the ills which afflict it from within and from external aggression. Its message to its target electorate has therefore emphasized the issues of security (by demanding tougher measures against crime and immigration), morality (through the battle against corruption, homosexuality and the defence of the 'natural' family and native traditions), and the living conditions of classes less protected by rival parties and trade unions (by advocating commercial protectionism and opposing punitive pension systems for the self-employed). Consistent with the idea of democracy cultivated by populists, the *Lega* appeals to a people held to constitute an idealized community in which class distinctions have no relevance. The people are a genuine, healthy and natural entity, free of the vices that contaminate the ruling class. They are honest and hard-working people, who are thus the polar opposites of those who illegitimately impose their will on them: politicians, bureaucrats, intellectuals, lobbyists and financiers. Despite the zigzags in its strategy over the years, this populist character of the Lega has not disappeared. Rather, it has adapted itself to change. Both in opposition and in government, the proclaimed aims of the movement have remained the same:

(a) to make the voice of the people heard and defend their rights against the arrogance and fraudulence of the powerful;
(b) to protect the people from the dangers that threaten them all around;
(c) to preserve their 'genuine' attributes and the traditions which serve as the basis for their identity.

Indeed, in order to keep its electoral space intact, the *Lega* 'in government' has been obliged to remain a party of continual struggle (Albertazzi and McDonnell, 2005). As a result, during its time in power, it ran the constant risk of destabilizing the administration it was part of by disagreeing with government decisions, such as its agreement with the EU's decision to offer membership to Turkey, a country seen by the *Lega* as a menace to Europe's cultural identity and another source of mass immigration.

...and *Forza Italia*, or the anti-political populism of the 'common man'

A quite different, but no less effective, form of populism is that represented by Silvio Berlusconi. This can be distinguished from the populism of the *Lega* by the fact that it presents itself as a personal attribute of the mentality and manner of the leader of *Forza Italia*, but not of the party itself, which rather has conservative connotations and includes amongst its middle ranks many who came from the old centrist parties which dissolved after the *Tangentopoli* scandal (Poli, 2001). From this point of view, the parallel often drawn between *Forza Italia* and other populist 'personal parties', such as Ross Perot's 'United We Stand', appears forced, because Berlusconi's party, whilst keeping a 'lighter' organization than its competitors, has progressively adopted a permanent structure and can count on a substantial core of activists, leaders and representatives in institutions at all levels of politics.

The style in which Berlusconi presents himself to voters does not leave room for improvisation or chance as the choice of populist tones and themes is carefully tailored to the public that he wants to reach. Nonetheless, it would be a mistake to claim that his relationship with populism is limited to the instrumental use of a communication strategy dictated by market research. Rather, there are, in his personality, way of thinking and behaviour, and in the image that has accompanied him since the beginning of his political adventure, particular traits which allow Berlusconi to fill the role of populist leader naturally and convincingly. The Milanese businessman is presented as a typical successful self-made man who has never severed his links with the middle classes from which he emerged. Despite his enormous fortune, he works hard to appear as one of the common people. He may well be luckier and better able to reap the rewards of his talents, but the message is that he is still made of the same stuff, as emphasized by the often-repeated phrase in speeches: 'I am one of you'. Paternalistic and reassuring, Berlusconi never misses an opportunity to proclaim himself as the interpreter and defender of the popular will. His ideal stage is not the platform of a rally, but the television screen which, as owner of the three most popular private networks, he knows perfectly. His model is not so much that of the crowd-seducer, but of the businessman who is taking on the difficult task of sorting out the accounts, delegating responsibility and ensuring the cooperation of all employees. He interprets and depicts his job as prime minister as that of the CEO of 'Italy plc', who cannot waste time on the burdensome rituals of parliamentary discussions and is obliged only to report to the company shareholders, or rather that part of the electorate which, with their vote, have placed absolute faith in him.

From the moment he decided to enter politics, Berlusconi has frequently reiterated that he is only on 'temporary loan' to politics. He has left the professional world, but wishes to return there once he has successfully completed his mission to 'save the country' from the abyss into which it would be led by 'old politics' (especially the parties of the Left). His pride in coming from outside the corrupt and inefficient elite is a key element in his populist repertory. He has consistently repeated that he is a businessman first and foremost, and was not afraid to claim in Parliament as Prime Minister: 'I do not, have not and will not do anything that is motivated by professional or party politicking' (Berlusconi, 2001: 43). What Hermet has defined as his 'post-ideological anti-politics' (Hermet, 2001: 395) expresses itself through his marked departure from the language and customs that characterize traditional political life. 'Abstract principles' and 'complicated ideologies' are, therefore, explicitly banned from *Forza Italia* which must remain 'a movement' and expresses an open 'aversion to party politics'. As the leader says: 'whenever I hear that *Forza Italia* is a party, I get shivers down my spine' (Berlusconi, 2000: 140). But it is not only the parties, their representatives and workers who are the object of Berlusconi's disdain. Even though he is always careful not to treat representative institutions with disrespect – unlike Bossi, who is regularly sarcastic and scathing towards them – and has declared an almost sacred respect for the Parliament, insofar as it is the prime institution of popular sovereignty, he has often lamented its indecisiveness, comparing it unfavourably with the efficiency of the private sector.

The value attached to the moral qualities of family and professionalism is another important feature of the populist rhetoric of the *Forza Italia* leader. For Berlusconi this serves not just to pillory professional politicians, but also to ensure that whoever is listening feels that he/she is on the same level as the man promising a better future. In order to create this impression, Berlusconi acts as if complicit with his audience, with the aim of appearing as the only sincere and worthy interpreter of what the man in the street thinks. Obviously, he knows his audience, and his celebration of the common man's virtues is targeted to tug the heart-strings not of an idealized and abstract community – like that of the Padanian people evoked by the *Lega Nord* – but of the ordinary public of shoppers and television viewers, i.e. the 'real country' as opposed to the politicians, functionaries and bureaucrats in the seats of power, the intellectuals in universities and newspaper headquarters. Aware that the identity of Italians and their style of life have been forged essentially on the basis of models proposed by the mass media, Berlusconi deploys simple and clear language that the common man will be familiar with from television, and which gives him the satisfaction of being finally able to understand something of the obscure and unsavoury material that is politics. This strategy is apparent in Berlusconi's praise for the common sense of 'the real Italy, the Italy that works', juxtaposed with the 'chattering Italy'.

Completing the picture of Berlusconi's populism are the concessions in his speeches to rhetoric aimed at the weak, the abandoned, the unemployed and the elderly – that is the most disadvantaged of the 'common people', whom the parties and unions of the Left have abandoned in order to defend the interests of those 'insiders' who are already protected. 'To help those left behind is a moral duty' read the slogan printed next to Berlusconi's smiling face in one of the many huge billboards plastered across the country in the run-up to the 2001 election, reminding us that 'compassionate conservatism' is not just an invention of George W. Bush. Indeed, it could not be otherwise for a man who, in the course of the same campaign, attempted to reconcile the seemingly contradictory self-images of the 'businessman President' and the 'blue collar President', both at the service of the nation.

The importance attached to the values of the 'little people', however, does not exhaust the range of Berlusconi's expressions. Whether in front of an adoring crowd or addressing Parliament, the leader frequently speaks of, and to, 'the people'. This is usually done with the aim of implying that politics would be better were it to incorporate some form of direct democracy: the state must serve the citizens and not vice-versa; the citizen must be sovereign; 'democracy will only return when we return to treasuring the real will of the people'; sovereignty belongs to the people, who are its sole possessors; and whoever ignores or tramples on the will of the people severs the roots which nourish the contract uniting citizens. The recognition of a 'demand for direct democracy', for an immediate and direct bond between the people and its leaders, is connected to an exaltation of the popular will that any populist would subscribe to. As Berlusconi says: 'We want the people to lead the state, not the state to lead the people. We want the popular spirit to fill these institutions' (Berlusconi, 2001: 174–5).

On other occasions, he has argued that an electoral mandate, once broken by those who have received it, becomes a dead letter. Interestingly, the first target of this criticism was Umberto Bossi, when the Lega left the government coalition in 1994. In such cases, the people, who have been tricked or fooled, must be able to revoke their mandate, as otherwise their right to decide their political future is *de facto* confiscated. Naturally, all of these statements are weighed and spun according to the needs of the moment. They can serve to reinforce the legitimacy of governmental action, or to deny the legitimacy of rivals when in opposition. Similarly, there are frequent calls for the people to remain united around an idea of the common good which rises above partisan disputes and societal ills like envy and class hatred. However, while not entirely absent, the emphasis put on the dangers that immigration, criminality and corruption pose for the 'healthy' people is much more marginal and sober compared to that found in the rhetoric of other European populists.

Along with the considerable media resources at his disposal, Berlusconi's plebiscitary-based populism played an essential role in enabling him to win over a large part of the electorate hostile to the Left, at a time when the Christian Democratic-dominated party system collapsed amid judicial investigations into corruption and fraud. Given his populist vision of politics and society, Berlusconi is convinced that the sovereignty of public opinion cannot, in a democracy, be limited, even by the actions of elected institutions. As a result, the activities of his government must not be obstructed by restrictive rules because, in expressing the wishes of the majority that elected it, the government must be free to grant those wishes, thus building a 'true' democracy. Woe betides those independent actors, not elected by the people, who interfere, such as the judiciary. Any intervention of this type is cast as impermissible interference which must be rejected, because, in cases of conflict between different branches of the state, 'the last word must always go to the legitimating power of the people' (Berlusconi, 2001: 255).

This plebiscitarianism can also be read in reverse: if a government led by political opponents obtains little support in newspapers and television opinion polls, then this is sufficient to deem that government illegitimate and to call for its replacement. Indeed, the same principle, in this 'audience democracy' vision of politics, applies equally well to both Parliament and the Head of State (Manin, 1997).

The 'appeal to the people' has been a constant and essential component of Berlusconi's discourse, both in opposition – when it served to discredit the legitimacy of those opponents who had forced him to resign by a First

Republic-style coup – and also in the years after he returned to government. As prime minister, he has continued to accuse the old political class of meddling in the affairs of businessmen and all innovative and creative citizens, and praised the simple and linear solutions practised by such 'men of action', contrasting them with the unfathomable alchemies of those who know no job other than politics. Similarly, he has criticized the intellectuals opposed to him, dismissing them as opportunistic layabouts. Justifying the actions of his government, he has claimed that it was 'the people' who demanded the laws approved by his parliamentary majority. The symbolic figure of 'the people' has re-emerged continuously in his speeches, sometimes to signify his supporters, but more often meaning the people, the owners and guardians of sovereignty, who have entrusted him with the sceptre, and ask of him that he exercise the responsibilities and prerogatives that accompany such a role. Moreover, there is no reason to believe that matters will change after Berlusconi's return to opposition following the elections of April 2006. If anything, the electoral campaign – with the strong resurgence of *Casa delle Libertà*, driven by the leader's numerous media appearances – has confirmed Berlusconi's capacity to speak to 'his' people and to convince them to pardon him for his many broken promises.

Populism in government, populism in opposition

Through the *Lega Nord* and Berlusconi, populism has emerged in two new forms in a society already structurally disposed to welcome its message. This double face of populism has been used to capture the sympathies of different sectors of public opinion, divided by socio-cultural characteristics, but attracted by certain common points of the political programmes of these two actors: the personality of the leader, the appeal to the people, the direct communication between leader and grass-roots supporters, the radical criticism of the traditional structures of representation (Diamanti, 2004: 47–8). The pact between the *Lega* and *Forza Italia* has created a positive electoral synergy, and the 2001 success was certainly in part due to the populist themes employed by the *Casa delle Libertà* such as:

(a) its attacks on the administrative inefficiency of a state still steeped in clientelism;
(b) its insistence on the need to deliver clear and strong responses to growing internal and international insecurity, starting with stricter controls on immigration;
(c) the promise to bring politics closer to the real needs of the people;
(d) the proposal to entrust the government of the country to a leader capable of instinctively knowing the needs of the community.

However, the performance of the Berlusconi government did not satisfy the expectations of all those who had voted for it in 2001 and the centre-right was defeated, albeit by a tiny margin (less than 24,000 votes) in the 2006 elections. One may ask, therefore, whether, once transposed from opposition to government, populist sentiments became less acceptable to Italians or whether, rather, it was their postponement or non-realization which disappointed part of the electorate.

Analysing the policies of the Berlusconi government, we can say that some of the issues which were held dear by the populist electorate were tackled, but in much more moderate terms than suggested by the parties' manifestos, especially that of the *Lega Nord*. On immigration, the Bossi-Fini law introduced more stringent procedures for checking up on and expelling illegal foreigners but, at the same time, also led to the regularization of hundreds of thousands of clandestine immigrants already resident in the country. It also enshrined the principle of annual quotas for immigrants from countries outside Europe with employment contracts (79,500 in 2005), thus negating the oft-repeated promise/threat of Bossi to send as many immigrants home as possible.

The hard-line positions taken by the *Lega* against Islam and multiculturalism, including protests in various cities against the construction of mosques, have not stopped the government from seeking dialogue with the Islamic religious community in Italy, even if the Berlusconi government has followed the Bush administration's hard line against Islamic fundamentalism. Similarly, the *Lega's* anti-globalization rhetoric and its calls to rebel against the 'Brussels superstate' of the EU have remained unheard by its coalition allies. The government has continued to support free international trade and to involve itself directly in the drafting of a European Constitution, rejected by Bossi, but signed by the Deputy Prime Minister Gianfranco Fini, who participated in the Constitutional Convention. On the theme of 'law and order' – the fight against crime, security issues in urban areas, drug-related problems and squatting – the government has been more committed, but without making concessions to the more extreme requests of the *Lega* such as the restoration of the death penalty for particularly violent crimes, bounties for the capture of criminals, preventing gay rights groups from demonstrating, etc. The decrease in the tax burden for families and small enterprises has taken place, but the reduction was much less than had been promised, although this was because of factors such as the weight of public debt and not due to a lack of will on the part of the Prime Minister, who had staked much on this issue. The transfer of power from the state to the regions and other local administrations, which should have brought politics closer to the common people and rendered it more transparent, was decided after a long and tortuous parliamentary debate, but a referendum (ironically, an instrument of direct democracy so dear to populists) abrogated the law little more than two months after the April 2006 general election defeat. The other 'anti-*partitocrazia*' measures promised, starting with the reduction in the number of parliamentarians and cost-containment in the ministries, Parliament and other institutions, were also left unfulfilled.

In terms of concrete policies, therefore, populism in Italy has hardly achieved any of the objectives which its standard bearers had set themselves. This is despite the fact that the two most obvious exponents of Italian populism, Berlusconi and Bossi, governed together from 2001 to 2006. This verdict does not hold true for populist *style*, however, which has reached new heights over the last decade. Indeed, it is not just Berlusconi, Bossi, and other members of the CDL centre-right government who have used this style, i.e. the media-heavy celebration of traditional national and popular virtues, continuous exposure of the vices of professional politics, repeated references to the common sense of the people, intolerance of the formal procedures that might obstruct and diminish the decision-making power of the prime minister. Some within the opposition have also chosen to arm themselves with the weapons of their adversaries, fighting populism with populism. This is not true of the main parties of the centre-left coalition, although they have attempted to follow the same path as the CDL by promising harsher policies on immigration and crime, and by criticizing the 'old politics' of corruption, the excessive power of the parties as opposed to government leaders, the inflated number of deputies and the unjustified privileges enjoyed by institutional representatives. Nor is it true of the parties of the radical Left, who have bitterly criticized both the ideas and the style of the populists, accusing them of subverting the democratic spirit. Rather, populist tactics have been embraced on the centre-left by spontaneous movements like the so-called *Girotondi* and Antonio di Pietro's *Italia dei Valori*, which have claimed a monopoly in expressing the feelings of the 'clean', 'honest' and 'virtuous' part of the population and have not hesitated to condemn professional politicians (Tarchi, 2003: 183–200).

Now that the Berlusconi government's time in office has come to an end, one might ask in closing whether populism is destined to disappear from the Italian political mainstream in the near future. The are many elements which suggest such a conclusion:

Berlusconi's image has been tarnished by defeat;
(a) the *Lega* has been weakened by the illness of its charismatic leader and the rejection by referendum of the constitutional reform package which was to introduce devolution;
(b) *Alleanza Nazionale*, whose origins lead it to be viewed as capable of assuming populist stances (that would certainly please many of its activists), is meanwhile seeking to move itself towards the centre in order to compete directly with *Forza Italia* for the moderate conservative sections of the electorate.

On the Left, the success of the *Unione* and the entry of Di Pietro into the Prodi government as a minister makes it more likely that his strongest anti-political impulses will be absorbed. At the same time, however, opinion polls continue to show that the majority of Italians hold very critical views of politics and politicians which are similar, if not identical, to those articulated by the leaders of populist movements throughout Europe. Moreover, anxieties about immigration, the creation of a multiethnic society, the end of religious and cultural homogeneity, the erosion of the sovereignty of the state versus the European Union, and the consequences of globalization, are all important dynamics in public opinion. For the political entrepreneurs of populism, therefore, both those of the present and those of the future, Italy remains a fertile terrain for populism.

7
Switzerland: Yet Another Populist Paradise

Daniele Albertazzi

A fundamental and traditional aspect of Swiss traditional culture is its distaste for popular leaders. (Kobach, 1993: 180)

If one overlooks the enormous influence of Christoph Blocher, it becomes impossible to understand the changes imposed by the Zurich branch of the SVP/UDC to the national party during the 1990s. (Oscar Mazzoleni, 2003b: 81, my translation)

The success of the Swiss People's party (SVP[/UDC]) in the 1990s is probably the most striking in the whole electoral history of the Swiss party system. (Ladner, 2001: 129)

Switzerland poses a significant challenge to the editors of this volume, as some of the country features that have often been seen as impediments to the growth of populism, and which are held to have distinguished Switzerland from its European neighbours, have evolved very considerably in the last few years.[1] Basing itself on the definition of populism provided in the introduction to this book, this chapter analyses the structure and agency interplay which has facilitated the success of this ideology in the country.[2] The chapter will, of course, discuss what is currently the largest western European populist party (in relation to national competitors), the *Schweizerische Volkspartei/Union Démocratique du Centre* (SVP/UDC – Swiss People's party). The SVP/UDC deserves special attention as it has radically affected Swiss political life over the last decade, rapidly doubling its national vote share (and government delegation) to become the country's largest party. Moreover, it has shown an impressive ability to take control of the national political agenda. The SVP/UDC has resorted to a rhetoric that is typical of populist movements across Europe and which has not been toned down, I will argue, even after the party's assumption of greater governmental responsibilities. Although discussing the SVP/UDC is thus useful (indeed inevitable) in this context, this chapter's main aim is to identify the reasons why populism has been so successful in Switzerland, rather than providing a full and comprehensive study of the SVP/UDC (or other Swiss populist movements), that readers can find elsewhere.[3]

In the way of the populists?

Despite Switzerland's traditional refusal to perceive itself as a country of immigration and its isolated position in Europe (factors certainly conducive to the kind of rhetoric employed elsewhere by Umberto Bossi and Jörg Haider), until recently one could have been forgiven for doubting that the populism that had fared well in neighbouring countries might also be successful here. Due to its growth after the Second World War, Switzerland is now one of the richest countries in the world, having enjoyed 'the lowest [unemployment] figures ever in modern history' (Lane, 2001: 204) during the 1960s and been blessed by a degree of political stability that is considered by some (McRae, 1964; Lijphart, 1984) to be one of the keys to its success. Its non-adversarial political culture, respect for its four national languages, attentiveness to special interests, sitting alongside the institutions of federalism and direct democracy, have been singled out as key factors in explaining such stability (Linder, 1998; Kriesi, 2005). Swiss citizens, it is alleged, have plenty of opportunities to influence the policy decisions of cantonal and federal executives. If, as Margaret Canovan (1999) says, there is always a tension between populism and democracy, as though populism wanted to 'remind' democracy of those promises (of self-determination and participation) that the system should, but often cannot, fulfil, then arguably this gap is much narrower in Switzerland than in the rest of Europe. In the context of such a wealthy and stable country – one in which whatever popular discontent there might be can be expressed in a variety of ways and where special interests can find a sympathetic ear – who would ever need populists?

The practice of 'power-sharing', here found in conjunction with the institutions of direct democracy and federalism, was established at national level in the nineteenth century to enable the governing Liberal-Radicals to co-opt Catholics and avoid having all decisions of the executive challenged by an alienated minority through the tools of direct democracy. The principle has been developed further and, as a consequence, major decisions are now always preceded by complex consultation processes and normally represent the outcomes of delicate balancing acts and compromises. As for the seven-strong collegiate executive, the Federal Council had the same composition between 1959 and 2003: the so-called 'Magic Formula'. In this period, the government was composed of two members from the Liberal-Radical Party (FDP/PRD), two from the Christian Democratic Party (CVP/PDC), two from the Social Democratic Party (SPS/PSS) and one from the SVP/UDC. This formula was only changed in 2003 when the SVP/UDC gained a second seat in government due to its electoral success (and at the expense of the shrinking Christian Democrats). The Swiss executive is a microcosm mirroring the nation with such accuracy that the selection of its members can become extremely difficult in certain circumstances, as the political, linguistic, religious, economic and gender cleavages all need to be represented and reflected by an accurately chosen and well-balanced governing team. The same principle applies to cantonal executives, federal courts and even the national football organization. In a country where power-sharing is so fundamental to the nation's political culture, how can any protest party credibly claim to be excluded (and, crucially, to speak *for* the excluded, as populists invariably do)?[4] Moreover, a homogenous, undifferentiated 'people' obviously does not exist in Switzerland since, even leaving aside those class, religious and urban/rural divisions that have been, after all, quite significant to its history, the country is divided into different linguistic regions. This begs the question: Who is the 'people' that a nationally based populist movement can address here?

Finally, this is a country where strong leadership has always been viewed with great suspicion; where many parliamentarians still serve 'part-time'; and where parties are loose federations of cantonal organizations, whose internal divisions run very deep. Parties are weaker and poorer than powerful interest groups, given that their public funding is limited (Gruner, 1984). As a consequence of all this, how can populist leaders, supported by an efficient, disciplined, professional and media-savvy party machine, emerge here, as occurred in Austria and Italy, also discussed in this volume?

Before returning to these questions, let us summarize (albeit very briefly) what has actually happened in Switzerland since the beginning of the 1990s.

The rise of populism

In his study of the SVP/UDC, Oscar Mazzoleni (2003b) divides into three phases the history of the small parties and movements that campaigned on identity issues, low taxation and anti-immigration platforms, thus preparing the ground for the nationally based SVP/UDC. The first comprised the period between 1960 and 1986 and was characterized by the campaigns of anti-foreigner movements such as *National Aktion* and the *Republikaner*. The second period, between the mid-1980s and mid-1990s, was one marked by the limited success of the *Parti des automobilistes* (Party of car drivers) and the Swiss Democrats. The former later became the *Freiheits Partei Schweiz* (Swiss Freedom Party) and still has branches in many German-speaking cantons, while the latter represents what remains of the xenophobic movements of the 1970s and still campaigns against EU accession. Notwithstanding their tactical alliance with the *Lega dei Ticinesi* (League of Ticinesi – LDT), the Swiss Democrats have very little influence and a highly limited following.

Finally, the decade beginning in the mid-1990s is when the themes and rhetoric of populists started to affect mainstream politics (Oscar Mazzoleni,

2003b: 14). The apotheosis of this process is undoubtedly the victory in 2003 by the SVP/UDC of an extra federal executive seat. It went to Christoph Blocher (see below), who is now in charge of the Justice and Police department (thus, importantly, has responsibility for immigration matters). The parties mentioned above developed a critique of the political class and immigration policies which was later adopted by the rebranded SVP/UDC. In the context of the present chapter, however, for reasons of space we are forced to focus only on the third of such phases mentioned by Oscar Mazzoleni, i.e. the sudden success of populism in the last fifteen years or so. We will do this by briefly examining the emergence of regionalist populism in Ticino and by considering the Action for an Independent and Neutral Switzerland (AUNS/ASIN) to see what they may have taught the SVP/UDC. This second section will conclude with an examination of the rise of the 'New' SVP/UDC.

The Lega dei Ticinesi (LDT)

The LDT, confined to the Italian-speaking canton of Ticino, is the only Swiss party to date which has been able to create a centre-periphery cleavage conducive to striking electoral success. Despite its triumph in the 1991 cantonal elections (in which it gained 15 per cent of the vote just a few months after its formation) and again in 1995 (in which it received 18.1 per cent and a seat in the collegial cantonal executive which the party still occupies), the LDT is nonetheless prevented by its very regionalist ideology from playing a major role in Swiss national politics. In terms of rhetoric and style, however, the party – which now suffers competition from the Ticino cantonal branch of the SVP/UDC – has provided inspiration to the would-be populists of Switzerland.[5] Elsewhere, I have defined the party as 'a paradigmatic embodiment of populism' (Albertazzi, 2006: 133) due to its unease with representative democracy, the crucial role played by the concept of the 'people' in its propaganda, the power of the leader within the organization and the party's chameleon-like tendency to borrow keywords and ideas from all political traditions. The LDT provided the SVP/UDC with an example to follow mainly by the way it disrupted a Ticinese political life which had been dominated for decades, if not centuries, by the same parties (and even the same families). It did so through its specific brand of regionalist, anti-centralization, no-global and anti-EU rhetoric – spiced up with constant attacks against the political class.

A factor that certainly helps to foster populism is the apparent anti-EU consensus in the country, particularly in the German and Italian-speaking regions. The LDT was thus very clever to identify the EU as the enemy of the Swiss (and Ticinese) traditional way of life. To see how the anti-EU consensus has developed, however, we also need to consider the activities of a movement that has recently constituted a considerable stumbling block in the way of any hypothesis of further *rapprochement* between the country and the rest of Europe.

The AUNS/ASIN (Action for an Independent and Neutral Switzerland)

AUNS, until recently led by the same Christoph Blocher who, as we will see, has been fundamental to the SVP/UDC's process of radicalization, brings together politicians of both Left and Right, and, importantly, economic organizations as well. This is not a political party, therefore, but a single-issue movement. Founded in 1986, it is now the most successful of all anti-EU Swiss organizations, although it is by no means the only one. AUNS now has over 46,000 members, a solid organization and enjoys access to more financial resources than many Swiss parties. The movement opposes Swiss participation in all international organizations, institutions and alliances, from the EU to the United Nations (UN), from NATO to the IMF. It also defends the *Sonderfall* (Switzerland's 'special case'), which is seen threatened by processes of economic and cultural globalization.

The first success of AUNS was the popular rejection in 1992 of entry into the European Economic Area (EEA) (with a 'no' vote of 50.3 per cent and a clear majority of cantons), on a very high turnout of 78.7 per cent, despite all political parties, except the SVP/UDC, advocating a 'yes' vote. Interestingly, the decision by the SVP/UDC to side with AUNS followed an internal struggle between the party's moderate and radical factions, eventually won by the anti-EU Cristoph Blocher. The 'no' vote was particularly high in German and Italian-speaking cantons, with the core opposition coming from conservative, less-educated, rural voters who tend to support the SVP/UDC in disproportionate numbers nowadays. Despite AUNS' determination not to be seen as dependent on a specific party, its good working relationship with the SVP/UDC becomes apparent if one simply glances at the list of its top activists.

There have been many more votes in recent years on the relationship between Switzerland and the EU (as well as other international organizations). In 1994, for instance, the people rejected the proposal to contribute forces to the UN blue-helmets, while in 2001 a popular initiative launched in favour of immediate negotiations on EU entry was heavily defeated by a 76.8 per cent margin – with the opposition again being led by AUNS. It is true that, on that occasion, AUNS also benefited from a temporary alliance with those who opposed the timing of entry, but not necessarily the principle itself, however again in 2002 the organization came very close to denying the necessary cantonal majority in the referendum on UN entry, despite most of the Establishment being, again, in favour. Admittedly, the battles by AUNS, the LDT and the SVP/UDC 'against' the EU have not always been successful. For instance, an initiative by the LDT demanding a popular vote before any kind of negotiations with the EU could even start, was rejected in 1997. However, the hyper-activism of anti-EU parties and organizations has pushed the issues of Swiss independence, freedom and neutrality to the very top of the political agenda and helped split the country right down the middle on international affairs. The anti-EU lobby does not waste any opportunities to voice anger and alarm at the Union's supposed interference in Swiss affairs (Church, 2003: 9) and, as long as these issues stay at the top of the agenda, there is only one nationally based party that can benefit from them. It is, therefore, to this party that we turn to now.

The SVP/UDC

The SVP/UDC as such was formed in 1971, as the product of a merger between the Party of Peasants, Craftsmen and Burghers (which had been a member of the national government and a critic of the then-dominant Liberal-Radical party since 1929), and the old Democratic Party. Since the beginning of the 1990s, the party has undergone a process of radicalization led by the Zurich-based leader, Christoph Blocher. Like the FPÖ in Austria, but unlike *Forza Italia* in Italy (see Reinhard Heinisch and Marco Tarchi in this volume) therefore, the SVP/UDC was not a 'new challenger' which had to find a political space at the expense of other established parties. Voters already knew the party when it started to radicalize by adapting a traditional, family orientated conservative ideology – in line with what was happening elsewhere in the Alpine region. The process was led by the Zurich party-branch and profoundly changed it (despite opposition from the Berne branch). However, such reorganization is not comparable to the challenge of creating a successful campaigning organization from scratch in a country where, despite increasing dissatisfaction in recent years with government performance, the ruling parties have attracted, on average, between a minimum of 68.7 per cent and a maximum of over 80 per cent of votes at elections held over the last four decades.

At present, the SVP/UDC's rhetoric insists on the following key ideas (see SVP/UDC, 2003; 2007). First, there is criticism of a political system (the 'elite', the 'political class', *'une clique'*) which Blocher depicts as self-serving, if not outright corrupt, and conspiring behind the backs of 'the people'. Switzerland does not 'belong' to this elite, as even its very creation as a nation is owed to a process generated 'from below' (Blocher, 2006). The people are sovereign and, together with parliament, have legislative power. Their ability, therefore, to take decisions affecting the life of the country should be guaranteed and not find any limitations in international treaties/ conventions, such as the European Convention on Human Rights. Fighting on behalf of the people also means questioning how public money is spent by the elite. Second come identitarian politics: anti-immigration and opposition to 'bogus' asylum seekers, with crime statistics being used to highlight the 'dangers' of the melting pot (SVP/UDC, 2006: 3). It is not by chance that the first referendum ever launched by the SVP/UDC in 1993 was concerned precisely with 'illegal immigration'. Third, there is the defence of the

Sonderfall, the alleged uniqueness, isolation, prosperity and neutrality of Switzerland, coupled with a stance *vis á vis* the EU and other international institutions and associations that closely resembles that of AUNS. Finally comes a marked conservatism in social affairs (i.e. law-and-order rhetoric), alongside the fight for tax cuts and public expenditure reductions (see Betz, 2005).

In terms of its ideology, therefore, the SVP/UDC closely resembles other right-wing populist formations covered in this volume. Like them, the party embodies some of contemporary Europe's most blatant contradictions: between hyper-modernism on the one hand, and the desire to protect native 'traditional' cultures on the other; between the perceived need for immigrant labour on the one hand, and the schizophrenic desire not to *see* and have to deal with foreigners on the other (as the party's slogan says: 'yes to foreign workers, no to immigrants'). The only aspect that partially differentiates the SVP/UDC from the 'ideal type' of populist party defined in the introduction to this volume is that, despite Blocher having gained a great reputation within its ranks as leader of the radicalization process, he remains just one of the party's leaders. Moreover, there are still two different visions of the party's future battling against each other (with the Bernese branch more moderate and conservative than the now hegemonic Zurich branch). Unlike *Forza Italia* in Italy, therefore, the SVP/UDC has never been purely and simply 'a personal party' (Calise, 2000).

The radicalization process has paid dividends in electoral terms, with the party nearly doubling its national vote share in about ten years, following sweeping successes in cantonal parliaments. This happened first at the expense of extreme formations such as the Swiss Democrats, and then other 'bourgeois' parties (FDP/PRD and CVP/PDC), while the Social Democrats (SPS/PSS) and the Greens have also benefited from a climate of increasing polarization – almost in the style of adversarial democracies. This is an interesting process in a country where the Left has traditionally been weak.[6]

Table 7.1 Federal elections results in Switzerland, 1995–2003 (percentage of valid votes)

Party	1995	1999	2003
SVP/UDC	14.9	22.5	26.7
Soc-Dem (SPS/PSS)	21.8	22.5	23.3
Rad-Lib (FDP/PRD)	20.2	19.9	17.3
Christian-Dem (CVP/PDC)	16.8	15.9	14.4
Greens (GPS/PES)	6.5	5.3	8
Others	19.8	13.9	10.3

Source: The Swiss Statistical office, data quoted in Selb and Lachat (2004: 1).

The salient aspects of the 2003 federal election (the most recent at the time of writing) are the following, as Peter Selb and Romain Lachat (2004) explain:

1. An increase in voter turnout of exactly 3 per cent from 42.2 per cent in 1995 to 45.2 per cent in 2003. After a campaign marked by rather aggressive tones and a high level of personalization, with the SVP/UDC having asked for an extra governmental seat for some four years, this election was perceived by voters of all political inclinations as important and, as mentioned above, this contributed to some considerable polarisation (with the Left gaining over 30 per cent of votes for the first time).
2. More young people bothered to vote: a factor in the SVP/UDC's favour.
3. Far from levelling out, the participation gap between men and women (who were only granted the right to vote in 1971), increased. This also worked to the SVP/UDC's advantage as in line with what happens elsewhere in Europe, the party's average voter is more likely to be male (see Alfio Mastropaolo's contribution to this volume).
4. Analysis of the vote also shows that the SVP/UDC now increasingly attracts voters from the FDP/PRD and CVP/PDC, while at the same time successfully maintaining its core constituency. The party is no longer confined to Protestant areas and attracts support from all social classes and especially from the poorly-educated. While 91 per cent of votes still come from German-speaking cantons, the party is slowly, but surely, growing in the Swiss Romande and has now shed its traditional image as a rural party. (Ladner, 2001: 138) Among blue-collar workers, support for the SVP/UDC has increased in 2003.

There is little doubt that the party has been able to articulate (and, at the same time, push further up the political agenda) fears and grievances that are now deep-seated within the Swiss electorate. We are therefore finally in a position to ask what has made the SVP/UDC's impressive growth at all possible by considering the interplay between structural factors and agency in contemporary Switzerland.

Opportunity structures

Consociationalism and direct democracy: a populist paradise?

There are three fundamental tools through which Swiss direct democratic rights are exercised: the compulsory referendum, the optional referendum and the initiative. Clive Church (2004b: 272 and 273) briefly explains the differences between them as follows:

A referendum must be held as regards both changes to the constitution and the ratification of certain types of treaties [compulsory referendum] ... referenda may also be used to challenge federal legislation [optional referendum]...At the same time the Swiss can call initiatives, calling for constitutional changes...if they can collect 100,000 signatures [the initiative].

Direct democracy thus 'provides efficient instruments to exert continuous pressure on policy making of the established political parties' (Skenderovic, 2001: 5).

Let us look at 'initiatives' for a moment. It is true that they are rarely passed when put to voters – since their introduction, their average success rate is a modest 10 per cent. And yet their importance should not be underestimated. First, more of them have proved successful in recent years (Linder, 2003b; Trechsel, 2003: 481) and, more generally, it is becoming less common for voters to 'simply' follow the lead of the government, come what may (Kriesi, 2006). Second, their very existence is in itself a constant reminder of who the ultimate sovereign really is, especially given that, unlike Italy (where a referendum can only repeal legislation *ex-post*), the initiative empowers voters to do much more than simply say 'no'. Third, honourable defeats still help considerably in pushing certain themes to the top of the political agenda and in enabling what are sometimes small groups and organizations to enjoy the limelight, attract supporters and increase their influence. This is why 'intense' minorities that launch (or become involved with) initiatives and optional referendums 'invest in the defence of their cause independently of their chances of success' (Kriesi, 2006: 611). Fourth, sometimes initiatives only fail (or else are withdrawn before being put to the vote) for the very reason that parliament has already been pressurized to act on a disputed issue, either by introducing new legislation or by putting a 'counter-project' to the people that addresses some of the worries informing the original proposal. A proof of the effectiveness of the tools of direct democracy is the fact that the government, despite often having it its own way (Trechsel, 2003: 495), has sometimes failed to win over citizens and prevail precisely in those referendums on issues particularly dear to populists: taxation, immigration policy and relationships with international bodies. Consultation and dialogue normally work in avoiding embarrassment for the government; however, on certain issues voters are not always willing to compromise.

Besides offering great opportunities to lobbies and campaigning organizations, direct democracy also exerts important effects on the political system. Such is its disruptive potential (especially in a divided country like Switzerland) that power sharing and negotiation become absolute necessities (e.g. Neidhart, 1970). As Hanspeter Kriesi comments: 'By forcing all the participants at every stage in the decision-making process to anticipate a possible popular veto at its very end...[referendums]...have stimulated the integration into the decision-making process of all powerful interest-associations capable of launching a referendum and/or winning a popular vote' (2005: 23).

Not only, therefore, do all major parties need to be involved in the decision-making process, but often interest and citizen organizations, too, as some of them have the organizational muscle to veto legislation (Klöti, 2001: 24). The system works so well, in fact, that since the introduction of the 'Magic Formula' the proportion of bills challenged by referendum has fallen to seven per cent (Papadopoulous, 2001: 40). Switzerland is thus characterized by a system of 'mutual accommodation' (Lijphart, 1984; Linder, 2003a) and must be studied alongside other 'populist paradises' such as Belgium and Austria where the growth of anti-politics (to use Alfio Mastropaolo's terminology) has been impressive.

Arguably, in fact, consociational practices, far from being impediments, provided very fertile ground indeed to the populist anti-system rhetoric of the SVP/UDC. As important as they certainly were, anti-immigration and law-and-order propaganda were underpinned by an idea that always provides the very foundation of populist ideology: immigration may (theoretically at least) cease completely and old foes may turn into friends; however, the claim that a party is ready to 'stand up alone', come what may, and defend the rights of the 'people' against a political system where all major political actors (from both Left and Right) are basically the same is the populist rhetoric's *sine qua non*. They are 'all in it', self-serving, plotting behind the backs of citizens and equally responsible for the ills affecting the country: this is indeed the philosophy that has provided the cornerstone of the SVP/UDC's recent propaganda (see the programme for the 2003 national elections, SVP/UDC, 2003: 12). Faithful to its mandate, the more its electoral weight increases, the more the party claims to be uninterested in the privileges and perks of office and only bent on delivering its programme against anyone else (ibid., 6 and 7).

Faced with a powerful, if collegial executive, the Swiss parliament does not even have the power to sack it. Moreover, parliament often lacks courage – because controversial decisions could easily be overthrown by popular votes – and is quite secretive in its proceedings, since most of the work required to strike compromises on legislation is done by restricted committees, where both the major parties and interest groups need representing. Furthermore, 'initiative entrepreneurs' – i.e. people who pursue their own agendas and use organizations such as AUNS to gain political clout (Kobach, 1993: 134–136) – fully exploit the weakness of political parties and can always threaten to take action if their grievances are ignored. Often such groups are more cohesive (and, importantly, wealthier) than the parties themselves, as discussed above. They can therefore afford to 'buy' the support of MPs, or exchange favours with them, not to mention that some MPs are sent to parliament precisely thanks to the support of business groups and/or associations. When several big groups (e.g. employer organizations, financial associations or the big unions) agree to something, the momentum created is irresistible (Mach, 2003). Far from being a democratic heaven, Swiss politics can thus be depicted and perceived as a matter for the usual powerful few to decide, following a certain amount of horse-trading and strictly behind closed doors.

What is interesting, of course, is that those who benefit from this slide towards 'corporatist democracy' are sometimes the very same people who vociferously complain that citizens are being ignored. Not only Cristoph Blocher, a wealthy businessman who can also count on the support of AUNS, falls into this category, but the founder of the LDT, too. Giuliano Bignasca is another politician who has used his financial muscle to advance his own political agenda, for instance by providing essential funding to his party's own medium, the newspaper *Il Mattino della Domenica*.

In a context in which identification with, and trust in, the governing parties has declined sharply since the beginning of the 1990s (Kobach, 1993: 90; Oscar Mazzoleni, 2003b: 56–59; Ladner, 2003), with all parties losing members year-by-year – up to 30 per cent since the 1960s – the SVP/UDC is the only organization whose membership has in fact grown. Despite various signs of detachment from the political system in fact – turnout at national elections being the lowest in western Europe – when people feel able to affect the course of events, more of them participate and turn out to vote. Controversial referendums such as that for the 'abolition of the Army' in 1989 (attracting a 68.9 per cent turnout), or on membership of the EEA (78.3 per cent), have been well attended. So, in the general climate of disillusionment with political parties, propaganda campaigns that touch on emotive issues such as crime, defence, immigration, the EU and political events that are seen as worth participating in, do generate higher turnouts.

Consociationalism makes it impossible for an opposition to offer a clear alternative to the electorate since there is no chance that parties will alternate in power and then pursue 'their own' programmes. As a consequence, in Switzerland, the role of opposition is often 'taken over' by direct democracy. The SVP/UDC has learned to exploit the opportunities this provides by breaking the rule of governmental solidarity and keeping one foot in and one foot out of government. This is more easily done here than elsewhere given how the Swiss system works: since it is understood that all members of the collegial government are expected to defend collegial decisions, their 'own' parties are not at all embarrassed at 'having to speak' against their own representatives in government. The same has happened to the LDT in Ticino, which has at times found itself supporting more radical positions than its own governmental representative. Furthermore, the SVP/UDC has sponsored or launched several referendums on foreign policy, illegal immigration and asylum and, in so doing, has reinforced its image as the 'odd one out' – a logic which, in part, recalls that followed by the *Lega Nord* in Italy (Albertazzi and McDonnell, 2005) – although the *Lega* must often satisfy itself with symbolic initiatives. Through the means of direct democracy, the SVP/UDC, even when ultimately defeated, can claim to have helped give voice to a constituency sometimes comprising 40/45 per cent of voters (i.e. often well above its own electorate) on issues of identity, 'Europe' etc.

To summarize: the logic of consociationalism prepares the ground for 'anti-system' propaganda, but also makes it almost inevitable that a large party will participate in government, even when it is very critical of its allies. At the same time, direct democracy – the very existence of which makes consociationalism and power-sharing a necessity – provides populists with invaluable tools to create an adversarial climate and tap into people's resentment, without even endangering the government's survival. We now need to see the 'new' version of the SVP/UDC in power for longer in order to understand whether such a 'double personality' can be sustained in the longer term (i.e. whether it is precisely this dialectic between 'responsibility', on the one hand, and 'radicalism', on the other, that makes it attractive to voters), or whether at some point the Swiss public will be tempted to call its bluff.

As Yannis Papadopoulos has argued (2005: 73) 'anti-party' feelings tend to go hand-in-hand with other motivations – often in recent years, the fear of immigration coupled with the willingness to defend a community that is perceived as being under threat. Having established the importance of the political system in the emergence and growth of the SVP/UDC, we now need to consider which elements of Swiss political culture could be exploited and made sense of in the context of a new political rhetoric. We need to turn, therefore, to the culture of localism and discuss how this has been affected by processes of globalization and immigration.

Political culture: localism, the 'militia system' and opposition to Europe

'In essence, the old Swiss Confederation was simply a series of alliances among thirteen small sovereign states, bound together by a common desire for security' (Codding, 1961: 24). Things have progressed since the seventeenth century, and it is now increasingly difficult for cantons to discharge their duties in splendid isolation. It is not by chance, however, that one gains Swiss citizenship by being accepted as a citizen of a certain *commune*, and, as a consequence, *canton*. To answer yet another question posed at the beginning: the 'people' of the populists can only be a very diverse and heterogeneous people in Switzerland. However, populist rhetoric can still work well. Crucially, in fact, it is the 'diverse' that 'we' know which is respected, the 'diverse' that has always 'been here', as 'Multicultural coexistence...has failed...to develop open attitudes toward *new* minorities' (Skenderovic, 2001: 7, my emphasis).

Cantons and communes are the entities with which all Swiss strongly identify, while nationalist feelings are more widespread in German-speaking areas. Moreover, in many cantons, the system of voluntary, non-remunerated self-administration by citizens (the 'militia system') is simply essential to the discharge of public duties, given the very small size of cantonal bureaucracies. The fact that even in the national parliament various politicians still serve part-time while keeping their jobs as lawyers, architects etc., is also explained by this culture of self-government and participation.[7] Besides its practical implications, this culture has obvious beneficial consequences, in so far as it can empower those citizens who are willing to take part. It has also been exploited to generate a very powerful narrative that pits the good, honest 'locals' (who know 'what is needed' for the good of their 'village', 'region' etc) against interfering bureaucrats from the capital (when not even Brussels). Freed from the yoke of various elites, these communities can preserve their purity and unique characters, can still be 'masters in their own homes' (to quote a famous slogan of the Italian *Lega Nord*). Or so the story goes. Since localism and voluntarism remain very powerful myths in Switzerland, it is not surprising that the SVP/UDC has been active in defending the 'militia system' at all levels and has posed strong resistance to all proposals to turn even the national parliament into a more professional body.

If anything, the awareness that 'the smaller rural and mountain municipalities continue to be the decisive social and institutional connection and are, therefore, identity-building collectives' (Wiesli, 2003: 375) now proceeds hand-in-hand with hard Euroscepticism, the strength of which can only be understood as one considers the 'broader popular uncertainties' (Church, 2004a: 271) that it is able to mobilize. Populist movements across Europe have elaborated a new 'ideology of home', a vision of the 'lost' homeland which, while often expressing nostalgia for what is, in reality, a radically 'reconstructed' past, nonetheless provides some sense of security against the advance of globalization, the 'European superstate' and the perceived loss of identity. To say it with Zygmunt Bauman, 'community' has become 'another name for paradise lost – but one to which we dearly hope to return, and so we feverishly seek the roads that may bring us there' (2001: 3).

Myths of independence and neutrality (Linder, 2003a: 15), localism and 'Swiss exceptionalism' are all present in the SVP/UDC's electoral publications (e.g. SVP/UDC, 2007). 'Lost' in an EU-sea, by which it is surrounded on all sides, yet mindful that its economic prosperity depends on it, Switzerland conceives of the EU as an imposition. In the hands of the LDT, AUNS and now also the SVP/UDC, the alliance between the small, 'natural', 'knowable' (Williams, 1973) democratic communities of the Swiss cantons becomes a myth through which identities are preserved and 'homogenization' is resisted.

What could pro-Europeans put forward in order to challenge such narratives in a country that has always seen itself as a special case? Justifying the idea of more engagement with the EU, or else international organizations such as the UN or NATO, by simply saying that 'there is no other choice', has understandably left a lot of people cold.

'First the Italians, then the Turks, now the Kosovars'

Since it is obvious that increasing immigration and the 'clash of civilizations' in which Christianity and Islam are said by some to be engaged have provided excellent opportunities for populist rhetoric (always in need of new enemies), this section will only touch briefly on the issue. Naturally, this needs to be seen alongside Switzerland's love of its uniqueness and splendid isolation.

Despite a decrease in the number of new migrants reaching Switzerland during the 1990s, the Swiss population now includes very large numbers of foreigners by European standards due to the arrivals of economic migrants in the booming period of 1946–75 as well as the increase in asylum applications in the 1980s: 23 per cent of the overall population in 2005. Immigration brought obvious benefits to the Swiss economy by offsetting the ageing of the natives. Switzerland has never been particularly keen to grant its foreign workers citizenship rights, even if, until recently, the majority of foreigners were coming from neighbouring countries, such as Italy. Starting in the 1980s, however, the number of non-EU migrants, and particularly those from Islamic countries, has risen very sharply. If southern Europeans had already upset the delicate balance between Protestants and Catholics among the population, the arrival of Muslims posed further problems of integration, acceptance and racism (testified by an increase in violent attacks on, and even murders of, foreigners throughout the 1990s).

The SVP/UDC has been quick to capitalize on the issue (e.g. SVP/UDC, 1999). Its rhetoric has resembled that of the far Right in other European countries, focusing in particular on the alleged link between immigration and criminality and the 'abuse' of the asylum system. On the other hand, preoccupation with what some perceive as an excessive number of migrants is not a 1990s novelty. Rather, just like the *Lega Nord* in Italy, the SVP/UDC only brought into the open and gave new legitimization to a resentment that had already been highlighted, as we have seen, by the number of initiatives called on the issue since the 1970s.

It's the economy, stupid...

The thesis that populist parties attract large crowds of 'modernization losers' (Betz, 1994; Kriesi, 1999) holds much water in the case of the SVP/UDC. Of all the factors mentioned at the beginning of this chapter that have changed considerably in recent years, the economic outlook of the country throughout the 1990s is the most apparent. Starting at the end of the 1980s, the Swiss economy entered a phase of uncertainty from which it has now only partially recovered. To mention but a few of the problems the country had to face: unemployment went up (from 0.6 per cent to 5.2, between 1990 and 1997) (Oscar Mazzoleni, 2003b: 46), casual and part-time work increased, exports suffered and economic stagnation caused the closure of companies that had symbolized Swiss success (e.g. Swissair).

Although the Swiss economy had started to recover in 1997 (e.g. OECD, 1999), 'growth of per capita income has been weak and considerably below the OECD average for a number of years' (OECD, 2006: 1). These economic difficulties, besides making the lives of some less secure (especially those at the bottom of the social scale, whose share of national wealth has decreased steadily throughout the 1990s), have also added to the worries of those spared the worst. The response of the executive to the crisis has been to push for greater 'modernization' and 'liberalization', which are inevitably paid for through even less job security. Moreover, the level of provision guaranteed by the welfare system is now increasingly under scrutiny in a country that shares with the rest of Europe the problem of an ageing population and a shrinking workforce and there is huge pressure on the executive to restrain social spending growth (OECD, 2006). All in all, the 1990s have provided definitive proof that Switzerland was far less special and less safe than some liked to believe. As a consequence, and mirroring what happens in other countries, those who earn a good wage now increasingly support the Social Democrats (Ladner, 2001: 138), while blue collar workers, as well as those who feel the economic situation has deteriorated, are instead increasingly voting for the party that wants to preserve Swiss exceptionalism.

Changing media

With about four in five participating voters (i.e. excluding abstainers) using newspapers and television to make up their minds during campaigns (Trechsel and Sciarini, 1998), the role of the media is here, as elsewhere, crucial. Luckily for Europhiles, unlike the UK, Europhobia is not a constant in the Swiss media. There are no campaigning tabloids (in the British sense) and papers are naturally restricted to the three main linguistic regions, thus striving to keep in tune with the area they serve (with the French-speaking characteristically being pro-Europe). Different regions are served very differently by the press, with the most populated being privileged in enjoying a choice of more than one daily paper.

Overall, newspapers and especially television (most of which is public service broadcasting) have not been enamoured with the language and rhetoric of the 'New' SVP/UDC. However, to some extent this has actually helped the party in its pursuit of its 'new course'. Given the 'us' against 'them' logic fostered by the party, when media criticism focuses on the SVP/UDC the other bourgeois parties can be accused of receiving preferential treatment. Adopting a typical populist strategy discussed by Gianpietro Mazzoleni in this volume, Blocher has turned to his advantage what he perceives as punitive treatment by the media, by accusing them of either being part of the usual 'elite' or of being dominated by left wingers. His party has also 'retaliated' against public television by putting forward proposals for a reduction of the licence fee and by suggesting in its most recent electoral programme that public service broadcasting could be privatized (see SVP/UDC, 2007: 70–73). The Zurich branch has also made use of more or less directly controlled media through its own party's paper, *Der Zurcher Bauer*, but also the SVP/UDC – sympathetic and anti-EU magazine *Schweizerzeit*. Furthermore, mirroring the *Lega Nord* in Italy, cantonal sections of the party have happily resorted to the cheap and still effective medium of the wall poster, especially as far as immigration and taxation were concerned.

The way the Swiss media are changing also works in the populists' interest. While the party press is disappearing and in the context of increasing media ownership concentration (all phenomena that, again, put Switzerland on a par with the rest of Europe), papers have come to rely very heavily on advertising and thus need to attract larger readerships in order to survive. The consequences have been increasing processes of simplification of messages, the personalization of reporting (focusing on the private lives of candidates, etc) and dramatization (whereby every piece of news is reduced to 'a clash' between easily identifiable entities of 'good' and 'bad'). All these processes make populists interesting from a media perspective, as their language and rhetoric already follows, and at the same time helps to foster, this very same logic. Following these trends, even public television now shows considerable interest in political campaigns and has talk shows where tabloidization processes of political communication are increasingly apparent (e.g. the programme *Arena*, in German-speaking Switzerland, which has greatly facilitated SVP/UDC confrontationalism).

Conclusions: naming the agent

The deeply ingrained culture of consociationalism and power-sharing – essential to the 'smooth functioning' of a divided country where direct democracy is so central to the political process – has provided the most important opportunity structure of all for the emergence of populism in Switzerland. While the wealth of the country during past decades, the possibility to 'export' unemployment (by sending guest-workers home) and the lack of a perceived external 'threat' have all stood in the way of the emergence of a significant populist challenge (despite the presence of widespread anti-foreigner and isolationist feelings), as soon as Switzerland awoke to a rapidly changing globalized world and its supposed uniqueness, the independence of its 'knowable' communities and its economic wellbeing could all be portrayed as having come under fire, the stage was set for a populist showdown. Since the beginning of the 1990s, some of Switzerland's neighbours such as Austria and Italy provided examples of populist movements having gone from strength to strength, even taking on major governing responsibilities, after having contributed to seriously disrupting previous political equilibria. Then there was proof of growing resentment *vis á vis* Europe provided by campaigning organizations. Processes of personalization of politics and changes in the logic of the media were also at hand.

Opportunities such as these are not always exploited, however, as Duncan McDonnell explains in this volume with reference to Ireland. Moreover, charisma is an increasingly required quality for leadership in mass mediated democracies (Mény and Surel, 2004: 145). A relaunch of the SVP/UDC – surviving on somewhere around 12 per cent at the end of the 1980s – and a 'conversion to populism' thus needed to follow the path of charismatic leadership.

A self-made man personifying the allegedly 'Swiss' virtues of determination and hard work who had managed to become the major shareholder of the company that had employed him (now Ems-Chemie Holding AG), Christoph Blocher also had the necessary ability to address people's concerns by using simple and media-friendly language. Furthermore, as in the cases of Silvio Berlusconi in Italy and Giuliano Bignasca in Ticino, Blocher's personal wealth was helpfully at hand to fund his ambitions, given that the SVP/UDC had a history of investing very little in political campaigns (Kobach, 1993: 127). The great autonomy that cantonal sections of political parties enjoy was also turned into an advantage as Blocher moved away from the traditional moderate line of his party embodied by the Bernese SVP/UDC. At the head of the Zurich branch since 1977, Blocher was able to build a solid power base in a canton where the far Right had traditionally been strong (and where certain slogans, therefore, were not perceived as being as offensive as they would have been elsewhere), attracting increasing numbers of votes, election-on-election until recently.[8] Under his leadership, the SVP/UDC of Zurich put considerable effort into improving its communication strategies and adopting professional marketing techniques, which, following their success, set an example to the party nationwide. So, if the party now campaigns to 'save' the tradition of running political and administrative affairs by means of a voluntary 'militia system', this has not prevented it from making sure that its own organization is run more professionally than in the past, in the context of an overall weak party landscape. Given the spreading of the Zurich example nationwide among party activists, this process provides us with an excellent example of how 'agency', in turn, does indeed affect 'structure'.

Unlike *Forza Italia* or the *Lega Nord* in Italy, the SVP/UDC was not born with its current most influential leader and is surely going to survive him. It does owe him a great deal, however, and if Blocher falls, the party will receive a considerable blow. It remains to be seen if other bourgeois political parties, badly bruised by the last two national elections, will be able to contain Blocher's challenge and possibly exploit the SVP/UDC's contradictions now that he sits in the country's executive. The signs are that the Liberal FDP/PRD is paying a high price for its cosy relationship with the SVP/UDC (http://www.gfsbern.ch).

Throughout the autumn of 2006 the populists have been very vocal in their criticism of the other governmental parties and there is no evidence that their rhetoric might have been toned down at all following Blocher's entry into government in 2003. On the contrary, all-out propaganda war against Brussels is still on the agenda and the party has even argued in favour of the abolition of legislation designed to prevent the spread of race hatred (SVP/UDC, 2007). In a September 2006 referendum, 68 per cent of voters supported new tough legislation on immigration and asylum proposed by Blocher, and yet the signs are that the SVP/UDC might have ceased to make gains at cantonal level after its poor performances in Zurich and Berne in 2006. The prediction at the beginning of 2007 is that the Greens, who have continued to grow in cantonal elections, might even reach 10 per cent in the forthcoming federal elections of the same year (http://www.gfsbern.ch/) and that support for the SVP/UDC will not change (which would, after all, still leave it as the largest party in the country). Knowing that its themes keep pole position at the top of the national agenda (with all major parties, for instance, now putting emphasis on the great need for more integration of immigrants), the SVP/UDC has already promised its members that it will fight to the death to keep Christoph Blocher in the national government (despite the Left arguing for his substitution by a more moderate SVP/UDC member).

If Blocher is not confirmed after the elections of 2007, the party is threatening to join the opposition, which would deal a very heavy blow to the tradition of concordance in the country and further embarrass centre-right parties (especially if this is accompanied by another good showing of the Left). Whether the SVP/UDC will continue to be a thorn in the side of the other governing parties from within government or whether it will eventually pull out, on the basis of what we have seen in recent years, and despite some limited setbacks in regional elections, Switzerland seems destined to remain yet another populist paradise for the foreseeable future.

Notes

1. I would like to thank Clive Church, Wolf Linder, Alfio Mastropaolo and Oscar Mazzoleni for their useful comments on the first draft of this chapter.
2. In the introduction Duncan McDonnell and myself define populism as: 'an ideology which pits a virtuous and homogeneous people against a set of elites and dangerous "others" who are together depicted as depriving (or attempting to deprive) the sovereign people of their rights, values, prosperity, identity, and voice'.
3. For a recent study of the SVP/UDC, see Oscar Mazzoleni (2003b); on its electorate, see Kriesi *et al.* eds (2005). A comparative analysis of the SVP/UDC and the *Lega*

dei Ticinesi (LDT) can be found in Oscar Mazzoleni (2003a). On the origins and rhetoric of the LDT, see Oscar Mazzoleni (1995, 1999 and 2005) and Albertazzi (2006).

4. As we say in the introduction, a fundamental characteristic of populism is the claim to speak on behalf of a virtuous majority which, despite its size and consequent 'rights', is being deceived and exploited by a self-interested elite.

5. The LDT achieved a mere 7.5 per cent of the vote within Ticino in the 2003 National Council elections (down from 18.1 in 1995), while the *Ticinese* branch of the SVP/UDC secured 7.4 per cent (up from 2.1 per cent in 1995). However, since then the LDT has recovered, by gaining 13.6 per cent of the vote in the Cantonal elections of 1 April 2007.

6. The FDP/PRD, CVP/PDC and SVP/UDC are often defined as the 'bourgeois' block in Swiss political commentary in order to distinguish them from leftist parties such as the SPS/PSS and the Greens. While both the FDP/PRD and SVP/UDC claim to draw their inspiration from liberalism, the CVP/PDC is a Christian Democratic party. As recent Selects studies reveal, despite the SPS/PSS having shed its profile of being essentially a 'workers party', the bourgeois and leftist electorates still differ very considerably in terms of their values and beliefs (Ladner, 2003).

7. The other side of the coin is that the system facilitates the perpetuation of a parliament of wealthy middle class professionals turned politicians, who can afford to take time off work to attend sessions (Wiesli, 2003: 383–389).

8. Incidentally, Blocher does not seem to mind the definition of 'populist' at all. On the official site of the 'Department of Justice and Police' that he now leads he is described as 'one of the founders of the populist student group Studentenring' (see http://www.ejpd.admin.ch).

8

Germany: Right-wing Populist Failures and Left-wing Successes

Frank Decker

Introduction

In Germany, unlike most other countries in Western Europe, organized right-wing populism has so far made little impression on party politics. While parties like the French *Front National*, the Flemish *Vlaams Blok* (now *Vlaams Belang*), the *Lega Nord* in Italy, the Danish People's Party and the Norwegian Party of Progress have established themselves and are now permanent and prominent features of the party-political landscape in their respective countries, the parties of the far Right in the Federal Republic of Germany remain in the shadows. The only major national success of challengers from the Right was in 1989, when the Republicans won 7.1 per cent of the vote in the European Parliament (EP) elections. For a comparable performance in a general election, we have to look all the way back to 1969, when the right-wing extremist National Democratic Party of Germany (*Nationaldemokratische Partei Deutschlands* – NPD) won 4.3 per cent of the vote, just short of the threshold for representation in the *Bundestag*. Its success at that time was part of the so-called 'second wave' of right-wing extremism in Germany, which brought the NPD further spectacular successes in state parliament elections, but quickly ebbed again during the 1970s.

Almost two decades were to elapse before a new third wave of right-wing extremism began to gather momentum as part of a wave that has not yet broken. It carried the Republicans, formed in 1983 by a splinter group from the Bavarian Christian Social Union (*Christlich Soziale Union* – CSU), into three state parliaments and the German People's Union (*Deutsche Volksunion* – DVU), a new party formed in 1987 by the far-right Munich-based publisher Gerhard Frey, into seven. The NPD, whose history stretches back to 1964, was not part of this wave in its initial stages, apart from a once-off success in local government elections in Frankfurt. Indeed, it was not until 2004 that this 'most notorious' representative of the far Right evoked memories of its heyday in the 1960s by winning a sensational 9.2 per cent of the vote in elections to the Parliament of Saxony. The party was unable, however, to repeat this success in subsequent state elections and, in the early national election of 2005, the total share of the vote for all representatives of the far Right remained as marginal (2.2 per cent) as it had been in 2002 and 1998 (1.0 and 3.3 per cent respectively).

More surprising than the absence of far-right electoral successes, however, is the lack in German politics of a more moderate right-wing populist force of the sort that we find in Italy, Austria, Switzerland and the Scandinavian countries. When the Schill Party, which took its name from Ronald Schill, a former local-court judge, registered the best-ever result achieved by a new right-wing populist party, obtaining 19.4 per cent of the vote in the election to the *Bürgerschaft* (state parliament) in Hamburg, journalists and academics feverishly speculated that the relative failure of Germany's right-wing parties might be coming to an end. The attempt to establish the Schill Party nationally, however, was almost as miserable a failure as the efforts to launch a federal version of the *Statt-Partei* (Instead Party), which had also emerged in Hamburg a few years previously. Meanwhile, other new parties such as the Free Citizens' League (*Bund Freier Bürger*) and the Pro D-Mark-Partei, formed in defence of the deutschmark, never left the starting blocks.

How can the relative weakness of right-wing populism in Germany be explained? If the rise and electoral success of far-right and right-wing populist parties is regarded as the product of a modernization crisis within society, as most writers tend to argue, then it must be assumed that there is also a breeding ground for right-wing movements and parties in Germany. If we look at the eastern part of German society, where many sections of the population were hit by social insecurity after the overthrow of the Communist regime and now regard themselves as being on the losing side of political and economic changes, the potential for a right-wing party of protest in this area of Germany would actually seem to be above average. This is not only suggested by developments in other former Communist countries, such as Poland, Hungary and Slovakia, where right-wing extremist and populist parties feature just as prominently as they do in western Europe, but is also demonstrated by the high incidence of acts of violence inspired by right-wing extremism and/or xenophobia. Whether there is any link between the level of violence, which is higher than in most other countries, and the relative weakness of right-wing extremist and populist political parties in Germany is a question, however, that has not yet been explored in any great depth by researchers. Explanations for the lack of success of parties of the Right must therefore be based on the same categories that are applied in other countries to describe the transformation of the party system. These will therefore provide the skeleton of this chapter.

As is customary when analysing the party system, a fundamental distinction must be made from the outset between structural factors and the agency of political players. As far as the former are concerned, the institutional framework, the history of the democratic system, the political culture underlying it, and the range of political matters that can be influenced in the short term, given the governing constellations and strategic abilities of the established parties, all restrict the scope for right-wing populism in Germany and thereby make life difficult for challengers. These restrictions will be discussed below. As will why right-wing extremist and populist actors have also failed to grasp those opportunities that have been presented to them. The spotlight here falls on organizational problems and a lack of professionalism within the new parties, in addition to the absence of charismatic leaders and, finally, the rivalry between them. I shall then try to gauge the extent to which the prospects for right-wing populism in Germany have been impaired by the emergence of a protest alternative on the Left, in the form of the PDS and The Left Party. It would have been equally consistent with the structure of the chapter to deal with this point previously, during the examination of the structural factors affecting the parties of the far Right. However, it owes its inclusion among the factors related to agency due to the fact that, in my view, the PDS and Left Party embody key populist attributes, some of which they share with the parties of the Right, and can therefore be analysed as populist players on the political stage.

This mooted existence of a left-wing brand of populism raises the question of whether populism is a concept that can be clearly and fully defined and what value it possesses as a label for a newly emerged family of political parties in Western democracies. I examine these questions later, focusing attention on the alleged affinity of populism with the ideological Right. This analysis culminates in a working definition of the concept of populism, which makes an analytical distinction between three levels:

(1) the social background from which populist parties emerge;
(2) their ideological characteristics;
(3) their organizational forms and the techniques deployed to appeal to voters.

Right-wing populism as a party label

Long established in academic discussion to denote a new breed of party and politician, the term 'right-wing populism' is now increasingly used by journalists and politicians too. There are probably two main reasons for this: first, right-wing populism is the sort of term that is equally at home as an explanatory scientific formula and as a political battle cry; second, the term is remarkably non-committal. Although it is employed in a critical sense, it is not truly condemnatory or stigmatizing. Indeed, this may be the reason why the accusation of populism is so ubiquitous in public debate.

The characteristics of populism as a political formula, however – namely its heavily value-laden nature and semantic imprecision – pose problems for its use as a scientific term. This, to be sure, seems especially true of the discussion in Germany, where the negative connotations of populism appear to be particularly pronounced. A cross-section of the definitions found in the relevant literature reveals that appeals to 'ordinary people' and criticism of the 'Establishment' are at the heart of the 'populist syndrome'. The underlying definition of the people may focus on a particular group or stratum within society, but generally it cuts across all classes. Whenever they refer to 'the people', speakers invariably mean those lowly people whose wellbeing is allegedly being trodden underfoot by the ruling elites. Populists see the world in black and white, as a battle between good and evil: on the one side are the righteous people; on the other, the wicked corporate combines, political parties, government machinery and other power blocs conspiring against the people's interests. This reflects a romanticized vision of a bygone age, the ideal of an organic and self-contained community protected by the state against infringements of its rights (Canovan, 1981: 290 onwards).

As we can see from even a peremptory review of the pertinent literature, it is clear that, on the basis of this definition, the most widely diverse groups, individuals, ideologies, behaviour patterns and forms of expression can be categorized as 'populist' (Ionescu and Gellner, 1969). Accordingly, before the term can be used meaningfully, it must be chronologically, spatially and materially restricted. The concept of 'new right-wing populism' does this. It relates to parties and movements on the right of the political spectrum that emerged and achieved their breakthrough in western democracies more or less simultaneously, from the mid-1980s onwards. As we know, parties with comparable political orientations are normally referred to in political science as a 'political family'. The basis of this assimilation is a categorization by ideological (Fascist, Conservative, Socialist, Communist, etc.) or orientation descriptors (Left, Right), from which certain conclusions can, in turn, be drawn about a party's voter base and organizational structure. On the basis of these three criteria, the general definition set out above can be extended and fleshed out as follows:

Social origins

Populist parties and movements are a product of modernization crises in society. They emerge when, in the wake of excessively rapid change or dramatic upheavals, particular sections of the population see their values being eroded, or suffer disorientation. This sense of loss, which may have economic causes, but is normally generated by cultural factors, is accompanied by a fear of declining status, uncertainty about the future and feelings of political alienation. Populist movements exploiting this type of situation have long existed – we need only think of the Populist Party, which emerged in the United States in the late nineteenth century and from which the phenomenon takes its name, or of the *Poujadistes* in the Fourth French Republic (Taggart, 2000). However, each of these forces took shape in a specific place at a particular time, whereas today's modernization processes are occurring in a world in which economic, cultural and political problems affect more and more societies at once. This is the main reason for the parallel nature of the changes in the party-political landscapes in various countries and also helps to explain why the new populists have not disappeared from the political arena as observers back in the 1980s expected (and often hoped) they would.

Ideology

The characteristic features of the political substance of populism are a precarious synthesis of the cult of the individual and collectivism and an 'ambivalent' interpretation of equality. On the one hand, populists rally the people against the ruling elite. On the other, they exclude perceived non-members of the people, namely those from other ethnic groups or foreign cultures. The main reason why such an 'exclusion mentality' is associated with the ideological Right is not its reactionary nature, but its anti-egalitarian element (Betz, 2001). This, however, does not preclude the existence of left-wing populism, as the editors have argued in the introduction to this volume. Like right-wing populists, those on the Left cultivate anti-elitist sentiments, opposition to the system and defence of the 'common people'. Unlike the populists on the Right, however, they do not extend the exclusion principle horizontally, instead remaining loyal to their egalitarian ideals and tending to be liberal, even libertarian, on value issues. Moreover, the polarized question of 'multiculturalism' versus 'nativism' pits them at the opposite extreme from the populist Right.

Public profile and organization

The most conspicuous formal characteristics of right-wing populist parties are that they take on the form of movements and rely on charismatic leadership. In addition, populism is characterized by its voter mobilization and recruitment methods. These formal elements cannot be isolated from the substantive ideology of populism. On the contrary, the two are closely intertwined. Populist parties see themselves as a movement and focus on a leader figure, which expresses both their belief in the homogeneity of the popular will and their rejection of representative party democracy in favour of decision-making by a majority of the people. At the same time, populist agitation reflects opposition to the Establishment and the exclusion of 'outsiders'. It is no exaggeration, in my view, to say that these formal attributes, even more than pure ideological substance, may be regarded as the real reason for the success of right-wing populist parties.

The limited scope for right-wing populism in Germany

Institutional framework

The basic institutional conditions within which a system of government works have a twofold effect on the election prospects of populist challengers.

First, they influence the competitive balance between parties and, hence, the scope for newcomers to make a breakthrough at the polls and/or gain a foothold in Parliament. Second, the institutional framework itself can serve as a motivating factor for populist parties, i.e. it can become a political issue in its own right. This applies especially in cases where the established parties have created a closed shop, which obstructs or totally blocks normal democratic change. Consequently, both competitive structures that are wide open and those that are tightly closed can be beneficial to newcomers.

The prospects of direct institutional access to the party system are determined by the electoral law. The system of proportional representation in Germany, with the rather restrictive clause requiring parties to obtain five per cent of the vote before they can enter Parliament, has proved to be a barrier, although not an insurmountable one, for newcomers (Harrison, 1997). Parliamentary representation is important, because it gives outsiders the media coverage that is indispensable in order to achieve sustained electoral success, not least because public broadcasters are legally required to provide representatives of all parliamentary parties with airtime to speak in pre-election broadcasts. In terms of electoral campaigning and public funding too, challengers in Germany are not unduly handicapped. The fact that half a percentage point of the vote in a general or one percentage point in a state election gives them access to public funds has been a source of general irritation, particularly in the case of the NPD. Attempts by the established parties to increase the threshold for access to public funds, however, were thwarted by the Federal Constitutional Court in 2004, which deemed it an unwarranted restriction of equal opportunities within the democratic system.

Germany's federal structure probably tends to diminish the prospects of new challengers. The presence of a second tier of government does benefit such parties in the short term, enabling them to develop their organizational structure more effectively in the smaller territory of a *Land* or city-state and to profit from the tendency for major parties to lose support in mid-term, subnational elections. Yet, it is precisely this syndrome that restricts their development prospects at the national level. It would seem that the opportunity for electors to give the established parties a black eye in regional elections reduces their incentive to register a protest vote in general elections. Moreover, parties almost inevitably become embroiled in conflicts when they seek to build successful state associations into national organizations – conflicts that perhaps could have been avoided had they originally constituted themselves as national parties.

The relative openness of the competitive structure, for its part, is the reason why the mobilization effect of the issue of partyocracy has remained minimal in Germany and why representatives such as the *Statt-Partei* and the Free Citizens' League, which tried to pursue a brand of anti-partyocracy populism, were only able to register minor successes in terms of public impact. Although, on the basis of the relevant indicators, such as recruitment of candidates for political offices, state funding of parties and appointment patronage, the Federal Republic can certainly be regarded as one of the most highly developed partyocracies in Europe, it would be wrong to say that political parties in Germany hold the sort of *de facto* monopoly on power that they have long enjoyed in Austria and Italy. That is precluded not only by powerful institutional counterweights such as federalism, the role of the Constitutional Court, the ministerial bureaucracy and the media, but also by the structures of inter-party rivalry, which, until recently, permitted a functioning democratic interchange between the CSU/Christian Democratic Union (*Christlich Demokratische Union* – CDU) and the Social Democratic Party of Germany (*Sozialdemokratische Partei Deutschlands* – SPD), with recourse to Grand Coalitions being limited to emergencies. In addition, the parties also managed to take the wind out of the populists' sails by means of target-orientated institutional reforms, such as the introduction of direct democracy instruments (Scarrow, 1997: 464).

Political culture: the shadow of the past

A far more serious handicap for parties of the Right is the set of restrictions arising from the historical burden that weighs on Germany's political culture. Because of the shadows of the Nazi past, there is a deeper stigma attached to right-wing extremism in Germany than in any other European country. This applies in both legal and social terms. Constitutional repression goes so far that it even impinges in some cases on the various instruments of 'militant democracy'. An illustrative example is that of the judicial proceedings for the prohibition of the NPD, which had to be abandoned after the Office for the Protection of the Constitution (*Verfassungsschutz*) refused to reveal the names of the undercover agents who had infiltrated the NPD.

From a social point of view too, the demarcation line separating the established parties and ruling elites from the far Right is absolute. It is reflected, for example, in the fact that right-wing extremists cannot expect any support whatsoever from the media. Consequently, challengers on the Right will only be able to achieve lasting success if they carefully avoid any convergence with National Socialism (Kitschelt and McGann, 1995: 203 onwards). That, however, is unlikely to alter either the basic instinct of the established parties to brand them as extremist or, conversely, the inclination of extremists to use non-extremist parties as a stepping-stone to avoid stigmatization. No new right-wing populist party in Germany has ever been immune to the risk of infiltration. As Roger Karapin observes,

> whenever a far-right party has gained votes in post-war Germany, neo-Nazi militants have been attracted to it, not least because of the strong chances of gaining local offices in the decentralised governmental system. The new activists pull the party toward neo-fascist positions and spoil its reputation among prospective voters. (Karapin, 1998a: 225)

This raises the question of appropriate counterstrategies. The resurgence of the NPD over the last few years is a clear indication that the social and constitutional stigmatization of right-wing extremism in Germany does not destroy its potential to woo voters and influence people's attitudes. On the contrary, this potential has been diverted into the dark recesses of violence and sectarianism, while the right-wing parties' prospects of success at the ballot box have remained slim. The fact that this situation has now changed is partly due to the heavy-handed use of the state's instruments of repression. For example, the bans imposed on 18 right-wing extremist groupings since 1990 might well have channelled at least some of the potential for right-wing extremist success back towards the NPD. Similarly, the collapse of the prohibition proceedings against the NPD itself boosted the standing of the extremist Right at the polls, especially in its stronghold of Saxony.

Opportunity structures in politics: government compositions and the strategic capabilities of mainstream parties

The restrictive environment within which right-wing extremism and populism operate in Germany does not rule out occasional electoral success. As a rule, however, these are linked to windows of political opportunity that can be exploited in the short term, but are liable to snap shut again very quickly. The term 'opportunity structure' is often used in political science to cover all the determinant factors that influence the emergence of new parties (Tarrow, 1991). These range from social cleavages and the institutional framework of the system of government (i.e. factors that only change over a long-term period) to circumstantial factors on the 'supply side' of politics. In order to differentiate between the two, I shall restrict my use of the term to the latter type of factor. In such opportunity structures, the favourability or otherwise of temporary circumstances depends on the one hand on the government composition and the party-political balance of power in a country, and, on the other, on the strategic abilities of the mainstream parties.

If government composition were the only relevant factor, the mobilization prospects of the right-wing parties actually ought to have improved during the 16 years of centre-right government led by Chancellor Helmut Kohl. Their poor performance therefore seems to indicate that the issues highlighted by these challengers in Germany either mattered little to the general public or were already well covered by the established parties. An international comparison shows that the new brand of right-wing populism attracts most of its support on the basis of three issues: partyocracy, the Welfare State and immigration (Decker, 2004: 195 onwards). The greatest appeal is exercised by those parties that take advantage of every issue on the political agenda and package their views into a sustained winning formula. The German representatives of populism are still far from that level.

Partyocracy, for example, may regularly generate controversy among intellectuals, but for the population at large it generally takes a scandal to make it a topic of discussion. As for the Welfare State, there is no reason why it should be a less significant issue in Germany than in other European countries. Nonetheless, during the 1990s, the new forces either did not seek to exploit it, or else did so half-heartedly. Another difficulty for the parties of the far Right stemmed from the consequences of the German unification process: not only did the former German Democratic Republic lack a sizeable middle class from which populist parties could have drawn support; the newcomers were also unable to benefit from the widely prevalent dissatisfaction there because the Party of Democratic Socialism (PDS) was already providing a genuinely East German alternative for protest voters.

It is more difficult to determine why the immigration-related problems in Germany did not provide the new right-wing parties with a passport to permanent success, as happened in countries such as France, Belgium, Norway and Denmark. Once the asylum problem had disappeared from the agenda in 1993, the rise in support for the far Right also began to dip again. The challengers were compelled to recognize that, in normal circumstances, the official policy towards foreigners offered them few lines of attack. Although Germany has one of the highest percentages of foreign-born residents in Europe, government policymakers managed over many years to maintain the view – critics would say the myth – that the Federal Republic was not a country of immigration and to resist multiculturalism in any form. The Kohl administration's haste to restrict the right of asylum by means of a constitutional amendment was understandable in view of the pressing nature of the problem. Beyond that, however, the government could not bring itself to make policy changes. There was no intensification of efforts to integrate immigrants who already lived in the country, nor were the CDU and CSU willing to incorporate into a general longer-term political strategy the immigration processes which were actually taking place and which, in certain cases, such as that of the repatriates of German origin, the CDU/CSU themselves had encouraged. They had no need to fear any significant resistance from the SPD to such an approach (Karapin, 1998b).

Since the late 1990s, the parameters of official policy towards foreigners in Germany have shifted (Kruse, Orren and Angenendt, 2003). A major watershed was reached when the 'Red/Green' coalition government of the SPD and Alliance 90/The Greens, which had taken office in 1998, tried, as part of a revision of the nationality law, to introduce the option of dual nationality. This project met with bitter opposition from the CDU and CSU and gave those parties the opportunity to demonstrate their ability to mobilize right-wing opinion through a massive campaign. The gratifying upshot, however, was a degree of convergence between the two sides. Just as the Social Democrats had to recognize that they could not consolidate the new course in the field of foreigners and immigration policy without seeking the support of the other mass party, the CDU and CSU began to acknowledge the reality of a society that was absorbing immigrants and thus stopped regarding the term 'integration' as a mere fig leaf. On this basis, and after long and arduous negotiations, the first reasonably up-to-date Immigration Act was jointly adopted in 2004. As far as the opening of new immigration channels and the legalization of existing residence qualifications are concerned, the law is still extremely restrictive. In conjunction with the relaxed naturalization conditions and improved integration measures, however, we can see a paradigm shift in the policy towards foreigners in Germany, which could present the parties of the far Right with new opportunities in the future. Firstly, we can assume that conflicts over the recognition of other cultures become pandemic and give rise to counter-mobilization in cases where immigrants are under heavy pressure to assimilate, as the French situation, for example, has demonstrated. Second, right-wing populists can exploit the fact that the anti-integration positions which once underpinned the aliens policy of the CDU and CSU, and which secured them the support of numerous xenophobic voters, have been superseded in Germany and that their proponents are increasingly isolated in today's party system.

Organizational and political failures of right-wing populist players

The fragmentation of the far right

The party-political fragmentation of the far Right in Germany is symptomatic of the inability of right-wing populism to assert itself. While success has been achieved in other countries by pulling together various strands of right-wing extremism and reorganizing them in a populist form, these threads are still frayed in Germany in the shape of various parties seeking to poach each other's voters. In such circumstances, floating voters generally tend to support the party that is believed to have the best prospects of success. When each of those new right-wing populist parties that have emerged, proved, without exception, to be a flash in the pan whose remnants swiftly faded into political insignificance, the main beneficiaries were the far-right DVU and NPD. The success of these parties in several state elections was not primarily due to their populist characteristics, which were rather underdeveloped, but to a combination of an existing protest mood and a long-term regional strategy. The latter had enabled the NPD in Saxony to build up a core voter base over many years and to consolidate its electoral strength.

In organizational terms too, the far Right has been catching up. Whereas the DVU members of the state parliaments in Saxony-Anhalt and Brandenburg, to which they were elected in 1998 and 1999 respectively, looked like incompetent amateurs in parliament, the NPD cadres in Saxony, most of whom were brought in from the West, initially acted in an uncommonly professional manner. This not only presented the established parties with a new scenario, but bolstered the efforts of right-wing extremists to coordinate their activities, culminating in the proclamation of a joint 'People's Front of the Right' by the two party chairmen, Udo Voigt of the NPD and Gerhard Frey of the DVU, at the end of 2004. The DVU and NPD agreed for the first time to run on a joint NPD list at the early election in 2005 and have planned a joint DVU list at the European elections in 2009. In addition, electoral pacts have been made for all state elections in the period up to 2009.

Even with the aid of better organizational cohesion, however, it seems scarcely imaginable that the NPD's three-pronged strategy of battling for the streets, hearts and minds and parliamentary power can yield much fruit, given the party's flimsy social base outside its Saxony strongholds. As long as the NPD continues to adhere to its neo-Nazi programme, this situation is essentially unlikely to change. Within the small area of a municipality or region, a party may succeed in tapping into a rich vein of protest votes with its ideology. In the context of national politics, however, such a strategy soon reaches its organizational limits and the extreme parties will not enjoy national success until they emerge from their present social isolation.

The failure of new parties from the Republicans to the Schill Party

However few the signs of ideological moderation on the part of the NPD, it remains equally unlikely that any other representatives of the far Right or of right-wing populism could challenge the current position of the neo-Nazis as the leading voice on the right of the political spectrum. The DVU does not have the organizational ability to mount such a challenge, although it polls more votes in general than the NPD, while other potential rivals have now dwindled into marginal forces, such as the Republicans, or have sunk into oblivion, like the *Statt-Partei*, the Free Citizens' League and the Schill Party.

The most credible contenders for the leadership role were the Republicans, a right-wing group which broke away from the Bavarian CSU in 1983 and which, in its heyday, from the mid-1980s to the early 1990s, embodied a potent blend of right-wing extremism and populism. The fact that this period of success coincided with the era of the recently deceased Franz Schönhuber, who chaired the party from 1985 until 1994, was no mere quirk of fate. Unlike Gerhard Frey, who rarely makes public appearances, Schönhuber excelled in the role of charismatic leader and conducted the Republicans' electoral campaigns almost single-handedly. This, however, was not sufficient to maintain control of the party, which was beset by constant personality clashes and power struggles. Originally conceived as an alternative to the CDU and CSU on the conservative Right, the Republicans strengthened their links with organized right-wing extremism under Schönhuber. His attempt to turn the party into a catch-all movement of the new Right, modelled on the French *Front National*, however, proved impossible to realize in the face of fierce opposition from the party rank and file, which rebelled against the chairman's authoritarian leadership style and ultimately deposed him (Winkler and Schumann, 1998).

Under Schönhuber's successor, Rolf Schlierer, the Republicans sailed into calmer waters. The return to the party's roots, however, was a bad move in electoral terms, since it robbed the Republicans of their populist impact. Their last major success in a state election came in Baden-Württemberg in 1996, and in the general election of 2005 the Republicans won 0.6 per cent of the vote, well below the 1.6 per cent obtained by their far-right rivals, the NPD. Just like the voters, party officials also began to jump ship, a trend that culminated in the defection of the entire Hamburg state executive of the Republicans to the NPD. Signs of meltdown have subsequently appeared in other regional associations, and these are likely to plunge the party into an even steeper downward spiral, probably resulting in its imminent disappearance from the German political scene.

Besides the Republicans, a number of other new parties have tried their hand at various forms of populism. The failure of any of these groups to make a political breakthrough was due in part to their concentration on a narrow range of issues. While the Republicans' fixation with the immigration issue mirrored the agenda pursued by the new right-wing populist challengers in other European countries, the one-off successes of the *Statt-Partei*, the Free Citizens' League and the Schill Party were based on a specific localized and/or ephemeral set of problems and were not easily transferable to the national political stage (Decker, 2004: 151 onwards). While the Hamburg-based *Statt-Partei* ('Instead Party'), a centre-right voters' association founded in 1993 by a CDU dissident, Markus Wegner, focused primarily on the politics of democracy and called for reform of the traditional partyocracy, the Free Citizens' League (*Bund Freier Bürger*), launched in the same year by Manfred Brunner, former chairman of the Free Democratic Party (*Freie Demokratische Partei* – FDP) in Bavaria, campaigned against the creation of the single European currency. The Schill Party, named after the former local court judge Ronald Schill, was also formed in Hamburg and devoted its 2001 electoral campaign entirely to the issue of law and order. Since the need to fight crime overshadowed all other political issues in the campaign for election to the Parliament of Hamburg, Schill captured 19.4 per cent of the vote, the best-ever performance by a newly formed party in any state election. The fact that this party of the centre-right, known officially as the Law and Order Offensive Party (*Partei Rechtsstaatlicher Offensive*) was able to rally considerably more voters to its cause than the *Statt-Partei* and the Free Citizens' League before it was due not only to the support it received, particularly from the Springer press group, which is particularly influential in Hamburg, but also to the fact that Ronald Schill, unlike Wegner and Brunner, possessed charisma and knew how to strike a chord with his populist pronouncements. For this reason, it seemed initially as though the former judge was destined to enter the ranks of Europe's successful right-wing populists (Faas and Wüst, 2002).

Only a few weeks after its triumph in Hamburg, however, the Schill Party saw its high-flown political ambitions begin to fall to earth. Its attempt to expand into a national organization fell victim to the same problems that had plagued the *Statt-Partei* back in 1994, i.e. gatecrashers from the far Right, a lack of professionalism in its political activities and internal strife. Moreover, Schill failed to broaden his political programme, even though the issue of law and order would certainly have served as a bridge to a broader right-wing political platform. What finished the party off, however, was its decision to take office in the Government of the City-State of Hamburg, which caused a massive loss of credibility among its supporters and mercilessly exposed the incompetence of its fledgling politicians (Hartleb, 2004). Here too, the fate of the *Statt-Partei* should have served as a warning to Schill. Very few right-wing populists have managed to make the transition from strong opposition to the pressures of government. Schill should never have tried. The escapades of the raw recruit in the office of Senator for the Interior are legendary. Not only did they see his popularity rapidly slip away, with the CDU dissolving the governing coalition after a year and a half, but they also led his own party and parliamentary group to distance themselves from their former figurehead. The break-up of the party and its debacle at the polls when the new state assembly was elected were the inevitable consequence.

Populist competition from the Left: the PDS and the new Left Party

The unification of the two German states meant that an additional party was able to establish itself on the federal stage after 1990: the Party of Democratic Socialism (PDS), successor to the Socialist Unity Party of Germany (SED), the official state party of the GDR. In the light of the poor election results of the SED/PDS immediately after unification, most observers assumed that the former Communists would disappear sooner or later from the party-political landscape. This assumption, however, proved to be mistaken. Instead, the PDS went from strength to strength in the new federal states, constantly expanding its voter base. Today, in the territory of the former GDR, it enjoys wide recognition as a major party, polling only slightly lower than the CDU and SPD.

Given the background to its creation, its internal heterogeneity and its ambivalent attitude to the prevailing democratic political system and free market economy, it would be wrong to label the PDS as an entirely extremist or left-wing populist party (Gapper, 2003). Nevertheless, in its methods and style, as well as in its ideology and political programme, the party has much in common with the anti-democratic forces on the Right. Anti-elite protest gestures, a high media profile thanks to its charismatic leadership, the pursuit of social protectionism and the cultivation of a feisty image are the main ingredients in its recipe for success. At the same time, in eastern Germany, the PDS presents itself as a pragmatic force which plays a constructive role in political decision-making and is part of governing coalitions in various municipalities and federal states.

Electoral analyses reveal that most of the voters wooed by the PDS belong to the same group of 'modernization victims' from which the parties of the Right also draw their support (Schoen and Falter, 2005: 37–38). What motivates these electors when casting their vote is a profound dissatisfaction with their own situation, for which they blame the prevailing political and social conditions. In this respect, the existence of a left-wing protest party which operates as a champion of the East has damaged the prospects of far Right parties in the new *Länder*. The PDS has not been able to curb right-wing extremism completely, because the far Right also draws on dyed-in-the-wool xenophobic voters, who are largely immune to the appeals of the former Communists, who take left-wing views on cultural issues. It is not impossible for this divide to be crossed on occasion, as was demonstrated by Oskar Lafontaine's remarks on immigration policy during the national election campaign in 2005 – when he referred to immigrants as *Fremdarbeiter* or alien workers, a term that was used by the Nazis in the 1930s and 1940s – which provoked fierce criticism from the ranks of his own party. The former SPD chairman, however, is probably right in thinking that there is no reason why the successful formula of culturally underpinned social protest should be the sole preserve of right-wing populists (Decker, 2006: 22 onwards).

There can be no escaping the fact, however, that the success of the left-wing populism practised by the PDS has been entirely confined to the new *Länder* over the past decade and a half. However much the reformist forces around Gregor Gysi and Lothar Bisky have tried to make the former Communists socially acceptable in the old West Germany, their efforts have been in vain. It took the emergence of a new left-wing force in the West, which was set up under the name of the Election Alternative for Work and Social Justice (*Wahlalternative für Arbeit und soziale Gerechtigkeit* – WASG) – in protest at the welfare and labour-market reforms of the SPD-led Federal Government – to bring the PDS closer to its long-cherished aim. It was also certainly a stroke of good fortune that, in Gregor Gysi and Oskar Lafontaine, who had left the SPD to join the WASG, the parties had two front men who were past masters of the populist approach to voters. More important, however, was the fact that, in strategic terms, an alliance between the PDS and the WASG represented a classic 'win-win' situation. The westward extension of its voter base enabled the PDS to stabilize its role in federal politics. In turn, the WASG benefited from being carried into the Bundestag on the backs of the former Communists (who were firmly established in the East), something it could scarcely have managed under its own steam.

The electoral vacuum created by the perceived defection of the Social Democrats to the neo-liberal mainstream and the refusal of the SPD to cooperate with the former Communists at federal level, coupled with the simultaneous weakness of right-wing populism and extremism, offers great opportunities for The Left Party, into which the PDS has now mutated, and will continue to do so (Lösche, 2003). Whether the party can take them, of course, depends primarily on its own agency, as in the case of the populists on the Right. From the resolution of the leadership issue following the foreseeable retirement of Gysi and Lafontaine to the culturally based differences in mentality between the more idealistically minded WASG in the West and the PDS with its pragmatic image in the East, to the internal power struggles that are something of a tradition in the PDS, there are so many imponderables and pitfalls that a firm prediction scarcely seems possible. It does appear likely, however, that left-wing populism will continue to find a more hospitable habitat than its right-wing counterpart in the German political system for some time to come.

The outlook for populism in Germany

Periods of economic downturn, structural crises, anxiety about the future and general pessimism create conditions in which populist formations on the Right and Left may thrive. This applies in Germany too, where the party system has hitherto been marked by a relatively high degree of stability. Many authors ascribe the lack of success of right-wing populist parties in Germany to the fact that populism is a constant in Germany, both within the established parties and in the media – the tabloid newspaper *Bild* being a prime example. And indeed the search for scapegoats for the fraught economic situation in 2005 induced not only members of The Left Party close to Gregor Gysi and Oskar Lafontaine, but also politicians from the mainstream parties such as CSU party leader Edmund Stoiber to engage in populist tub-thumping.

In Germany, then, it is by no means impossible to mobilize public opinion on typically right-wing populist issues, from immigration policy and law and order to criticism of the European Union. In the past, however, the mainstream parties have managed to take the sting out of these issues or have incorporated them into their own policy positions, thereby leaving potential challengers with little room for manoeuvre. Moreover, right-wing populist parties in Germany have faced two other obstacles: first, they operate in an extremely sensitive area in which, because of the country's Nazi past, they are wide open to stigmatization by the public and the media. Second, they have to deal with serious organizational problems, which can at best be temporarily sidestepped through the presence of a charismatic leader. Significantly, no such charismatic figures had emerged until very recently.

The prospects for left-wing populism seem rosier by comparison, since it possesses at least three advantages over its counterpart on the Right. First, it benefits from the charismatic qualities and talents of its two chief matadors, Gregor Gysi and Oskar Lafontaine. Second, through the PDS, which is firmly rooted in eastern German society and has an excellent organizational network, it possesses the resources needed to compete successfully with other parties and to cope with the probable imminent retirement of Gysi and Lafontaine. Third, it does not suffer to the same extent from the problem of stigmatization. Although the PDS is still burdened by its GDR past and the suspicion of extremism, these factors are no longer powerful enough to do lasting damage to the legitimacy of a party that has the support of almost a third of all voters in eastern Germany. This hypothesis is made all the more valid by the fact that the PDS seems to be second to none in its ideological opposition to right-wing extremism. Because it is immune in every respect to any suspicion of fascism, The Left Party can afford, at little risk to itself, to engage in vote-catching by addressing issues and resorting to methods that are normally associated with right-wing populism.

As the PDS has demonstrated in the *Länder* of eastern Germany, a pragmatic policy of power-sharing can indeed be pursued without the need to sacrifice populist appeal. Such a tightrope walk presupposes, however, that the party remains in opposition in the *Bundestag*. If it were to become part of a national governing coalition, it would no longer be able to adhere to its present line and would probably then have to back down from the positions to which it owes much of its populist magnetism. In that scenario, along with the Social Democrats, the parties of the Right that have hitherto been marginalized could then reap a rich harvest.

9
Sweden: The Scandinavian Exception

Jens Rydgren

Introduction[1]

The last two decades have seen a resurgence of the radical right in Western Europe. These parties, which hereafter will be called radical right-wing populist (RRP) parties, share a fundamental core of (a) ethno-nationalist xenophobia – manifested in strong anti-immigration stances and opposition to multiculturalism; and (b) anti-political establishment populism – expressed by presenting themselves as the only alternative to the corrupt elite, of which all other political parties are part. This ideological core is embedded in a general socio-cultural authoritarianism, which stresses themes like law and order and family values (Rydgren, 2005).

The emergence of RRP parties was preceded by the foundation of right-wing populist parties in Denmark and Norway in the early 1970s. These parties emerged primarily in opposition to bureaucracy and a tax take that, in their opinion, had escalated out of all proportion. They were not, however, ethno-nationalist and did not mobilize against immigration until the 1980s. In Sweden, however, populist parties have never managed to attract more than three per cent of the electorate, with the exception of the 1991 election, when the newly formed New Democracy gained 6.7 per cent of the vote. However, since the collapse of New Democracy in 1994, no Swedish populist party has won a parliamentary seat. Even given the relative success of today's leading RRP party, the Sweden Democrats, in the 2006 general election (in which it increased its vote share from 1.4 to almost three per cent and won over 250 seats on different local councils), Sweden's RRP parties appear marginalized in a comparative Western European perspective.

As the Scandinavian countries share several important traits – such as welfare regimes, secularism, histories of Social Democratic dominance, and so on – the fact that radical right-wing populism has been highly successful in Denmark and Norway, but largely failed in Sweden since the mid 1990s is counterintuitive. The main aim of this paper is to present possible explanations to the questions this fact gives rise to. The chapter will therefore examine some of the explanatory mechanisms that have been profitably used to explain the emergence of populist parties in other countries (Rydgren, 2003b; 2005). Political opportunity structures will be discussed and the ways in which the Sweden Democrats have tried to take advantage of favourable political opportunities will be analysed. First, however, we will look briefly at the 'rise and fall' of the one successful populist party in Sweden so far: New Democracy.

The rise and fall of New Democracy: right-wing populism in Sweden before 1994

While tax populist parties emerged in Denmark and Norway in the early 1970s, the Swedish five-party system remained intact until the electoral breakthrough of the Green Party in 1988. The absence of a Swedish 'Progress Party' on the national political arena inspired a great deal of debate, especially in light of the growing lack of confidence in politicians amongst the Swedish electorate at the time. One common explanation for this absence is that the non-socialist parties had remained an untried alternative in Sweden up until 1976, leaving Swedes, unlike their Danish and Norwegian neighbours, with no experience of right-wing government. General tax discontent and political distrust might consequently have been directed primarily at the sitting government party, which had been in power for generations. In addition to the absence of referendums, Jørgen Goul Andersen and Tor Bjørklund (1990), note the lack of major issues that cut across established party lines and loyalties and thus release floating voters. This is true insofar as no referendum on EC membership was held in Sweden during the 1970s (whereas Denmark and Norway both held referendums in 1972, just before the electoral breakthrough of each country's Progress Party). However, this reading of events overlooks the importance of the environment and nuclear power as political concerns. In the 1970s, much of the populist current was propelled by these issues and was channelled through the Centre Party, which thus became something of a surrogate populist party, draining the market of resources that otherwise might have facilitated the rise of a new party (Fryklund and Peterson, 1981). Furthermore, as a result of the 1980 referendum on nuclear power, the Green Party was founded in 1981.

It was only after 1982, following six years of non-socialist rule and when concerns about the non-socialist parties' failure to reduce taxes and the new political issue of immigration had started to take hold, that populist voices had any kind of political impact in Sweden, albeit initially only at local level. Nationally, no Swedish right-wing populist party emerged until the 1990s, when New Democracy won 6.7 of the vote in the 1991 general election. The party was founded in February 1991, and traced its short-term roots to an article in November 1990 by Bert Karlsson and Ian Wachtmeister which appeared in one of the leading Swedish newspapers, *Dagens Nyheter*.

Both Karlsson and Wachtmeister were already well-known to the Swedish public. Karlsson was a fun-fair and record company owner, and had gained political visibility by criticizing food prices. Wachmeister was a businessman, who was associated with the Right-wing think tank *Den nya välfärden* (The New Welfare), and had written popular books in which he ridiculed Swedish politicians and bureaucracy (Taggart, 1996).

The main reasons behind the sudden emergence of New Democracy lie in the fact that a new area of opportunity for populists had opened up among the Swedish electorate: the anti-immigration niche within a developing socio-cultural dimension. The party was also helped by a general shift to the right in the socio-economic sphere and by the emergence of a pure protest dimension. If we look at subjective explanations of party choice among the electorate, for instance, we find that no less than 53 per cent of those who voted for New Democracy made reference to 'fresh new approaches,' the need to 'shake things up,' and the claim that the party 'speaks the mind of the common man.' Moreover, 19 per cent of them referred to the immigration and asylum question, twice that of those who voted for other parties. Finally, 11 per cent attributed their choice to the party's policy on tax, although this was half as many as among Conservative Party supporters (Gilljam and Holmberg, 1993: 89–93).

In the second half of the 1980s, voter opinion started to shift to the socioeconomic Right, a process that gained in strength around the turn of the decade. Traditionally speaking, since the Second World War, there had always been more voters identifying themselves with the Left than with the Right. This gap disappeared in the 1980s when the numbers became fairly evenly balanced (35 per cent for each side in the 1988 election, for example). In the 1991 election, however, the proportion of voters considering themselves on the 'Right' suddenly increased to 44 per cent, at the expense of the 'leftists,' who declined to 27 per cent (Gilljam and Holmberg, 1993: 137). This swing in public opinion also becomes apparent if we look at attitudes to the Welfare State: the proportion of voters who said that they would like to see a smaller public sector increased dramatically between 1989 and 1990 from 42 to 56 per cent.

This socioeconomic shift to the Right was the product of several interacting factors. First, we should not underestimate the effects of the fall of Communism in Eastern Europe, which led to the 'triumphal advance of the market economy', nor should we forget the impact of the powerful boom economy at the end of the 1980s. In addition, there was an ideological offensive led by the Swedish Employers' Confederation and its information and propaganda agency Timbro during the 1980s. This campaign, inspired by the successes of the new Right in the USA (under Ronald Reagan) and Britain (under Margaret Thatcher), was designed to break the leftist hegemony in Swedish ideological debate and agenda-setting and, as Kristina Boréus (1994; 1997) shows, neoliberalism made a clear mark on public political discourse during the 1980s. It should be stressed, however, that the Swedish 'right-wing wave,' unlike that elsewhere, was built exclusively on neoliberalism and 'neo-conservatism', as it has come to be known, did not appear until the 1990s (Boréus, 1997: 277).

Second, as will be further discussed below, at the time of New Democracy's rise, resources had been freed up in the form of 'party disloyal' voters and a protest dimension in Swedish politics had been established alongside a shift to the Right on the economic cleavage dimension. These processes combined to create favourable opportunity structures for a party such as New Democracy.

Finally, we can add that an anti-immigration/anti-immigrant niche had been exposed, which coincided with the politicization of the immigrant/refugee question. In the 1991 election, the contours of an alternative cleavage dimension began to surface. These returned to a state of latency for the rest of the decade, before appearing again in the 2002 election, as we will see below. The cleavage dimension between xenophobia and cosmopolitanism, and the 'open' and 'closed' society, can be seen as a component of the more general socio-cultural cleavage dimension, which has been central to the growth and establishment of populist parties throughout Western Europe.

In the late 1980s and early 1990s, the Swedish electorate grew more hostile towards the accommodation of refugees, asylum and development aid and the immigration issue became an increasing political concern for many voters (Gilljam and Holmberg, 1993). At the same time, all the mainstream parties were more or less in agreement that Sweden would continue to accept refugees, even if their immigration and integration policies were at variance with each other. These factors exposed a niche in which a party of immigrant and immigration sceptics could attract voters.

Nonetheless, New Democracy's success was short-lived. The party gradually fell apart during its parliamentary term, before disappearing from the *Riksdag* with a meagre 1.2 per cent of the vote in the 1994 general election (see Table 9.1). The first cracks started to appear shortly after the 1991 election and when Ian Wachtmeister resigned as party leader in February 1994, its disintegration was inevitable. Although the main reason for the party's demise was its lack of an organizational backbone, the deep recession into which the country had been plunged had also turned public opinion away from New Democracy's political profile.

As we saw above, one of the catalysts behind the growth of the party was the powerful shift to the Right in the socio-economic dimension before the 1991 general election. Gradually, however, this slowed down and was replaced by a shift to the Left as the economic crisis began to take hold. New Democracy found itself increasingly out of step with the times and, in contrast to the period around the 1991 general election campaign, its political profile was not well suited to the niches and political opportunity structures

Table 9.1 Swedish election results, 1982–2006 (in percentages)

Year	LP	Soc. D.	Gr. P.	Cen. P.	Lib. P.	Christ. D.	Con. P.	New Dem.	Swe. Dem.
1982	5.6	45.6	1.7	15.5	5.9	1.9	23.6	–	–
1985	5.4	44.7	1.5	12.4	14.2	–	21.3	–	–
1988	5.8	43.2	5.5	11.3	12.2	2.9	18.3	–	–
1991	4.5	37.7	3.4	8.5	9.1	7.1	21.9	6.7	–
1994	6.2	45.3	5.0	7.7	7.2	4.1	22.4	1.2	–
1998	12.0	36.4	4.5	5.1	4.7	11.7	22.9	–	0.5
2002	8.4	39.9	4.6	6.2	13.4	9.1	15.3	–	1.4
2006	5.9	35.0	5.2	7.9	7.5	6.6	26.2	–	2.9

Source: Statistics Sweden (www.scb.se).

that presented themselves for the 1994 election. The economic crisis also contributed to the shrinking size of the anti-immigrant/immigration niche by making traditional issues relating to political economy and the Welfare State more salient, at the expense of those belonging to the socio-cultural dimension (Rydgren, 2002; 2003b; Holmberg, 2000: 114).

New Democracy's problem, as we shall also see below, was that these changes made it more difficult, if not impossible, for the party to keep its three supporter categories (neoliberals, opponents of immigration/immigrants, and protest voters/populists) happy all at the same time. This was an historic coalition of voter groups and one that was only possible during the late 1980s and early 1990s. In the mid-1990s, however, a combination of populism, xenophobia and 'left-wing economics' (combined in a protectionist welfare chauvinism) would have been much better suited to mobilize voters. Most RRP parties, such as the *Front National* in France, moved in this direction during that period (Rydgren, 2003b). However, New Democracy was neither able nor willing to undergo such an ideological and rhetorical change. This rendered the party even more out of step with the times from the perspective of vote maximization.

Another badly timed strategic error by New Democracy was to persist in its defence of the EU. Opposition to Swedish membership rose sharply from 17 per cent to 62 per cent between 1990 and 1992, and even though opinion swung again in the year before the 1994 referendum (in which 52.2 per cent voted for and 46.9 against – Lindahl, 1995: 139), the heavy politicization of the issue presented possibilities for mobilization, in particular for Eurosceptics. Unlike many populist parties in other countries, New Democracy thus missed its chance to combine EU opposition with nationalism, xenophobia and populism, which could have appealed to a significant number of anti-EU voters who did not share the other political values of the Eurosceptic camp – made up of the Left, Centre and Green parties (Rydgren, 2002).

These political developments made it more difficult for New Democracy to win over voters based on the ideology pursued in the run-up to the 1991 election. As a result, elements within the party and its executive appealed for urgent changes of direction and, in so doing, highlighted the lack of mechanisms possessed by the party for dealing with internal conflict. Ultimately, the party's collapse and electoral failure in 1994 was due to these organizational factors. Having been formed only a few months before the 1991 election, New Democracy had had no time to establish and consolidate an efficient organizational process (Rydgren, 2006).

Explaining the relative failure of radical right-wing populism since 1994

Dealignment and realignment processes

Dealignment and realignment processes provide favourable political opportunity structures for emerging populist parties. Several cleavage dimensions always co-exist simultaneously (Lipset and Rokkan, 1967; Rokkan, 1970), with most of them ultimately based on social identity or interests. While these cleavage dimensions, whether manifest or latent, exist side by side, their salience increases and declines during certain periods (Hout *et al.*, 1996: 55–6). Contemporary Western European democracies are characterized by two major cleavage dimensions: (a) the economic cleavage dimension, which pits workers against capital, and relates to the degree of state involvement in the economy; (b) the socio-cultural cleavage dimension, which concerns issues such as immigration, law and order, abortion, and so on. The relative strength of these two cleavage dimensions influences the potential of populist parties for successful electoral mobilization. For instance, we may expect that the relative strength or salience of the old socio-economic cleavage influences the possibilities to mobilize on issues and frames connected to the new socio-cultural cleavage (Kriesi *et al.*, 1995).

Moreover, political discontent and alienation can have both direct and indirect influences by sowing the seeds of political protest and releasing voters from their ties with mainstream parties. In this respect, the declining degrees of party identification and class voting are particularly important.

In this sense, Sweden is no exception. In fact, confidence in political institutions has declined more in Sweden since the end of the 1960s than in most other European countries (Möller, 2000: 52). Swedish voters now have little respect for political institutions. Indeed, in 2002, a mere one per cent of those polled expressed full confidence in political parties, and 13 per cent fairly high confidence. By contrast, 41 per cent of voters stated that they had little or no confidence in the parties (Holmberg and Weibull, 2003b: 44). Moreover, just two per cent of them replied that they had strong confidence, and 27 per cent that they had rather strong confidence, in national politicians (Holmberg and Weibull, 2003b: 56).

That said, we can also observe how voters in Sweden have become more content with how democracy in the country operates. In the mid-1990s, Swedes were no more satisfied than other Western Europeans. In fact, they were much less satisfied than their Danish counterparts and roughly on the same level as the French and Austrians (all countries whose electorates had voted in significant numbers for populist parties). However, from the mid-1990s to 2002, the proportion of voters who claimed to be 'very or fairly pleased with democracy in Sweden' increased to 74 per cent, making the Swedish electorate among the most contented in Europe as regards the democratic process (Holmberg and Weibull, 2003a: 13). This suggests, therefore, that in recent years the niche for the mobilization of discontent has contracted.

Nevertheless, while it may be limited, for some time there has been scope for protest mobilization by a populist party through the incitement of popular discontent with the mainstream political establishment – provided that it is not perceived as challenging democratic principles. This situation also implies that more voters have been released from their political loyalties, and thus are available for voter mobilization in the electoral arena. That this is the case is even more obvious if we consider the declining degree of party identification.

As mentioned above, party identification and class voting are two key indicators of political stability. The term 'party identification' denotes the psychological affinity an individual has for a certain party (Campbell *et al.*, 1960). Even though the level of identification can vary in strength, it is usually assumed that it constitutes a relatively stable factor in the voting patterns found within any political system.

Traditionally speaking, party identification has always had a powerful influence on voting behaviour and the number of voters expressing strong party identification has declined in Western Europe in recent decades (Putnam *et al.*, 2000: 17). This has also been the case in Sweden, where the relevant figures dropped from 53 per cent in 1960 to 34 per cent in 1982 and 21 per cent in 1991, declining further to 19 per cent in 1998 and 18 per cent in 2002 (Holmberg, 2000: 41; Holmberg and Oscarsson, 2002: 186). Consequently, Swedish voters have become increasingly mobile, with the numbers of voters shifting from one party to another increasing dramatically. In 2002, 31.8 per cent of voters opted for a different party than in the previous election in 1998. It is interesting to note, by way of comparison, that the corresponding figure between 1985 and 1988 was 20.2 per cent. Similarly, the proportion of voters stating that they did not decide how to vote until the election campaign (approximately one month before the election) has also increased from 40 per cent in 1988 to 57 per cent in 2002 (Holmberg, 2000: 19–22; Holmberg and Oscarsson, 2002: 134–7).

Class voting is also a relatively stable factor in the analysis of voter behaviour and, as measured by the Alford index, has declined in Sweden. It should be noted, however, that Swedish class voting had been unusually high and remains well above that of many other countries. It should also be pointed out that this trend did not continue into the 1990s, and class voting is still high among working class voters (albeit slightly less so than during the 1990s). Hence, 75 per cent of industrial workers and 63 per cent of other workers voted for either the Social Democrats or the Left Party in the 1998 election (Holmberg, 2000: 68). In the 2002 election, the share among industrial voters had decreased to 68 per cent, but increased among other workers to 65 per cent (Holmberg and Oscarsson, 2002: 146). Exit polls in 2006 indicate that class voting may have decreased between 2002 and 2006, possibly due to the weak election campaign of the Social Democrats.

These statistics are important because we know from previous studies that working class voters are one of the groups over-represented amongst the supporters of RRP parties (cf. Rydgren, 2003b: chapter 2; Betz, 1994). Having said this, the proportion of non-voters is also high in this group: 26 per cent of industrial workers and 23 per cent of other workers did not vote in the 1998 election, along with 40 per cent of the unemployed (Holmberg, 2000: 68, 100).

Thus, even though class voting has declined in Sweden, it remains fairly high (especially amongst the working classes) and this may obstruct the emergence of a strong Swedish populist party. Moreover, these figures, in conjunction with the fact that trade union membership in Sweden is higher than in any other EU country (Kjellberg, 2000), suggest that there is still a relatively strong sense of class affinity in Sweden. Indeed, the proportion of manual workers who identified themselves with the working class was slightly higher (53.6 per cent) in 1995 than it was in 1980 (Sohlberg and Leiulfsrud, 2000: 54). This indicates that 'traditionally provided and sustained collective identities' (Betz, 1994: 29) have not been eroded or destroyed in Sweden to the extent that Hans-Georg Betz claims, and that the socio-economic cleavage dimension still dominates Swedish politics.

As mentioned above, there is also much to suggest that the economic crisis in Sweden boosted the relative importance of conventional issues of political economy and the Welfare State rather than those of a socio-cultural nature, such as immigration and law and order. While questions concerning the economy and employment dominated the crisis years around the mid-1990s, healthcare and education have moved higher up the electorate's agenda since the final years of that decade. In fact, since the mid-1990s, healthcare has emerged as a particularly critical issue. Thus, while in 1995 only 15 per cent of voters gave it any serious priority, by 1999 this figure had risen to 41 per cent. The same can be said of education, which jumped from 7 per cent in 1995 to 32 per cent in 2002. These figures indicate a continuing high salience of the socio-economic cleavage dimension and suggest that realignment processes have not been much of a factor in Swedish politics (with the exception of issues concerning the environment and the EU).

Politicization of new issues

Following Ian Budge and Dennis Farlie (1983), we may assume that parties try to profit from issue-voting not so much by opposing each other's issue positions as by attempting to shift public (and media) attention from one issue to another. Hence, agenda-setting, politicization, and framing play crucial roles for modern parties. The immigration issue, in particular, has been important for the emergence of populist parties. While not all voters who hold anti-immigration attitudes vote for a new radical right-wing party, most voters who do vote for these parties also hold such attitudes.

Sweden has long been a country of net immigration, in that more people have migrated in than migrated out. Non-European immigration increased in the 1970s, 1980s and 1990s, and today 11 per cent of the Swedish population consists of people born abroad. Moreover, during the last of these decades, the average number of asylum applications was 29 for every 1,000 Swedish citizens, as opposed to 18 in Belgium, 16 in Austria, five in France and one in Italy (van Holsteyn and Rydgren, 2004). Thus, as Herbert Kitschelt has shown, immigration on its own cannot explain why populist parties have been successful in some countries, but failed in others (Kitschelt, 1995: 62).

On this point, it is interesting to note that a majority of Swedish voters in the 1990s were in favour of reducing the number of asylum-seekers. These attitudes peaked at 65 per cent in 1992, falling steadily thereafter for the remainder of the decade. In 2002, however, the number of anti-immigrant voters rose again from 44 per cent to 50 per cent (Demker, 2003: 85).

Nonetheless, the existence of xenophobic attitudes does not automatically lead to the growth of an RRP party. Nor is it sufficient for the immigration issue to be considered important and prominent. Rather, the key factor is that it must be seen as a politically important issue. This means that it must first be politicized, or 'translated' into political terms. Although an issue is already politicized to a certain extent when seen as important by both politicians and voters alike, it is only really fully politicized when it affects their political behaviour (Rydgren, 2003b: chapter 2 and 6; cf. Campbell *et al.*, 1960). Seen from this perspective, therefore, we can say that the immigration issue was not fully politicized in Sweden during the 1990s and did not prove particularly important (in terms of party choice) for the Swedish electorate – with the possible exception of 1991 when New Democracy made its electoral breakthrough. However, in the 2002 election, in which immigration played a central role (due to the liberal party's agenda-setting efforts in calling for tougher citizenship legislation), 10 per cent of voters stated that the immigration issue was one of the principal factors influencing their choice of how to vote (Holmberg and Oscarsson, 2002: 173). In the 2006 election campaign, however, the salience of the immigration issue seems to have once again decreased.

We have thus found that Sweden has about as many xenophobic and immigration-sceptic voters per head of the population as other Western European countries. Some 50 per cent of voters favour taking in fewer asylum-seekers and a relatively large proportion accords high priority to the issues of asylum and immigration. As Marie Demker (2003: 89) has shown, the proportion of voters holding anti-immigrant sentiments was higher (60 per cent) amongst those who ranked refugee and immigration issues as one of the top three social problems. This means that 11 per cent of voters want a tighter immigration and asylum policy and consider this more important than most other issues. It is amongst such voters that RRP parties can hope to mobilize support, leaving us to conclude that there is a relatively large niche available for a Swedish anti-immigration party to take root. At the same time, however, immigration has not been a particularly salient political issue, in the sense that it has not significantly affected voting behaviour, as has been the case in countries where RRP parties have enjoyed success.

Party convergence

The degree of party convergence can also affect the political opportunity structure for emerging parties (Kitschelt, 1995). Convergence may fuel political distrust and alienation by aggravating the sense that there are no significant and relevant differences between the parties. It thus creates an atmosphere in which political discontent can be articulated and mobilized. It can also serve to create niches in the voter arena. Equally important is that it can trigger the depoliticization of a formerly dominant cleavage dimension, such as the socio-economic dimension (Schattschnieder, 1975; Rydgren, 2005), by rendering it less engaging and thus less relevant for voters and the media. In its place, a new, alternative cleavage dimension (such as the socio-cultural) may then flourish, which in turn can facilitate the rise of a new populist party.

Swedish political space, however, did not see any major convergence between 1994 and 2003. When asked to place the parties on a Right-Left scale (on which 0 represented the far Left and 10 the far Right), voters gave the Conservative Party a score of 8.9 in the 1979 and 1982 elections, 9.0 in 1985, 8.9 again in 1988, 8.7 in 1991, 8.8 in 1994 and 8.9 once more in the 1998 election. Similarly, the Left Party was consistently placed between 0.9 and 1.4 between 1979 and 1998. The Social Democrats, however, have migrated to the Right since the mid 1980s (with the exception of the 1994 election), and between 1994 and 1998 drifted from 3.2 to 3.8 (Holmberg, 2000: 124).

Nonetheless, this method tells us nothing about how voters actually interpret the terms 'Left' and 'Right' and we can surmise that they base their distinction of the parties' respective positions on socio-economic considerations. At the same time, however, we know that the socio-cultural dimension (which comprises issues of nationality and nationalism, immigration, abortion, law, security and so on) is more fundamental to the emergence of populist parties (Rydgren, 2003b). Accordingly, going by the above polls, we cannot categorically exclude the possible presence, now or in the past, of convergence on the socio-cultural dimension.

There are tentative indications that this might be the case (or, at least, that it was the case at the time of the 1998 election). When voters were asked about their attitudes to 'the multicultural society' and invited to place themselves on a scale from 0 (strongly disapprove) to 100 (strongly approve), Conservative Party voters scored an average of 58, Centre Party voters 59, Social Democrat voters 60, Christian Democrat voters 61, Left Party voters 65, Green Party voters 71 and Liberal Party voters 73 (Holmberg, 2000: 134). This suggests that there might be a vacant niche of voters who are opposed to the concept of the multicultural society, although we should not forget that the socio-cultural cleavage dimension has played a subordinate role in Swedish voters' choice of party (cf. Oscarsson, 1998).

Moreover, since 2003, the Conservative Party has moved significantly toward a centre position. The party has ceased talking about 'system change' and no longer proposes to dismantle the Welfare State. Indeed, it presented itself as 'the new workers party' during the 2006 election campaign. It remains to be analysed what effect, if any, this convergence had on levels of political trust and to what extent it contributed to the electoral gains of the Sweden Democrats.

The presence or absence of elite allies, increased legitimacy and/or increased visibility

The decision by one or more of the mainstream parties or other actors on the political field to work together (at any level) with an emerging populist party can also have a profound impact on its likelihood of achieving an electoral breakthrough. This is because such collaboration can legitimize the party in the eyes of voters (which is extremely important for marginalized extremist parties) and give it, through the media attention attracted, greater political visibility (Rydgren, 2003a). Similarly, whenever mainstream parties appropriate the policy ideas held by the emerging party or adopt a similar political language, they are also contributing to its legitimization.

It should be noted, however, that this can conflict with other opportunity structures discussed above. After all, any collaboration between one or more mainstream parties and the emerging populist party can serve to shrink the niches available for continued mobilization on the electoral arena (Rydgren, 2005). Such collaboration might also hamper the emerging party in its use of the populist antiestablishment strategy and its self-representation as the only genuine opposition to the entire 'political class.' These different mechanisms must therefore be carefully weighed up against each other. I would suggest that a working partnership with established parties creates favourable opportunity structures for an emerging RRP party, in particular those whose roots lie in extra-parliamentary right-wing extremism. In such cases, the necessity of reducing electoral stigmatization by increasing legitimacy may be well worth the price that possibly has to be paid for shrinking niches on the political arena.

Unlike many other Western European countries (not least Denmark), the mainstream parties in Sweden have effectively erected a *cordon sanitaire* against the Sweden Democrats, avoiding any kind of collaboration. They have also tried explicitly to avoid appropriating the political programme of this or any other anti-immigrant party.

The ideology and rhetoric of the Sweden Democrats

The rest of this chapter will discuss the ways in which the Sweden Democrats have tried to take advantage of mobilization opportunities.

The Sweden Democrats party was formed in 1988 as a direct successor to the Sweden Party, which in turn was the outcome of a merger in 1986 between the Swedish Progress Party and the BBS (Keep Sweden Swedish) (Larsson and Ekman, 2001). The Sweden Democrats trace their roots back to Swedish Fascism, and there were, particularly at the end of the 1980s and for the first half of the 1990s, distinct overlaps between them and openly anti-democratic, Nazi and Fascist groupings (Larsson and Ekman, 2001). During the latter half of the 1990s, however, the party worked hard to erect a more respectable façade. A ban on uniforms was introduced in 1996 by new leader Mikael Jansson (who had previously been active in the Centre Party) and, in 1999, the Sweden Democrats openly renounced Nazism. Furthermore, some of the more provocative paragraphs in the party manifesto were toned down or eventually deleted (in particular those dealing with capital punishment, and the banning of both abortion and non-European adoption). However, and notwithstanding the remarkable continuity in the party manifesto up to 2002, this softer profile precipitated a split in the summer of 2001 when a disgruntled 'traditionalist' faction broke away to form the National Democrats.

If we look at the Sweden Democrats' manifesto and examine its political rhetoric, it is clear that the party has been increasingly influenced by the electoral successes of other European RRP parties. While the British National Front was one of its larger sources of inspiration during the latter half of the 1980s, the French *Front National* made a profound impression on the ideological and strategic direction taken by the Sweden Democrats during the 1990s along with, to a lesser extent, the Austrian FPÖ, the Danish People's Party, the German *Die Republikaner* and Italy's *Alleanza Nazionale*. Indeed, the leader of *Die Republikaner*, Franz Schönhuber, appeared as a guest speaker at a Sweden Democrats election meeting, and the French *Front National* made substantial contributions to the party's 1998 election campaign fund. The party has also been explicit about its desire to work more closely with other RRP parties (Johansson, 2002: 5). Like most of these parties, the Sweden Democrats is a pronounced culturalist party, whose programme is based on ethno-nationalism and xenophobia. Like other populist parties, it also makes frequent recourse to an anti-Establishment strategy. If we look at the party's 2002 manifesto, we find that its primary stated political goal is 'to defend our national identity' (*Sverigedemokraterna*, 2002 on line). This ambition rests upon an ontological relationship with the terms 'people' and 'culture' (that is, to the notion that each nation embodies one ethnically determined culture) and a nostalgic belief in 'the myth of the golden past' (Rydgren, 2003b), a yearning for an imagined *gemeinschaft* free from conflict and social problems. This philosophy thus treats cultures as unique, yet fragile, and when different cultures come together in one and the same state, the integrity of the unique, dominant national identity is therefore jeopardized. Consequently, the Sweden Democrats advocate ethnic segregation. In the words of the former party secretary, Torbjörn Kastell, the party wants 'a multicultural world, not a multicultural society' (2002: 130).

According to the Sweden Democrats, immigration, supranationality (such as the EU), cultural imperialism (mainly from the USA) and globalization (they also want a check on economic globalism) were the greatest threats to the unique Swedish culture and by far their greatest concern was immigration. Consequently, the party advocates a highly restrictive immigration policy that effectively denies access to all non-Europeans and imposes a citizenship condition of 10 years' residency and knowledge of Swedish language and history.

As with other RRP parties, the Sweden Democrats' discourse on immigration and immigrants is constructed around four separate themes: first, as we saw above, immigration is considered a threat to Swedish culture and national identity. Second, immigration is considered to be at the root of crime and, in particular, offences of a violent or sexual nature. Hence, the Sweden Democrats' official journal *SD-kuriren*'s website has regularly published accounts of crimes committed by people with immigrant backgrounds in an attempt to promote an image of immigrants as the main cause of criminality.

Third and fourth, immigration is seen as a cause of unemployment and of the financial constraints and problems of the Welfare State. Immigrants are generally depicted as illegitimately competing for scant resources, which in the rhetoric of the Sweden Democrats should go to 'ethnic Swedes.' Like the French *Front National*, the Sweden Democrats have promulgated the principle of 'national preference', by which they mean that 'Swedes' are to be given priority access to childcare, jobs and healthcare. This strategy is conducted under the motto of 'Swedes first!', a highly potent slogan that plays on jealousy and identifies a convenient scapegoat for the problems faced by many people in their everyday lives.

The Sweden Democrats also adopt socio-cultural right-wing authoritarian positions on issues related to family policy and law and order. Like other RRP parties, the Sweden Democrats consider the family to be the most fundamental unit of society besides that of the nation, and are therefore horrified over what they see as today's 'moral disintegration', as represented, for example, by divorce and abortion. Yet, it is in this area where we find the greatest changes taking place over time. Since the release of the party's first manifesto in 1989, capital punishment and an abortion ban have been struck from their list of demands (with effect from the late 1990s), although internal debate on these issues has continued. The shedding of these calls and its more toned-down posture together represent an attempt by the party to erect the respectable façade it needs to forestall voter alienation.

We also find that the Sweden Democrats are populist through their use of the antiestablishment strategy: all other political parties are lumped together into one political class, and any significant differences distinguishing them are rarely acknowledged (even if the Left – in the broad sense of the term – is arch enemy number one). Party member Jimmy Windeskog, for example, views all political opponents as being part of the 'liberal-Marxist establishment' (1999: 8). This is, then, what the Sweden Democrats place themselves in opposition to, posing as the party that has not only witnessed reality, but also has the courage to describe it. Like the French *Front National*, the Sweden Democrats boast about 'saying what common people think, and saying it loud' (cf. Larsson and Ekman, 2001: 277) rather than using politically correct rhetoric. Moreover, given that they consider demographic (ethnic) homogeneity a necessary condition for a peaceful and functional democratic society, all the mainstream parties (that in one way or another favour immigration and asylum) are therefore, by contrast, depicted as the gravediggers of democracy. In this way, the party portrays itself not as the enemy of democracy, but as its greatest champion. The Sweden Democrats also claim to be the victims of a 'doctrinal dictatorship' created by a process 'that gives "approved" internationally oriented politicians leading positions in society', thanks also to an 'extremely homogenous media [and] TV and radio monopoly' (*Sverigedemokraterna*, 2002 online).

The main task facing the Sweden Democrats, however, has been not to appear overly extreme or too closely associated with openly anti-democratic groups. As we have seen, the party has its roots in the extra-parliamentary far Right and, for the first half of the 1990s there was no clear distinction between the Sweden Democrats and various skinhead and Nazi organizations. Indeed, overlap of membership was not uncommon (Larsson and Ekman, 2001). We can see this proximity in the pressure felt by Mikael Jansson, as newly appointed leader, to impose a uniform ban in 1996 and to urge members repeatedly not to wear uniforms at party meetings up to 1999. Nevertheless, the party did not explicitly renounce Nazism until 1999/2000 after events in the small town of Malexander (when two policemen were killed by three armed criminals with links to Nazi movements) and the murder of trade unionist Björn Söderberg, which also brought the Sweden Democrats media scrutiny and much adverse publicity (Larsson and Ekman, 2001: 171). In 2003, the party took a further step towards ridding itself of the stigma of extremism by announcing that the UN Declaration of Human Rights was to form a cornerstone of its policies. This process of change has continued since 2005, when Jimmie Åkesson became party leader. The party logo featuring the Swedish flag as a burning torch – a direct derivation of the British National Front's emblem and very close to those of both the French *Front National* and Italy's neo-fascist *Movimento Sociale Italiano* (MSI) – was replaced in 2005 by a more neutral flower. Although the increased support for the Sweden Democrats in the past few years is partly due to the effectiveness of these changes, there is much to suggest that the party is still seriously hampered by its extremist image amongst a large portion of the electorate. Not only are these changes comparatively new (and will probably only have a full effect, if at all, in the future), there are also clear signs that not everyone has taken them to heart and that they have not been properly implemented throughout the organization. Numerous statements have been made that have stepped over the official 'respectable' line, and since many of the party's leading members were already active during the early 1990s, it is hard to give a credible explanation why they, as confirmed democrats, chose to join an extremist party in which one in three members of the executive had Nazi links (Larsson and Ekman, 2001: 165). There have also been voices from within the organization opposing the abandonment of old ideological principles, and this has caused serious problems for the party.

Conclusions

This chapter has shown that Sweden shared several important opportunity structures with other West European countries, in particular those related to anti-immigrant sentiments and feelings of disenchantment towards political institutions. However, Sweden diverged in a number of important ways. First, the socio-economic cleavage dimension was still highly salient in Swedish politics. Second, and related to the first point, the issue of immigration has not been fully politicized in Sweden. Although this started in the 2002 election campaign, the issue was less salient in 2006. In Sweden, questions relating to the socio-economic dimension still dominate politics. Finally, the Sweden Democrats have been heavily stigmatized as a result of their Fascist origins and links. The party has thus found it very difficult to create a respectable façade, although its progress can be largely explained by its ability to present itself as increasingly more respectable. The party doubled its electoral share between the 2002 and 2006 elections to almost three per cent of the vote, and it continues to make inroads in local politics. It remains to be seen, however, if the Sweden Democrats possess the organizational tools needed in order to survive a phase of expansion without provoking internal splits. However, given that the party has proved successful at keeping its organization together, the results of the 2006 election present it with new opportunities. The party will be entitled to state subsidies, which will give it the economic resources required to conduct a more ambitious election campaign in 2010. Finally, the growing presence of the Sweden Democrats in local politics is also likely to give the party increased visibility, not least in the mass media.

Note

1. This chapter draws from Rydgren (2002 and 2004) and Chapter 5 in Rydgren (2006).

10
The Netherlands: Populism versus Pillarization

Paul Lucardie

Introduction

Until recent times, populism was not a significant political phenomenon in the Netherlands. That all changed in February 2002, when Pim Fortuyn founded a populist movement that became the country's second largest parliamentary party just three months later. Following its leader's violent death and its entry into coalition government, however, the *Lijst Pim Fortuyn* (LPF) rapidly disintegrated. This chapter will examine the swift and spectacular rise of Fortuyn's movement in terms of (a) the structural conditions within which it emerged and (b) the agency of the LPF and its leader. In particular, the chapter aims to provide answers to the following questions:

(1) can existing theories about the emergence of new parties explain the LPF's sudden success?
(2) how can we account for the equally rapid decline of the movement?
(3) has Dutch populism disappeared or does it survive as a sleeping volcano that could erupt again at short notice?

The emergence and electoral success of the LPF: structural conditions

This section will analyse the structural conditions which facilitate or hinder the emergence and success of new (populist) parties in the Netherlands: the electoral system and other institutional factors, the party system, political culture and the media. Subsequently, we will assess the political and economic conditions that might have favoured the rise of the LPF in 2002. Finally, we will look at the resources mobilized by Fortuyn: his personality, his political project and ideology, the organization and funding of the LPF, and his relationship with the media.

The institutional context

The electoral system in the Netherlands is a pure example of proportional representation: seats in the lower house of parliament are distributed among parties according to the number of votes gained across the whole country. The country is divided into 19 electoral districts only for administrative purposes. The upper house is not elected directly by the people, but carries less weight than the lower house. As the lower house contains 150 seats, a party needs only 0.67 per cent of the popular vote (at present about 60,000 votes) to obtain a seat. There is no legal threshold (as exists, for example, in Germany and Austria). Obviously, this makes life easier for any new party. New parties do have to fulfil a few conditions, however: they must register with the Electoral Board, pay a deposit and persuade 30 citizens in each electoral district to sign a declaration of support. If a new party manages to do this in all 19 districts, it is allocated a few minutes of airtime on public radio and television, subsidized by the government – the only funding a party is entitled to before it has won seats in parliament. These requirements may not appear particularly burdensome, compared to those in other European countries, although they do discourage independent candidates. Between 1946 and 2003, 18 new parties have gained entry into parliament. Other institutional factors, such as the parliamentary system and the unitary character of the Dutch state, seem less relevant to the rise of new parties.

The party system, pillarization and depillarization

Because of pillarization (and facilitated by the electoral system), the Dutch party system is fairly fragmented. Pillarization implies the close ties between political elites and the masses through networks of ideological organizations – referred to as pillars or columns. Almost every religious denomination and social class produced its own political party. Most Catholics and Calvinists voted for Catholic or Calvinist parties (Lijphart, 1968: 26–58). Socialists were less pillarized, and Liberals least of all. As a result, since 1894, no party has ever won an absolute majority of seats.

The number of parties in parliament since 1946 has fluctuated between 7 and 14. Giovanni Sartori regarded the Netherlands as an example of moderate pluralism rather than extreme pluralism, because the number of relevant parties did not rise above five in his opinion (Sartori, 1976: 148–50; cf. Andeweg and Irwin, 2005: 48). The five identified by Sartori were the three religious or confessional parties – these would merge into the Christian Democratic party (CDA – *Christen Democratisch Appèl*) in 1980 – and two secular, class-based parties: the Liberal party (VVD – *Volkspartij voor Vrijheid en Democratie*) and the Labour party (PvdA – *Partij van de Arbeid*). The confessional parties dominated practically all coalitions between 1918 (when proportional representation and universal suffrage were introduced) and 1994, while the Liberals and Social Democrats (Labour) alternated in government.

The hegemony of the Christian parties was steadily eroded, however, in the 1960s and 1970s, by social and cultural processes which are usually described by terms like secularization, depillarization and individualization – processes which occurred almost everywhere in the modern world, but had a particular impact in the Netherlands (Andeweg, 1999: 112–21). Gradually, a non-pillarized public domain emerged. This encompassed not only newspapers and radio and television stations, but also environmental organizations and other social movements which refused to commit themselves to a particular political or religious belief system (Koole and Daalder, 2002: 29–30; see also Pennings, 1997).

The 1994 elections demonstrated the fragility of the Christian Democratic hegemony as the CDA lost more than a third of its electorate and 20 of its 54 seats. Its coalition partner – and main rival – the PvdA, suffered an only slightly less dramatic loss (12 out of 49 seats). The main winners were the least pillarized parties, in particular the VVD and the leftwing liberal Democrats 66 (D66). For the first time in Dutch history, the two Liberal parties entered coalition with the Social Democrats, thus consigning the Christian Democrats to the opposition benches. The coalition was called 'purple', because it mixed the 'blue' conservative liberalism of the VVD with the 'red' socialism of the PvdA. Lacking a colour of their own, the liberal Democrats, who had taken the initiative, soon became invisible. Yet the 'red' of socialism also turned out to be rather pale. Wim Kok, the PvdA leader, proved keen on 'shedding the ideological feathers' of his party and his government mainly pursued liberal policies in both socio-economic and socio-cultural spheres. It reduced the public deficit and the tax burden for citizens and companies, privatized energy, transport and telecommunications; and introduced a rather liberal law on euthanasia as well as on same-sex marriage. Helped by an economic boom, the purple coalition won 97 seats (out of 150) at the parliamentary elections of 1998 – five more than in 1994. Only the Democrats lost ground, as their charismatic leader retired from politics and their main aim in government, constitutional reform, had not been achieved. In fact, politics continued to be consociational, or at least consensual, even after the disintegration of the pillars – a paradoxical situation, according to some observers (Koole and Daalder, 2002: 36–40; Thomassen, 2000: 206–9; Pennings, 1997: 15–21).

The ideological distances between the parties have diminished over time, especially during the 1990s (Volkens and Klingemann, 2002: 156–7). As Jacques Thomassen predicted in 2000, the ideological *rapprochement* between the established parties in the Netherlands would offer a golden opportunity for populist parties of the Right or Left (2000: 206–9).

Populist parties had emerged from time to time in the Netherlands, often as a reaction against pillarization, but rarely managed to mobilize the masses. In the 1920s and 1930s, as well as in the 1960s, agrarian populist movements mobilized farmers (Lucardie, 2003, 178–80). In the 1980s and 1990s, the Centre Party and its offshoot, the Centre Democrats, combined nationalism with populism and won a few seats in parliament (Mudde, 2000: 131–41; Lucardie, 1998).In 1994 the Socialist Party (SP) gained entrance to parliament with a rather populist campaign slogan of 'vote against, vote

SP!'. This appealed especially to working-class voters disappointed at how the PvdA had reduced social security (Van der Steen, 1995). Founded in 1971 as 'Communist Party of the Netherlands/Marxist–Leninist', the SP was inspired by Mao Zedong and his 'mass line', interpreted in a populist sense. Before taking a position on specific issues, the SP would often consult 'the masses' by door-to-door polling in working-class neighbourhoods (Voerman, 1987: 138). In the 1970s, its admiration for Mao waned, but not its emphasis on 'the masses' and 'the people'. In 1999, the SP redefined socialism in vague humanist terms: 'human dignity, equality and solidarity' (Socialistische Partij, 1999: 7). Gradually, the party seemed to shift from populism to social democracy – thus opening up the space for a new populist party.

In the 1990s, populism penetrated local politics. Independent of each other, many local parties had emerged in protest against the professionalization and technocratic nature of municipal politics. Often, they reacted against large-scale urban renewal projects, arguing that 'small is beautiful'. Emphasizing civic virtues and quality of life (with a new Dutch term: *leefbaarheid*, 'liveability'), they adopted names like *'Leefbaar Rotterdam'*, *'Leefbaar Hilversum'*, or *'Leefbaar Utrecht'*. In 1999, leaders of the latter two local parties decided to set up a similarly named national party: *Leefbaar Nederland* (Liveable Netherlands). In June 2001 the new party held its founding congress. In November 2001 a second congress discussed the party programme and elected a leader called Pim Fortuyn. With Fortuyn's rising popularity, the party's future looked quite bright. Yet in February 2002, three months before the parliamentary elections, the leader left the party, after alienating the party executive with provocative statements about discrimination – which he considered less important than freedom of expression. With a new relatively unknown and uncharismatic leader, *Leefbaar Nederland* won only two seats in the May 2002 general election. Internal squabbles did not improve the party image and, in the January 2003 general election, *Leefbaar Nederland* lost both its seats. More importantly for our purposes here, however, it had paved the way for the *Lijst Pim Fortuyn*.

The media and public opinion

With depillarization, formal and even informal ties between political parties on the one hand and newspapers and radio and television networks on the other weakened or disappeared altogether (Kleinnijenhuis and Scholten, 1989: 436–9). Moreover, the media that had belonged to the pillars lost popularity, due to competition from commercial television stations, the emergence of new media and government interference with broadcasting (Bakker and Scholten, 2003: 124–37). Commercial media and new media are rarely linked to ideological pillars – with the exception of political party websites, of course. Partly as a result of depillarization and commercialization, as well as growing competition, most media usually now try to report about politics in an objective and non-partisan mode (Kleinnijenhuis *et al.*, 1995: 80–3). Avoiding sensitive and contested interpretations of ideological questions, they focus increasingly on spectacular events and personal stories. This can be exploited by a new populist party, provided it is fronted by a colourful personality who performs well on television and radio and engages in 'spectacular politics'.

Today, journalists are often accused of spreading cynicism and distrust of politicians, as they focus on 'horse races', conflicts and 'strategic games' (Brants, 2002). Even if these accusations may be exaggerated, opinion polls and voting studies did indicate increasing cynicism and distrust of politicians among Dutch voters in the last decade of the twentieth century, and especially after 1998 (Van Holsteyn and Den Ridder, 2005: 84–90; Van Praag, 2003: 110). Nonetheless, even in 2003, most Dutch voters still trusted politicians and institutions such as parliament and political parties with about 70 per cent expressing 'a great deal' or 'quite a lot' of confidence in parliament and 56 per cent doing so with regard to political parties (Van Holsteyn and Den Ridder, 2005: 91). Thus, an overwhelming majority of citizens appeared to be satisfied with the way democracy worked in the Netherlands.

Turnout at parliamentary elections has remained fairly high in the Netherlands. Although it declined from 88 per cent in 1977 to 73 per cent in 1998, it rose again to 80 per cent in 2002, 2003 and 2006 (probably due to the presence of new populist parties). Membership of political parties also diminished, from almost 750,000 in 1960 (more than 10 per cent of the electorate) to hardly 300,000 (2.5 per cent) in 2000.[1] Political participation outside political parties and general interest in politics have not really fallen, however (Irwin and Van Holsteyn, 2002: 40–3). Indeed, many voters said they wanted more participation, for example, in referendums or direct elections of mayors and Prime Ministers (Irwin and Van Holsteyn, 2002: 46–8).

One might conclude from all this that Dutch voters at the beginning of the twenty-first century were not really alienated from the political system, but simply less loyal to the traditional parties and ready to give the benefit of the doubt to new parties and politicians. In turn, new populist leaders could use this potential and benefit from the increased objectivity of the media as well as the tendency to personalize and dramatize political news.

Precipitating factors: economic stagnation and immigration

In their campaigns for the 2002 elections, the governing parties concentrated on the economic achievements of the purple coalition. Growth had been quite impressive since 1994, although it began to slow down in the first years of the twenty-first century (CBS, 2002: 15–27; CBS, 2003: 15–28).

After the booming 1990s, exports and consumption stagnated, investments declined and, in 2002, unemployment began to rise. Given the relative weakness of opposition to the purple coalition – the largest opposition party, the CDA, was hamstrung by internal conflicts and leadership changes – the economic problems offered a potential opportunity to be exploited by a new populist party. However, when Dutch voters went to the polls in May 2002, they may not yet have felt the full effects of recession. Wages continued to rise in 2002 (CBS, 2003: 22) and most voters evaluated the government's economic performance quite favourably (52 per cent), particularly in the area of employment (66 per cent) (Van Holsteyn and Irwin, 2003: 54–5).

Nevertheless, the governing parties should not have expected gratitude from the voters. When asked to name the two most important political issues at the time, only six per cent mentioned (the lack of) economic growth (Van Praag, 2003: 108; see also Kleinnijenhuis *et al.*, 2003: 50). Rather, voters expressed concern about questions such as crime and security (53 per cent mentioned it as one of the two most important policy areas), health care (38 per cent) and asylum policy (21 per cent).[2] Unfortunately for the PvdA, VVD and D66, they had neglected these areas – at least in the eyes of many journalists and voters (Kleinnijenhuis *et al.*, 2003: 49–53, 128–30). The press tended to emphasize the failures of the government, rather than its achievements, and focused on hospital waiting lists, teacher shortages and street crime.

Insecurity was often associated with immigrants – perhaps not so much by journalists as much as among the public at large. A growing number of native citizens expressed negative feelings about immigrants, multicultural-ism and Islam (Gijsberts, 2005: 193–7). Most Dutch Muslims were migrant workers (or their descendants) from Morocco and Turkey or immigrants from the former Dutch colonies of Indonesia and Surinam. A smaller number were refugees from Iran, Iraq or Somalia. The number of Muslims had increased from 0.4 per cent of the population in 1971 to four per cent in 1995 and almost six per cent by 2005 (Shadid and Van Koningsveld, 1997: 20–1; CBS 2006). At first, many of them may have intended to return to their country of origin after earning some money in the Netherlands. However, most immigrants ended up staying and adapting – with some dif-ficulty and often reluctantly – to Dutch society. Some set up Islamic schools, student clubs, an Islamic broadcasting association and (local) political par-ties (Shadid and Van Koningsveld, 1997: 161–82, 208–13; Landman, 1992: 255–9, 260–9, 273–5). One might say they were trying to build an Islamic pillar, in line with Dutch traditions. However, due to inexperience and ethnic/religious differences (Sunnites, Shi'ites, Ahmadiyas, and so on), they achieved only modest success (Shadid and Van Koningsveld, 1997: 172).

In spite of its slow and uneven growth, the small Islamic pillar-under-construction might have worried Dutch people who felt pillars belonged to the past and that religion should disappear from the public realm. These feelings were articulated in scathing and violent terms by the maverick sociologist, Pim Fortuyn, in his regular columns in a conservative weekly and in a book with the provocative title 'Against the Islamization of our culture' (2001).

Pim Fortuyn takes the stage

Summing up the above, one might say there was a fairly favourable opportunity structure for a new populist party in the Netherlands at the turn of the millennium. The stage was set, as it were. Even so, in order to gain a foothold in the political system, any new party would have to mobilize sufficient resources, i.e. it would need not only a popular leader, but also a promising political project, personnel, funds and publicity (Lucardie, 2000: 178–9). The *Lijst Pim Fortuyn* managed to do all this in the space of three months, between 14 February and 15 May 2002.

Personal leadership and charisma

Wilhelmus 'Pim' Fortuyn was born in 1948, into a lower middle-class Catholic family. As a sociology student in the late 1960s, he turned to Marxism and became active in the student movement. Gradually, however, he lost his faith in Marxism and other kinds of socialism. In 1989 he left the PvdA, for ideological as well as personal reasons – he felt ill at ease in the culture of the party and sold short by the party leader, Wim Kok (Fortuyn, 1998: 236). In the 1990s he developed a reputation as a public speaker at meetings of business clubs, veterans' leagues and other organizations. At the same time, he wrote rather outspoken columns in *Elsevier*, the largest and most conservative weekly magazine in the Netherlands. While rather controversial, he had become a well-known national figure when nominated by the leaders of *Leefbaar Nederland* to lead the party in the 2002 general election. In November 2001, the party congress elected him with an overwhelming majority and the beaming winner ended his speech with a military salute and the words 'At your service!'. In a few months, he gained a massive following from across the political spectrum.

Fortuyn's flamboyant personality, dandyism and provocative statements marked him out from other Dutch politicians (cf. Pels, 2003: 247–76). So too did his theatrical and unusual life style – he made no secret of his visits to gay dark rooms. He was proud to speak his mind, boasting: 'I say what I think'. His narcissism, passion and religious sense of mission reminded historians of the late nineteenth-century, when charismatic leaders mobilized new social movements and mass parties that would become the foundation of the pillars (Te Velde, 2003). No doubt Fortuyn had charisma, in the original quasi-religious sense as defined by Max Weber. To be clear: charisma should not be confused with popularity or the pseudo-charisma manufactured by party machines and public relations agencies. Charismatic leaders feel they

have a special mission; they attract strong emotional support from their followers, who believe their statements and comply with them even if it
involves personal sacrifice (Eatwell, 2006). When interviewed, Fortuyn's
supporters would say things like: 'through Fortuyn I regained faith in politics', 'Pim says what I think'; 'I knew one day a man would come to redeem
our people. Fortuyn has opened my eyes' (Banning, 2002; Van der Horst,
2002). Indeed, Irena Pantelic, a Croatian immigrant, put her title of Miss
Netherlands 2001 on the line because she decided to work as a volunteer at
the party office. As she said, 'if I had to choose between the LPF and [my
title] Miss Netherlands, I would opt for Fortuyn' (*Chorus*, 2002). Even the
fact that Fortuyn was very open about his homosexuality did not deter his
supporters.

Of course, not everybody loved Fortuyn. Before his violent death on
6 May 2002, Fortuyn scored lower than all other party leaders in the
Netherlands on the 'feeling thermometer' (Van Holsteyn and Den Ridder,
2005: 140–1). Following his death, his score went up, but even then it did
not equal that of the leaders of the CDA and SP. Hence, he was not a 'charismatic giant' like Franklin Roosevelt or Adolf Hitler, but more of a 'charismatic luminary' who could turn indifferent masses into euphoric followers,
at least temporarily (Schweitzer, 1984: 237–72). Through charisma, a leader
can mobilize people with little interest in politics and a low sense of efficacy
(Madsen and Snow, 1991: 11–35; see also Van Herwaarden, 2005: 85–100)
and supporters of Fortuyn did have a lower sense of efficacy than others
(Van Praag, 2003: 109–12).

The political project

Fortuyn's project and ideology could be considered an eclectic – but not
necessarily incoherent – mixture of liberalism, nationalism, communitarianism and populism (Pels, 2003: 16–21; Lucardie and Voerman, 2002). It
was not a very strict populism, as defined in the introductory chapter of this
volume, however. Hence, it corresponds more to Margaret Canovan's definition rather than Cas Mudde's. Canovan defined populism as 'an appeal to
"the people" against both the established structure of power and the dominant ideas and values of the society' (1999: 3) while Mudde insisted on the
homogeneity of the people vs. the elite (2004: 543). Fortuyn, however, was
too much of a sociologist to use 'the people' and 'the elite' in the sense of
two homogeneous and antagonistic groups. He may have implied this in
some of his political writings, but in his more scholarly work he distinguished between at least three classes: the upper class or elite which controlled the government and corporations; a middle class that dominated the
political parties and an underclass of immigrants and native Dutch people
who were no longer represented by anyone (Fortuyn, 2001: 27–35; 2002a:
203–4).

In his more political works, Fortuyn argued that bureaucrats, technocratic managers and 'partycrats' governed the Netherlands without heeding the interests of 'us' ordinary citizens and that it would be difficult to wrest control from the political managers and bureaucrats who controlled the parties and all political positions. Nonetheless, it was Fortuyn's ambition to restore democracy and return power to 'the people in the country' (1993; 2002b: 151, 184–6). How? First of all, public officials like mayors and the prime minister should be elected directly by the people. In addition, parliament and cabinet should become more independent of each other, and of political parties (Fortuyn, 2002b: 141–3). In this worldview, small is beautiful: small schools, hospitals and municipalities are able to govern themselves without bureaucrats and managers taking control (Fortuyn, 2002a: 207–16; Fortuyn, 2002b: 39, 63, 147–8). Most populists would add to this the use of referendums and/or people's initiatives, but Fortuyn showed no enthusiasm for direct democracy. In his view, politicians should listen to their constituents, but not shy away from their own responsibilities. They should inspire public debate and exercise leadership (Fortuyn, 1993: 131, 211).

Fortuyn sometimes defined his ideology as 'modernized liberalism' (1991: 11). Other than managing the public sector, he argued that the state should not intervene in a modern, open economy. In Fortuyn's modern 'contract society', every citizen would be an entrepreneur and wage-earners would be entrepreneurs of their own labour, negotiating pension plans and disability payments directly with their employers, rather than depending on trade unions to do it for them (Fortuyn, 1995). Fortuyn was a liberal with respect to both socio-economic and moral issues and hence was a strong advocate of equality, irrespective of gender and/or sexual orientation (an area in which the state should not interfere). Similarly, he believed that drugs should be legalized, although, in general, Fortuyn advocated a conservative rather than liberal approach in the fight against crime, emphasizing repression rather than prevention and social reforms. His proposal of a universal social service for all Dutch citizens at the age of 18 also seems more inspired by conservative or communitarian concerns than by liberalism as this social service would help young immigrants (or their children) integrate in Dutch society (Fortuyn, 2002b: 176).

Integration of immigrants had been Fortuyn's main concern since the 1990s. It was the main factor behind both his break with *Leefbaar Nederland* and his growing popularity in urban areas where immigration was perceived as a problem. Fortuyn favoured a very restrictive immigration policy and assimilation of immigrants into 'Dutch culture', while rejecting charges of nationalism (2001: 105). However, Tjitske Akkerman shows convincingly that Fortuyn was a militant (albeit liberal) nationalist, although not an ethnocratic or ethnic nationalist (2005: 345–8). This nationalism chimes with his – almost romantic – opposition to a federal Europe which would 'lack a soul' (Fortuyn, 1997). In view of the aversion of most Dutch voters to unmitigated nationalism and conservatism, Fortuyn's blend of liberal nationalism, moderate populism and a little communitarianism offered an attractive alternative to the dominant ideology (varieties of liberalism, social democracy and Christian democracy). It was thus difficult to portray him as a rightwing extremist, although some politicians and activists of the Left tried to do this.

Personnel and funding

Although formally a voluntary association, the LPF in May 2002 was really not much more than an executive committee, with a small office, a secretary and a handful of regional volunteers. The volunteers were required in order to collect thirty signatures in each of the 19 electoral districts, but played a rather modest role in the campaign. Fortuyn personally selected the candidates for his list, with the help of one executive committee member. Almost all candidates were businessmen (and a few businesswomen), professionals and civil servants without political experience – and soon, some would prove rather controversial. Three of the candidates were nonwhite immigrants – purportedly showing that Fortuyn was not a racist. Members were not registered until July 2002, at which time the party claimed to have 1,000 members (Chorus and De Galan, 2002: 213). Funds were provided initially mainly by real estate dealers and a few other *homines novi* or *nouveaux riches* (Chorus and De Galan, 2002: 206–13) who donated/ lent almost a million Euro in 2002. Most of the loans would never be paid back.

Publicity

Fortuyn attracted considerable attention from the media. On the night of the March 2002 municipal elections, he confronted the leaders of the established parties for the first time with his aggressive, dramatic and exuberant style of debating. A second important event was the presentation on 14 March of Fortuyn's programme, entitled *The Mess of Eight Purple Years*. This 186-page book was a rather idiosyncratic mixture of autobiographical elements, dry statistics and political demands. Although it was ridiculed by various journalists and political leaders, it became a political bestseller and sold out within a few days. The televised presentation of the book was disturbed, however, by leftwing and green activists who threw three pies into the author's face.

In April, media interest declined. Yet on average, 18 per cent of the news in the campaign period was devoted to Fortuyn and his party, less than to the PvdA and VVD, but more than to the CDA and all the other parties (Kleinnijenhuis *et al.*, 2003: 37–47). Moreover, during the campaign, journalists tended to focus on the failures rather than the successes of the purple coalition, thus unwittingly promoting the same image Fortuyn was trying to sell to voters. Hence, the media did have a substantial effect on the outcome of the elections, in combination with the very successful campaign work of Fortuyn himself (Ibid.: 122).

Electoral success

Turnout at the 2002 elections was relatively high with close to 80 per cent of the electorate voting, five per cent more than in 1998. Of these, almost 1.7 million voted for the LPF, giving it 17 per cent of the popular vote and 26 seats in parliament. As a result, it became overnight the second-largest party in the country, surpassing the PvdA and the VVD (See Table 10.1).

Was it mainly a condolence vote? After all, Fortuyn had been shot nine days before by an animal rights activist. However, exit polls and the Dutch Parliamentary Election Study suggest that most LPF-voters had not changed their mind after 6 May when Fortuyn was shot, but intended to vote for him anyway (Obbema and Van Praag, 2002; Kleinnijenhuis *et al.*, 2003: 123; Van Holsteyn and Den Ridder, 2005: 169).

Socio-structural variables seem to explain a rather small amount (seven per cent) of the vote. Young men, the less educated and secular Dutchmen were somewhat over-represented among LPF voters, who were concentrated in the urbanized western part of the country. They were more cynical and felt less politically competent or efficacious than other voters (Van Praag, 2003: 109–12). Yet even these variables explain only a modest part of the vote. When added to socio-structural variables, political efficacy and cynicism explain 13 per cent of the variance (Van der Brug, 2003: 96). In fact, ideological agreement with Fortuyn about immigration and related issues seem to have been the main reason for voting LPF and explains 33 per cent of the variance (Van der Brug, 2003: 96–8). Studies have since shown that voters were conscious of this agreement. Fortuyn had proved able 'to change the political agenda and move issues related to asylum-seekers, immigrants and criminality to the forefront' (Van Holsteyn, Irwin and Den Ridder, 2003: 84). Analysing the Dutch Parliamentary Election data, Wouter van der Brug concludes that people voted for the LPF not because they were cynical about the system to begin with, but rather that they became cynical because they agreed with Fortuyn's ideas and noticed how the established parties reacted to him (2003: 98–101). However, Eric Bélanger and Kees Aarts show that LPF voters were already more cynical and discontented than others and held more negative opinions about refugees in 1998 (2006: 14–5).

The aftermath: consociationalism conquers populism?

In the Netherlands, elections condition, but do not determine, government formation. Even the dramatic 2002 election results allowed for several options, such as a Scandinavian-style minority government led by the largest party or a 'Flemish option' of a grand coalition of the CDA, PvdA and VVD imposing a *cordon sanitaire* on the LPF (see Table 10.1). However, all these options were incompatible with the consociational political culture of the Netherlands. Consociationalism required reconciliation of the emerging conflict between the populist opposition and the elitist government, in other words: the LPF had to be brought into coalition, in order to soothe the unrest and discontent mobilized by Fortuyn, and exacerbated by his violent death. Thus, no one was surprised when the Queen appointed a Christian-democratic lawyer to prepare the way for a majority coalition of the CDA, VVD and LPF (Dutch Government, 2002: 115–6). On 1 July, the three party leaders reached agreement on a government programme and three weeks later the cabinet was sworn in by the Queen.

Obviously, the LPF was ill-prepared for this. In fact, it was not prepared for anything at all. It lacked a coherent programme, a formal party organiza-tion and real leadership. The very day after the death of its founding father, the remaining members of the executive committee began quarrelling over his succession (Chorus and De Galan, 2002: 239). With the party executive committee practically impotent, only the parliamentary group could exer-cise some leadership within the LPF. On 16 May, it elected as chairman Mat Herben, an amiable civil servant and press officer at the Department of Defence, and number 6 on the list of candidates. While his position was challenged right from the start, he was perceived as the only person who could keep the party ranks closed (Chorus and De Galan, 2002: 281). The

Table 10.1   Parliamentary elections in the Netherlands, 1998–2006

	1998		2002		2003		2006	
	%	Seats	%	Seats	%	Seats	%	Seats
CDA	18.4	29	28.0	43	28.6	44	26.5	41
PvdA	29.0	45	15.1	23	27.3	42	21.2	33
VVD	24.7	38	15.4	24	17.9	28	14.7	22
D66	9.0	14	5.1	7	4.1	6	2.0	3
Green Left	7.3	11	6.9	10	5.1	8	4.6	7
Protestant Parties	5.1	8	4.2	6	3.7	5	5.5	8
SP	3.5	5	5.9	9	6.3	9	16.6	25
LPF	–	–	17.0	26	5.7	8	0.2	0
LN	–	–	1.6	2	0.4	0	–	–
PVV	–	–	–	–	–	–	5.9	9
Others	1.9	0	0.8	0	0.9	0	2.8	2

Notes: (1) In 1998 there were three Protestant parties. In 2000, two of them merged into the Christian Union; (2) In 2006, the LPF presented itself as 'List Five Fortuyn' (*Lijst Vijf Fortuyn*); (3) The Animal Rights Party (*Partij voor de Dieren*) won two seats in 2006.

Source: CBS *Verkiezingsstatistieken* 1998, 2002 and 2003; Electoral Board Press released on 27 November 2006: http://www.kiesraad.nl/nieuwsberichten.

LPF members of parliament therefore allowed Herben to conduct negotiations about a government coalition with Christian Democrats and Liberals.
Very few in the party preferred the option of opposition. After all, Fortuyn
himself had advocated a coalition of the LPF, CDA and VVD – even if he had
preferred a 'business cabinet' composed of professionals. However, Herben
was frequently criticized for his perceived weakness in the negotiation process. Over the summer of 2002, his leadership was questioned by different
factions within the parliamentary group and, in August of that year, he
resigned. His successor Harry Wijnschenk did nothing to reduce the tensions within the party. On the contrary, by allying himself with a member
of the cabinet, he managed to intertwine the conflict within the parliamentary group with already existing tensions between two LPF ministers.
Moreover, he antagonized the (provisional) president of the party, the real
estate tycoon Ed Maas, accusing him of manipulating the party with real
estate interests in mind. No one had the authority to mediate, and the party-
in-statu-nascendi lacked the formal/informal rules and institutions to handle
conflicts. When the ministers failed to resolve their dispute and refused
to resign, the leaders of CDA and VVD decided to end the coalition. On
16 October 2002, the prime minister therefore tendered the resignation of
his cabinet to the Queen.

When elections were held on 22 January 2003, the LPF obtained 5.7 per
cent of the popular vote and lost 18 of its 26 seats (see Table 10.1 above).
Grudgingly, the party joined the opposition benches. However, the internal
conflicts continued and were followed by further electoral decline. At the
2003 provincial elections, the LPF won only 2.9 per cent of the popular vote
and at the 2004 European elections it received just 2.6 per cent – not even
enough for a single seat. The parliamentary group finally fell apart in 2005
and when (early) parliamentary elections were held in November 2006,
there were three parties laying claim to the legacy of Pim Fortuyn. None of
them won any seats.

The legacy of the LPF

The rapid demise of the Fortuyn movement might suggest that it would not
have any great legacy in Dutch politics. Most observers would disagree,
however. True, the LPF did not succeed in introducing any institutional
reforms and its policy output was rather modest. Nonetheless, directly or
indirectly, it contributed to a tougher immigration policy in the Netherlands
and a greater emphasis on the integration of immigrants through language
courses, naturalization ceremonies and civics exams for marriage partners.
Moreover, this issue will remain on the political agenda for the foreseeable
future.

The LPF also changed the political culture of the Netherlands, for the time
being anyway. Accommodation and consensus made way for polarization

and confrontation, at least by Dutch standards. Personal leadership and an 'authentic' personal style have also become more important and new parties are taken more seriously, both by the media and by politicians. When the Dutch Sports Federation and Dutch Olympic Committee elected as president a relative 'outsider' rather than the candidate of the Establishment, journalists attributed this to 'the ghost of Pim' (Kranenburg, 2003). No doubt the ghost would not be very happy about the impact of his movement, but he need not be too sad either.

Conclusion and epilogue

With charisma, a liberal-nationalist ideology and an effective media campaign, Pim Fortuyn managed to become the first successful populist leader in the Netherlands. The time was ripe: the pillars had disintegrated and the political elites had lost the loyal support of the masses and neglected salient issues like immigration. Parties had shed their ideological distinctiveness, while the media focused increasingly on colourful personalities and on the failures of the ruling coalition rather than on its successes. However, the rise of Fortuyn's party came to a swift end after his violent death and posthumous election victory. The LPF failed to resist the consociational temptation to enter government and soon fell victim to internal bickering and mismanagement. Thus, even without pillars, consociationalism prevailed over populism.

The fall of Dutch populism with the LPF's demise may only be temporary, however. At the 2006 general election that sounded the death-knell for the LPF and its successor parties, a new populist party – the *Partij voor de Vrijheid* (Freedom Party) – won nine seats. Founded by Geert Wilders, a maverick MP who had left the VVD in 2004, the party combines economic liberalism with nationalism and demands for the direct election of public officials. Although, like Fortuyn, Wilders does not refer to the 'people' as a morally perfect homogeneous group, he does regard the political class as a homogeneous and nefarious body. Similarly, he advocates cutting taxes and shrinking the civil service (while hiring more policemen and nurses). He also embraces Euroscepticism, arguing that the Netherlands should retain its independence and reduce its contributions to the European Union. Indeed, it should even take the drastic step of leaving the Union in the event of Turkish accession. The party also espouses a hardline position on immigration, arguing for a five-year ban on immigrants from countries like Turkey or Morocco and the denial of welfare and other state benefits for the first ten years of their stay. In fact, in this area, Wilders goes further than Fortuyn by opposing the construction of new mosques. Likewise, he is also more conservative than his populist predecessor with regard to drugs and crime. What Wilders lacks, however, is the sense of humour and charisma which Fortuyn possessed in abundance and only time will tell, therefore, if he and his allies will be able to build a stable and disciplined populist party following their electoral breakthrough in 2006. Yet even if they fail, Dutch populism will probably make a comeback sooner or later. Most of the conditions favouring the rise of populist parties are still present in the Netherlands: an open electoral system; a consociational and consensus-orientated political system without substantial ideological differences between parties; parties that are no longer supported by a loyal mass media and mass organizations, growing numbers of floating voters and an increasing presence of Muslims who are perceived as 'dangerous aliens' by many indigenous Dutch people and who, as a consequence, may feel encouraged to meet these expectations and indeed behave as 'dangerous aliens'. In other words, populism may be the inevitable companion of consociationalism in a polity where pillars no longer link political elites to the masses. We may conclude, therefore, that populism has come to stay in the Netherlands.

Notes

1. Figures reported by the parties themselves, either in party documents (see Voerman, 1996) or directly to the Documentation Centre for Dutch Political Parties.
2. Surprisingly, perhaps, European integration and the introduction of the Euro did not play a significant role either.

11
France: The *FRONT NATIONAL*, Ethnonationalism and Populism

Jens Rydgren

Introduction

The *Front National* (FN) has been one of the most successful of all populist parties in Western Europe. Indeed, during the 1980s and 1990s, the party became a model for others through its combination of 'fervent nationalism, opposition to immigration, and a populist hostility to the political establishment' (Eatwell, 2000: 408). The *Front National* shares an emphasis on ethnonationalism with other radical right-wing populist (RRP) parties which is rooted in myths about the distant past and its programme advocates strengthening the nation by making it more ethnically homogeneous and returning to traditional values. Individual rights are generally viewed as secondary to the goals of the nation. Like most populists, the FN accuses the elites of putting internationalism ahead of the nation, and of prioritizing their own narrow self-interests, and various 'special interests' over those of the people (Rydgren, 2007). The above elements of ethnonationalism, xenophobia and populism are fundamental, therefore, in explaining why the *Front National* emerged as an electoral force during the 1980s.

This chapter will be structured as follows: first, a short account of the history of the FN and of right-wing extremism and populism more generally in France will be presented. We will then discuss the factors behind the FN's emergence and electoral success, focusing in particular on ethnonationalism, xenophobia and political discontent. This is followed by an analysis of the ideology and strategies of the *Front National*. Finally, given that the fortunes of a populist party also depend on the behaviour of other political actors, we will briefly examine the relationship between the established political parties in France – in particular the parties of the mainstream Right – and the *Front National*.

The *Front National* and the history of right-wing populism in France

The recent wave of Right-wing populism in France began in 1983–84 when the *Front National* first received 16.7 per cent of the vote in the 1983 local election in Dreux and then gained 11.2 per cent at the 1984 European Parliament elections (Perrineau, 1997). Right-wing populism was not entirely new to post-war France, however. In 1956, the Poujadist movement, a populist anti-tax and anti-modernization movement, captured 11.6 per cent of the vote and sent over 50 deputies to the National Assembly. However, the movement fell apart in 1958 and disappeared as quickly as it had emerged. During the 1960s, there were occasional outbursts of Right-wing extremism in connection with the war in Algeria. At an electoral level, these sentiments were manifested in the 1962 referendum on Algerian independence, in which 9.2 per cent voted 'No' and in the 1965 presidential election when Tixier-Vignancour, a former star lawyer from French Algeria, got 5.2 per cent of the vote (Mayer, 1998: 16; Perrineau, 1996: 37–38). It is interesting, therefore, to note that the leader of the FN, Jean-Marie Le Pen, was a deputy in the National Assembly for the Poujadist movement in 1956, and then served as campaign president for Tixier-Vignancour in 1965 (Marcus, 1995: 27–52). There are also a number of ideological similarities between the Poujadist movement, Tixier-Vignancour and the *Front National*. This is not surprising, of course, since these three political movements all have a common tradition of pre-war French Right-wing extremism and radical nationalism to draw from, including General Boulanger, Maurice Barrès and Charles Maurras (cf. Chebel d'Appollonia, 1996; Girardet, 1966).

Nevertheless, after 1965 the French far Right was highly fragmented and marginalized until the *Front National* was founded in 1972. During the first ten years of its existence, however, the FN was unable to escape electoral marginalization either. However, as we saw above, in 1983 the *Front National* finally made its electoral breakthrough in a local election, and in 1984 enjoyed national success in the European parliament elections. This was the beginning of a new, more prosperous era for the party and the FN has received vote shares of around ten per cent or over in all national elections since 1986 (see Table 11.1).

In addition to its improved performances at national level, in local contests in 1995 the party gained a majority of the vote in three cities, and was thus able to take political power in Marignane, Orange and Toulon (Perrineau, 1997: 82). In addition, in a partial local election in February 1997, the FN won control of a fourth city, Vitrolle (Perrineau, 1997: 91–92).

Yet, just when the Front National's fortunes appeared at their highest, the party split because of internal rivalries (cf. Hainsworth, 2000). In 1998–99, the rivalry between Le Pen and the *de facto* party number two, Bruno Mégret, escalated into an open conflict for power and control of the FN. Mégret founded a rival party, the *Front National-Mouvement National*, which later changed its name to *Mouvement National Républicain*. However, the schism was not the beginning of a terminal decline for the FN, as many commentators predicted. On the contrary, in the aftermath of September 11, and following an election campaign that had focused on issues of security and law

Table 11.1 *Front National* results in French national elections, 1973–2002 (in percentages)

Election	Vote share
1973 Legislative	0.6
1974 Presidential	0.8
1978 Leg.	0.8
1981 Leg.	0.3
1984 European	11.2
1986 Leg.	9.8
1988 Pres.	14.6
1988 Leg.	9.8
1989 Euro	11.7
1993 Leg.	12.5
1994 Euro	10.5
1995 Pres.	15.1
1997 Leg.	14.9
1999 Euro	5.7 (9.2)
2002 Pres.	16.9* (19.2)
2002 Leg.	11.3 (12.4)

* The result is from the first round of the presidential election. In the second round Le Pen received 17.8 per cent of the vote.

Source: Simmons (1996: 267); Perrineau (1997: 9); Eatwell (2000: 410); Hainsworth (2000: 20); www. electionworld.org. For the elections from 1999, the results presented within brackets indicate the sum of the FN and the Mouvement National Républicain (MNR) total vote.

and order, Le Pen saw his support rise in the opinion polls. This was confirmed when he received 16.9 per cent of the votes in the first round of the Presidential election in April 2002 and thus qualified for the second round (eliminating the Socialist Party candidate Lionel Jospin). After a massive bipartisan campaign in favour of Jacques Chirac, Le Pen was only able to increase his share in the second round of the election to 17.8 per cent of the vote.

Ethnonationalism

The *Front National* can in part be seen as a resurgence of French ethnonationalism, whose mobilization has been facilitated by a number of factors more or less particular to France. First, the declining size and impact of the French Communist Party (PCF) and the Gaullist movements, which had strong ideologies, left an ideological gap that could be filled with a substituting ideology. Second, there was in France a sophisticated far Right intelligentsia (for example, GRECE and *Club l'Horloge*), which facilitated the FN's success in transforming and reframing the social and political crises of the early 1980s into a crisis of national identity. Third, French citizenship policy was challenged in the late 1970s and early 1980s due to the fact that 400,000 young second-generation Algerian immigrants had the automatic right to obtain French citizenship (Brubaker, 1992: 139–142). This event triggered an intense debate about citizenship laws and provided the opportunity for nationalist actors – not least the FN – to criticize the existing legislation for 'turning foreigners into Frenchmen on paper without making sure that they were "French at heart" (*Français de cœur*)' (Brubaker, 1992: 143). An increasing proportion of the second-generation Algerian immigrants were free to choose between military service in France or in Algeria. Yet, although they had to serve two years in Algeria, but only one in France, many chose nonetheless to do military service in Algeria (Brubaker, 1992: 145). This had a provocative and mobilizing effect on people who believed that 'citizenship should possess dignity and command respect. It should not be sought for convenience or personal advantage. It should possess intrinsic, not merely instrumental, value. It should be sacred, not profane' (Brubaker, 1992: 147).

As Michel Winock (1998: 24–25) has demonstrated, ethnonationalism has re-emerged periodically in France (cf. Jenkins and Copsey, 1996: 106; Koopmanns and Statham, 2000: 38). The ideology of French ethnonationalism has also often been mixed with an anti-republican and anti-democratic tradition, not least because of its distinction between the 'essence' of France or the 'real France', on the one hand, and the 'legal France' with its political institutions, on the other hand. Within this tradition, the political institutions have typically been seen as a negation of the essence of the 'real France', and as a cause of degeneration.

The ethnonationalist message

For the FN, the rights of the nation transcend those of the individual (Davies, 1999: 130) and the equilibrium of the nation is considered to be more important than the possibilities for individuals to pursue their own liberation, emancipation and self-realization. In its 1985 programme, the party defines the nation as

> the community of language, interest, race, memories and culture where man blossoms. [A man] is attached to it by roots and deaths, its past, heredity and heritage. Everything that the nation transmits to him at birth already has an inestimable value. (Front National, 1985: 29–30, quoted in Davies, 1999: 82)

Support for the *jus sanguinis* – only those born to French parents can obtain French citizenship – provides one of the main pillars of the FN's nationalist discourse while another pillar is the principle of 'non-automatic' naturalization procedures.

The FN's main argument for its closed nationalism is the threat to French national identity posed by economic, political and cultural openness. According to the FN, only those rooted in a particular culture have the ability to show responsibility and due respect for its heritage. Others are assumed to act irresponsibly and with no regard for the laws and customs of France. Multinational corporations operating in France and immigration were thus both identified as enemies within the FN's strategy to defend French national identity (cf. Betz, 1994: 128).

One of the *Front National's* catchwords is 'the right to be different'. For the FN, the only way to preserve national 'differences', seen as a prerequisite for national identity, is to keep different 'people' separated. The party's defence of ethnonational identity thus inevitably implies an exclusion of 'foreign' elements (cf. Orfali, 1996: 130). As a natural corollary, the solution to the challenges facing French identity is national and ethnic isolationism. More specifically, the politics of 'national preference' implies policies that would afford special treatment to ethnic French citizens while discriminating against immigrants and French citizens of non-French ethnic origin. In addition, the FN advocates 'national preference' in the labour and housing markets, healthcare, etc. The politics of 'national preference' can be summed up in the party's slogan: 'The French first!'. During the late 1990s, the FN increasingly tried to present itself as a 'party of welfare'. However, true to the politics of welfare chauvinism, welfare should be distributed only to the ethnic French.

Recently, the European Union (EU) has also occupied an important place in FN discourse. Like a number of populist parties in western Europe, the *Front National* has changed its position on the European Union over the past decades, moving from a neutral or even pro-EU position during the 1980s to a strongly anti-EU stance during the 1990s. More specifically, the Front National has made great efforts to frame the question of European integration in xenophobic and ethnonationalist terms and thus interlinks its opposition to the EU with its concerns for French national identity (cf. Rydgren, 2003a).

Xenophobia and anti-immigration

One of the factors underpinning the electoral successes of RRP parties has been their strategy of linking a broad array of policy areas to the same two issues: ethnonational identity and immigration (cf. Bréchon and Mitra, 1992). Xenophobic and anti-immigration statements have been crucial mobilizing tools for the FN and for other RRP parties (cf. Marcus, 1995: 105;

Kitschelt, 1995: 103, 276), not least because of the increased salience of the immigration issue in several Western European countries (Solomos and Wrench, 1993: 4). For FN voters, immigration has always been first on their list when asked to explain their party choice and electoral studies regularly show that anti-immigrant attitudes are a key factor in predicting who will vote for the party (see e.g., Rydgren, 2003b; Mayer, 1999; 2002).

The fact that immigration was politicized, which increased popular xenophobia to the point where it came out into the open, clearly created a favourable situation for RRP parties. Moreover, according to many surveys, a majority in most West European countries have held immigration-sceptic views since the early 1990s (Betz, 1994: 103; EUMC, 2001). In France, this situation was already apparent in 1985. In a survey, nearly 75 per cent agreed with the statement that 'one does not feel secure in areas with many immigrants', 50 per cent agreed that 'immigrants are an important cause of criminality in France', and nearly 50 per cent agreed that 'every time a foreigner takes a job in France, it is at a Frenchman's expense' (Ignazi, 1996: 70). Furthermore, in two polls taken by SOFRES in November 1984, 68 per cent wanted to stop further immigration, 25 per cent wanted immigrants to 'go back where they came from', and 66 per cent thought that there were 'far too many North Africans in France' (Bréchon and Mitra, 1992: 68). These attitudes remained at roughly the same level throughout the 1980s and 1990s (Mayer, 1999: 137). However, it should be noted that the proportion of voters that favoured the departure of immigrants before integration decreased by almost 10 percentage points to 38 per cent between 1998 and 2002 (Balme, 2002).

The politicization and framing of the immigration issue

The *Front National* did not, of course, politicize immigration all by itself. Although it incorporated anti-immigration themes within its ideological core in the 1970s, the party was far too small and marginalized to be able to politicize the issue. In addition, although the intellectuals of the *Nouvelle Droite* (in particular Alain de Benoist) formulated a xenophobic ideology of 'the right to be different' during the late 1970s, they too were not in a position to politicize the immigration issue by themselves.

After liberation in 1945, the question of immigration hardly entered the public realm for three decades. Instead, immigration policy was worked out in collaboration between experts and politicians. Immigration policy was a technical issue rather than a politicized one. However, the consensus to keep immigration a 'technical issue' started to change in the 1970s. In 1974, shortly after Valéry Giscard d'Estaing had been elected president, the government announced that further immigration would temporarily cease. Three years later, it confirmed that this temporary suspension would be made permanent. In addition, the government sought to reduce the existing immigrant population in France. In order to encourage non-EC immigrants to return 'home', a system called *l'aide au retour* (repatriation assistance), which provided financial incentives for voluntary repatriation, was launched in 1977. However, the programme was rather unsuccessful (Hargreaves, 1995: 19). In its place, the government designed a proposal in which immigrant workers and their families could be forced to return 'home' if they were deemed to be superfluous to the labour market. The measure required radical legislative changes and the proposal failed to gain majority support when it was put before parliament in 1979–1980 (Hargreaves, 1995: 20; cf. Weil, 1991: 107–138).

These actions by the mainstream Right government had two, possibly unintended, effects: first, it challenged the tradition of consensus and the rule of experts (in other words, it initiated a politicization of the immigration issue). Second, it heralded a framing of the immigration issue in which immigrants and immigration were characterized as 'problems'.

This diagnostic frame was further developed by the French Communist Party. On Christmas Eve 1980, a group a PCF sympathizers, led by the elected Communist mayor of Vitry, used a bulldozer to destroy the power supplies and staircases of a hostel used by immigrant workers. This brutal action was later supported by the PCF's national leadership, when George Marchais wrote that he approved of the Vitry mayor's 'refusal to allow the already high number of immigrant workers in his commune to increase', and linked immigration to the housing crisis, the cost of social services, schooling problems etc. (Marcus, 1995: 77–8). As Martin Schain (1988: 606) has argued, this was the first time during the post-war era that an established French party had defined the immigration issue as a cause of social and economic problems. Indeed, it could be argued that this event greatly helped to formulate and establish a general diagnostic frame – that immigration and immigrants are a problem – which could be drawn upon and further developed by the *Front National*.

Turning to the ideology and strategy of the FN, the party has framed immigrants as a 'problem' in four different ways:

(1) they pose a threat to French ethnonational identity;
(2) they cause unemployment;
(3) they are a major cause of criminality and insecurity;
(4) they abuse the generosity of the Welfare States of Western European democracies.

We can easily find examples of all these frames in the party programmes and public statements of the *Front National*. French ethnonational identity is said to be threatened by 'a veritable invasion' (Le Pen, 1985: 289) of immigrants who pose a 'deadly menace to the French nation' (Le Pen, 1985: 51). According to Le Pen, 'more integration is impossible. The only possible course of action is resistance or else submission to the invasion sooner or later' (Le Pen in *Présent*, 13–14 November 1989; quoted in Duraffour and Guittonneau, 1991: 132). Immigration from Muslim countries is believed to be particularly dangerous, because Muslims are so culturally different that it is impossible to assimilate and integrate them into French culture (cf. Davies, 1999: 148). In addition, the FN argues that Muslim immigrants pose an even greater threat than others because they insist on maintaining their own religious, and therefore cultural, characteristics.

The second main frame employed by the *Front National* in its anti-immigration discourse is the strategy of linking the immigration issue to the issue of insecurity and criminality. This is an important mobilization frame because of the emotional elements inherent in the issue of insecurity. The FN and Le Pen argued that 'uncontrolled immigration leads to disorder and insecurity' (*Le Monde*, 9 March 1983, quoted in Marcus, 1995: 54) and the party's weekly newspaper regularly published a column on criminal acts committed by immigrants during the previous week (Winock, 1998: 30). Since criminal acts committed by non-immigrants – or, of course, a list of immigrants that have not committed criminal acts – are not also presented, readers are clearly encouraged to believe that immigrants in general are criminal, and that immigration is a major cause of criminality.

As we saw above, the *Front National* uses two important anti-immigration frames that are built on the same logic, namely the competition for scarce resources. These frames have a strong mobilizing power because of the perceived clashes of interests and, in particular, because of the emotional stress of unemployment (whether one is directly or indirectly affected). The first of these two frames is very simple: unemployment is caused by immigration. From this perspective, the problem of unemployment has a simple political solution: expel the immigrants and/or 'reserve job priority in this country for the sons and daughters of France' (Le Pen, speech 16 September 1984, quoted in Souchard *et al.*, 1997: 156).

The fourth anti-immigration frame (that immigrants exploit welfare systems) used by the *Front National* is also built on the idea of competition for scarce resources. The mobilizing power of this frame is its appeal to envy and resentment. The FN seeks to promote feelings of xenophobic welfare chauvinism by depicting immigrants as lazy parasites living on state subsidies. The problem of public housing is of particular importance in the French case as the waiting list for these apartments creates a fertile breeding ground for envy and resentment, which the FN has attempted to turn to its advantage by framing the problem in xenophobic terms.

Political discontent and the appeal of populism

The electoral breakthrough of the *Front National* between 1983 and 1985 occurred at a time when loyalties to the established parties had decreased and political alienation and discontent had increased to a critical point (cf. Ignazi, 1996: 77). This situation facilitated the emergence of the *Front National* for two reasons. First, loyal voters with a high degree of party identification are unlikely to vote for a new party even if they agree with its ideas. However, as a result of diminished party identification and loyalty in France, more people became issue-voters, which in turn opened up possibilities for the FN. Second, growing political alienation and discontent had created an audience receptive to 'anti-system' and 'anti-establishment' messages (cf. Ignazi, 1996: 77) and thus provided an opportunity for the FN to mobilize protest voters. Employing populist strategies, the *Front National* tried to stir up a public sense of alienation from the political process and resentment towards the established political parties and politicians (cf. Betz, 1993: 419). One such strategy was to depict all political parties as constituting a single, homogeneous political class. This 'anti-Establishment' strategy was facilitated by the decreasing importance of the economic cleavage dimension and by the fact that an increasing number of voters perceived no essential difference between the political Right and the political Left (cf. Mény and Surel, 2000: 115).

The proportion of French voters who claimed they had 'no ties to any party' soared from 29 per cent in 1978 to 42 per cent in 1984. During the same period, the proportion of voters claiming that they were 'very close' or 'fairly close' to a political party declined from 29 per cent in 1978 to 17 per cent in 1984. Since this decline in party identification did not coincide with a corresponding decline in interest in politics, it is clear that an increasingly large number of French voters were becoming available for political mobilization (Schain, 1988: 610). At the same time, according to surveys conducted by CEVIPOF, the proportion of voters who believed that 'politicians do not care about people like us' increased from 62 per cent in 1978 to 73 per cent in 1995, and to 80 per cent in 1997 (Mayer, 1999: 138). Thus, when asked in 1999 to describe their feelings about politics, 57 per cent of the French public answered 'distrust', 27 per cent 'boredom', 20 per cent 'disgust', and just 7 per cent 'respect' (Mény and Surel, 2000: 25–26). It is important to note, however, that although French voters deeply distrust political institutions and politicians, they do still support the democratic system (Mény and Surel, 2000: 25; cf. Dalton, 1999: 70; Klingemann, 1999: 44).

There are several possible reasons for this increased political discontent and heightened sense of alienation. First of all, the political parties and other political institutions have found it difficult to adapt to profound economic and social changes which have left many voters feeling that politics and politicians are divorced from the 'reality' in which 'ordinary people' live (Mény and Surel, 2000: 24). Second, as Pascal Perrineau (1997: 28) has argued, although the economic difficulties in France began in the mid-1970s, it was not until the early 1980s that people really began to realize the depth and extent – as well as the persistence – of the problem. Up until the early 1980s, many had regarded the situation as a 'normal' temporary recession, but in 1982 many understood that they might be witnessing the beginning of the end of the post-war 'Golden Years' period of unbroken economic growth. This changed perception was partly caused (or at least reinforced) by the victory of the Left in the 1981 elections. Until then, the Left had been an untried alternative (at the time, both the Socialist and Communist parties advocated a 'break with capitalism'). When it became apparent that the Left could not cope with the economic difficulties either – in other words, it had no 'miracle solution' – many people awoke to the sad reality of the economic crisis (Perrineau, 1997: 28). This situation was marked by increased pessimism and the proportion of people who said that 'things have a tendency to get worse' increased from 40 per cent in 1981 to 51 per cent in 1982, and 62 per cent in 1983. Distrust in political institutions also rose during this period. Third, the increasing complexity of the political process, combined with the declining political autonomy of the nation-state, has made political decision-making processes more opaque (see Poggi, 1990; Sassen, 1996). Fourth, the real or perceived convergence between the mainstream parties has caused a widespread feeling that no real differences exist between the political Right and Left. In France, there has been a dramatic increase in the number of voters who believe that 'Left and Right have little meaning in terms of political parties today': from about one-third in 1981 to approximately 50 per cent in 1984, and over 60 per cent in 1996 (Mayer, 1999: 29). This feeling of blurred distinctions may have been reinforced by the experiences of 'cohabitation', i.e. the co-existence of a president from one side of the Left/Right divide and a government from the other (Marcus, 1995: 169; cf. Ivaldi, 1998: 19). Finally, numerous political scandals, and cases of political corruption in particular, have had a negative effect on public confidence in politicians and political institutions (cf. Mény and Surel, 2000: 24; Pujas and Rhodes, 1999). In France, more people (61 per cent in 1999) believe that the politicians are 'corrupt rather than honest' than that they are 'honest rather than corrupt' (Mayer, 1999: 138; Mény and Surel, 2000: 25–26). Among young people between 18 and 24 years of age, the figure reached 75 per cent in 1999 (Mény and Surel, 2000: 25–26) – a group in which FN voters were over-represented (Rydgren 2003b: chapter 3; cf. Perrineau, 1997: 67). Unsurprisingly, the FN has frequently accused established politicians of being corrupt and has presented itself as the only political party that offers 'clean hands' (cf. Marcus, 1995: 167).

In addition, there are indications that the level of 'political satisfaction' has a major effect on whether voters who have the same xenophobic attitudes as the FN will vote for the party. Of those voters who agreed with the statement that there are too many immigrants living in France, but who also expressed a high degree of 'political satisfaction', only 13 per cent voted for Le Pen in the 1995 presidential election. By contrast, of those voters who expressed the view that there are too many immigrants and who also expressed a low degree of 'political satisfaction', 27 per cent voted for Le Pen.

Populism and the power of the 'anti-political establishment' strategy

The *Front National* holds a clearly populist view of society as 'ultimately separated into two homogeneous and antagonistic groups, the "pure" people versus "the corrupt elite"' (Mudde, 2004: 543) and its populist anti-Establishment strategy has been crucial to the success of the party. Populism is characterized by

(a) hostility towards the idea of representative democracy (within a democratic context, this may manifest itself in calls for direct democracy);
(b) an image of 'the people' as a harmonious and homogeneous community, pitted against 'the political class' or 'the Establishment';
(c) the idea that the populist party or leader represents 'the voice of the people'.

In Weberian terms, populist movements are charismatic, and try to base their appeal and legitimacy primarily on emotions rather than on rational considerations (cf. Weber, 1978: chapter 3).

Populist ideology and rhetoric accord an essential role to the idea of 'the people'. However, the term is ambiguous. The lines of inclusion are often very fuzzy and populists are typically clearer about which groups are to be excluded. As Paul Taggart (2000: 96) has suggested, the lines of exclusion often correspond to ethnonationalist or ethnoregional identities. This implies that populists often are ethnonationalist (which does not necessary mean that all or even most ethnonationalists are populists).

However, although the party's conception of democracy is a form of populist *Herrenvolk* democracy, or ethnocracy, the *Front National* differs from earlier French Right-wing extremist parties and movements in its self-proclaimed acceptance of democracy (cf. Marcus, 1995: 102). Rather, the FN is critical of existing, representative democracy, which it argues, is 'a democracy of appearance'. According to the party, there is a deep gulf between the people and the political elite, and it is ultimately because of the existence of this gulf that it rejects the idea of representative democracy (Souchard *et al.*, 1997: 135–136). In common with most other RRP parties, therefore, the *Front National* supports direct democracy (cf. Mény and Surel, 2000: 61).

In order to mobilize protest votes, the *Front National* has used the 'anti-political-establishment strategy'. A party using this strategy tries to construct an image of itself in opposition to the 'political class', while simultaneously trying not to appear anti-democratic. A party that is viewed as anti-democratic runs the risk of being stigmatized and marginalized as long as the overwhelming majority of the electorate is in favour of democracy *per se* (Schedler, 1996; cf. Mudde, 1996a: 272). However, if, in the eyes of the voters, an RRP party succeeds in detaching itself from anti-democratic currents, it can attract voters beyond the small, marginalized groups of voters that are prepared to support straightforward anti-democratic parties.

Part of the populist anti-establishment strategy is often also to criticize the established parties for focusing on obsolete issues, while at the same time suppressing political issues associated with the 'real' conflict between national identity and multiculturalism. Moreover, the populist anti-Establishment strategy makes it possible for parties to present themselves as the real champions of true democracy and as a new kind of party which considers the worries and interests of 'the common man' (see, e.g. Betz and Johnson, 2004; Mudde, 2004).

If we look at the FN in terms of the first part of the above strategy, we can clearly see that the party dismisses differences between socialist and established non-socialist parties, in order to group them together into one 'political class':

> The rotation of power, which in the 5th Republic represents a rule impossible to evade, only involves, or is only expected to involve, the RPR, the UDF and the PS. This rotation is false, since there are no differences between the two components of French politics. The Left has long since abandoned its generous ideas in order to administer the bourse and enjoy caviar. The Right, on the other hand, without doubt influenced by the freemasonry that today is a dominant feature in their ranks, has abandoned the defence of national values in favour of 'Europe-ism', 'globalism', and cosmopolitanism. (Le Pen, speech published in *Présent*, 4 October 1995; quoted in Souchard *et al.*, 1997: 142)

Moreover, the victory of the Left in the 1981 election and in particular the fact that the PCF participated in the Pierre Mauroy Socialist-led government, resulted in the Communist Party losing its traditional role of 'anti-political-establishment' party (cf. Bell and Criddle, 1994: 220). The *Front National* could thus fill a vacuum and role that nobody else was occupying.

With regard to the second part of the 'anti-political-establishment strategy', it is also important to note that the FN underwent an ideological transformation during the late 1970s, when many of the old neo-fascist member groups within the party were expelled or isolated, and the FN got rid of much of the old political 'baggage' of the French extreme Right (Marcus, 1995: 12). This was a necessary step in order to achieve the political legitimacy required to break the marginalization that had dogged it since its foundation in 1972.

Finally, other political actors have a considerable impact on whether a populist party is able to acquire public legitimacy. In this sense, the ambivalence shown by the mainstream Right parties in France, through local agreements and cooperation with the FN, together with an appropriation of policy proposals and rhetoric style, contributed to the legitimization of the *Front National*. Various leading representatives of the mainstream Right tried to borrow from the FN's policy proposals on immigration and law-and-order, as well as, occasionally, imitating the FN's anti-immigration rhetoric. Immediately following the electoral breakthrough of the FN, in 1983–1984, the established Right parties seem to have been taken by surprise, and they instinctively tried to win back voters by using similar anti-immigration frames to those of the *Front National*. In October 1984, for instance, Chirac remarked that 'if there were fewer immigrants, there would be less unemployment, less tension in certain towns and lower social costs', and in November of the same year, he linked France's decreasing birthrate to the threat of large-scale immigration (Marcus, 1995: 136). Moreover, in 1985, Charles Pasqua stated that immigrants were not in their own home and should behave accordingly (Marcus, 1995: 93). However, the strategy to win back voters by speaking the same language as the *Front National* seems to have failed. Indeed, if anything, these remarks served simply to legitimize the ideas and discourse of the FN.

Discussion

Before concluding this chapter it is worth briefly mentioning two important factors that have not yet been discussed: the electoral system and the mass media. Various scholars (Swank and Betz, 2003; Jackman and Volpert, 1996; Golder, 2003; Veugelers and Magnan, 2005) have argued that support for new radical right-wing populist parties tends to be higher in countries with proportional electoral systems (see also, however: Van der Brug *et al.*, 2005; Carter, 2002). This contention seems to be contradicted by the French case where, normally, a majority voting system is used. That said, it should be noted that a proportional voting system was in force in *Front National*'s two break-through elections: the 1984 European Parliament election and the 1986 legislative election. In the latter case, François Mitterrand introduced a proportional voting system in order to split the mainstream right. The unintended consequence of this measure, however, was to enable the *Front National* to send 35 deputies to the National Assembly. As a result, the party succeeded in increasing its political visibility and legitimacy. By the time the majority voting system was reinstated, in the following election, the *Front National* was already well established enough to do well electorally, despite the fact that the voting system was now once again working to the party's disadvantage.

Researchers have also argued that the mass media plays a pivotal role in the emergence of new populist parties. As Ruud Koopmans (2004: 8) has contended, for instance, the 'action of gatekeepers [within the mass media] produce the first and most basic selection mechanism ... *visibility*.' The media also play a role in their own right, by participating in agenda-setting and the framing of political issues. Furthermore, there is a growing tendency to personalize issues within the media, which may benefit populist parties which give the leader a pronounced central role (Eatwell, 2003, 2005). As the battle for readers and viewers has intensified due to new technologies and the growing privatization of the mass media in many countries, there has also been an increasing tendency to focus on the most scandalous aspects of politics which, in turn, may contribute to anti-establishment sentiments (Mudde, 2004). It is thus interesting to note, as Roger Eatwell (2005) has pointed out, that the *Front National* achieved its electoral breakthrough shortly after Le Pen was allowed access to state television.

In conclusion, we can see that the *Front National* has now been a significant political force in French politics for over two decades. Although many thought the party was on the wane after the split in 1999, Le Pen showed in the 2002 presidential election that there is still a demand for the mixture of ethnonationalism, xenophobia and populism that the FN offers. According to Koopmans *et al.* (2005: 5), many people have experienced a loss of identity as a result of globalization and, because there 'is nothing beyond the nation-state that can serve as a new anchor for collective identities and can renew the sense of control', they turn to nationalism as a way to find such an anchorage. If this is true – and if populism is fostered by the increasing complexity of the political process, the declining political autonomy of the nation-state and the growing opaqueness of political decision-making processes – then it is unlikely that the demand for this political message will disappear in the near future. Similarly, there are few indications that issues related to immigration and citizenship will become less salient in the near future. On the contrary, they are likely to become more important, especially as the French mainstream Right (with Nicolas Sarkozy as a prime example) also seeks to exploit them.

The future prospects for the *Front National*, however, hinge on more than just demand-centred factors. As was noted above, populist movements are charismatic in the sense that they try to base their appeal and legitimacy on emotions rather than on reason. The *Front National* is no exception and Jean-Marie Le Pen's personality and appeal fit the description of a 'charismatic leader' very well (Eatwell, 2005). Indeed, the *Front National* satisfies several of the criteria of Angelo Panebianco's (1988: 145) definition of a 'charismatic party': the party leader has an extremely strong influence over appointments to central positions within the organization; he/she is the main interpreter of the party's political doctrine; the party includes a dominant group united by its loyalty to the leader; internal career paths are closed to those not favoured by the party leader, partly through elite recruitment and partly through the imposition of a high degree of centralization; the party is usually an anti-party party that presents itself as an alternative to all others. However, because charismatic parties are highly dependent on singular individuals, they tend to be vulnerable in the long term – and it remains an open question how the *Front National* will handle life after Jean-Marie Le Pen. As Max Weber (1978) famously noted, the 'routinization of charisma' is an extremely difficult process and, in the case of the FN, may therefore lead to severe splits within the party organization.

12
Britain: Imperial Legacies, Institutional Constraints and New Political Opportunities

Stefano Fella

In contrast to many other Western European countries, no real populist movement has been able to emerge and have a lasting impact on party political competition in Great Britain. A prominent factor often identified to explain this is Britain's majoritarian first-past-the-post electoral system (FPTP), which severely limits the opportunities for new political forces to make an impact in terms of winning parliamentary seats and altering the balance of party competition. Nevertheless, the recent success enjoyed by new political forces, such as the UK Independence Party (UKIP), under the proportional voting system introduced for European Parliament elections since 1999, indicates a degree of potential for populist parties in Britain. Moreover, the gains made by the extreme-right British National Party (BNP) in local elections (albeit in very limited pockets) also suggests that there is a market to be tapped into for a populist party of the extreme-right variety. Both UKIP and the BNP can be analysed in terms of the categorization of radical right-wing populist (RRP) parties that has emerged from the literature on the far Right and contemporary (neo) populism (Betz, 1994; Rydgren, 2005). However, while discussing this phenomenon in British politics, this chapter will move beyond this limited categorization and examine the extent to which populism, or elements of it, has found its way into the discourses, programmes and strategies of the existing mainstream parties, most notably the Conservatives and Labour. The chapter will begin by surveying the structural conditions and key characteristics of the political framework that shape the opportunities for populist movements to emerge in Britain, in particular the nature of the electoral system, participation in elections and key policy controversies such as the country's relationship with the European Union (EU) and immigration.

Opportunity structures for populists in Britain

The definition of populism provided by the editors in the introduction to this volume presents a juxtaposition between 'the elite' and 'the people', with the former caricatured by populists as corrupt and self-serving and the latter as pure and righteous. The 'common sense' of the people should thus prevail and not be obstructed by constitutional checks and the trappings of pluralist democracy. In this sense, the nature of the British unwritten Constitution, with its absence of a constitutional check on the absolute sovereignty of parliament, could theoretically provide fertile ground for populists, particularly given the FPTP electoral system which often gives parties a large majority in parliament (despite the absence of an absolute majority of votes) and thus allows strong leaders with a loyal party behind them to exercise considerable power. In the past, this has led to a great deal of academic discussion on the potential that the British Constitution provides for 'elective dictatorship'. However, while the political system provides potential for populists within the main parties to wield considerable influence over events, the electoral system makes it rather difficult for new political forces (populist or otherwise) to make an electoral breakthrough. Nevertheless, the decline in identification with, and support for, the two main parties in elections since the 1970s (and more dramatically in 2001 and 2005) suggests that there is potential for new political movements to emerge and enjoy some electoral success, particularly given the new opportunity structure provided at the end of the twentieth century by the switch to proportional electoral systems in European elections and in the new devolved administrations in Scotland and Wales, as well as the institution of directly elected mayors in London and other local authorities.

Indeed, as well as UKIP in European elections, New Labour's constitutional innovations have provided the framework for the emergence of new movements that have sometimes been characterized as populist, such as Tommy Sheridan's Scottish Socialist Party (SSP) which has won a small number of seats in the Scottish parliament, and Ken Livingstone's independent candidature for the London mayoralty in 2000 (which he won and then retained in 2004, the latter contest after returning to the Labour party). The SSP has appeared more of a genuine populist movement, combining attacks on the political establishment with Scottish nationalism and conventional socialist politics. However, it appeared to fall apart in 2006 after key party figures testified against Sheridan in a well-publicized court case.

Livingstone's style falls short of the definition of populism offered by the editors of this volume in which a virtuous people are pitted against a self-serving Establishment elite and various other dangerous 'others'. Aside from his consistent attacks on the international economic system and US foreign policy, Livingstone's programme is fairly pragmatic and he has shown a willingness to do deals and work with a variety of groups and individuals within the political Establishment. Other figures worth mentioning include George Galloway, who won a parliamentary seat with his Respect movement in 2005. Again, Galloway combines conventional socialist politics with populist anti-Establishment rhetoric. However, the (limited) strength of his movement has rested on alliances with an array of Marxist and Muslim groups and appeals to voters (often Muslim) disenchanted with British foreign policy (particularly the war in Iraq). The appeal of this movement, therefore, may not outlive the anti-war, anti-Tony Blair ferment of 2002–2005. A more convincing UK populist with long-standing appeal is, of course, Ian Paisley, leader of the Democratic Unionist party (DUP) in Northern Ireland. This movement benefits from the rather special circumstances of Northern Ireland politics, characterized by an entirely separate party system and political cleavages dominated by the religious divide.

For reasons of space, however, this chapter will focus on Britain (rather than the UK as a whole) and on mainstream populism as found in the two main parties (Labour and Conservative) and the radical right populism of UKIP and the BNP. Echoing the strategies of other radical right parties in Europe, the latter two parties have focused on the twin issues of EU membership and immigration/asylum in order to claim that the British people have been betrayed by their political leaders. Moreover, they exploit a general public apathy or disillusionment with their political elites which has been egged on by a populist press.

Within the mainstream parties, the leadership of the Conservative party since 1997 has also adopted a populist strategy in seeking to exploit concerns about immigration and the EU, albeit through a more circumspect political discourse. Both main parties operate in the shadow of the Thatcherite legacy, with New Labour under Blair having accepted many of the tenets of Thatcherism in moving to the political centre ground while the Conservatives have struggled to reproduce the election-winning success of the Thatcher governments. This chapter will explore similarities between the Blairite and Thatcherite approach to politics, both of which have often been described as populist. The two leaders each sought to appeal to 'the people' over the heads of their own parties, appealing to the values of middle England in particular, while drawing support from the middle and upwardly mobile working classes alike. These approaches also stemmed from a decline in class identification with the main parties and a blurring of class distinctions which provided an opportunity for the Thatcherite Conservatives and a challenge for the old Labour party (which saw its traditional working class base eroded). Nevertheless, these shifting approaches also meant that what remained of the traditional working class and, more broadly, those left behind by the restructuring of the economy associated with the Thatcherite period (which led to a spiral of ever increasing wealth disparities which has not been reversed by Blair) were more susceptible to populist platforms alleging sell-out by the mainstream political Establishment. As will be explored below, the BNP in particular has sought to capitalize on the apparent abandonment by New Labour of its traditional working class base.

The public, politicians and the media

Reporting in the survey of British Social Attitudes, shortly after electoral turn-out reached its nadir of 59.1 per cent in 2001 (it rose again slightly in 2005 to 61.2).[1] Catherine Bromley and John Curtice (2002: 161) suggested that this was attributable to the choices being offered to electors not being 'sufficiently interesting' and because 'those who were already less motivated to vote stayed at home'. One could argue that this related to the perception that there was little difference between the main parties and that there was therefore little point voting. There certainly appears a case for arguing that there has been an ideological convergence between the two main parties, particularly since the Labour party under Blair moved to occupy the centre ground. Analysis of the Conservative and Labour manifestos in 2001 showed that they were closer to each other ideologically in 2001 than at any time since the 1950s (Bara and Budge, 2001, cited in Bromley and Curtice, 2002). Moreover, data cited by Curtice from the annual surveys of British Social Attitudes shows a dramatic decline since the 1980s in the percentage of people in Britain who felt that there was a great deal of difference between Labour and the Conservatives. In 1983 and 1987, the figures were 88 and 85 per cent respectively, while in 2001 and 2005 they had fallen to 17 and 21 per cent respectively (Curtice, 2005: 776–779).

In their study of the 2001 election, Bromley and Curtice also noted a dramatic decline in levels of political trust, with a significant number of respondents having negative perceptions regarding various indicators of 'system efficacy'. Thus, 27 per cent of those surveyed in 2001 strongly agreed with the statement that political parties 'are only interested in people's votes, not in their opinions'. A similar proportion (25 per cent) agreed that, generally speaking, 'those we elect as MPs lose touch with people pretty quickly' while 18 per cent agreed that it 'doesn't really matter which party is in power, in the end things go on much the same' (Bromley and Curtice, 2002: 144–145). The figures for the first two questions were around 15–16 per cent in 1987 and 1991, while for the first question they were 7 and 11 per cent respectively. Widespread public feeling that politicians are corrupt or out of touch with ordinary people is, of course, likely to encourage populist sentiments. However, as Cas Mudde (2003: 553) asks: are the elites of today more corrupt than they were before the 1990s or is it simply that corruption is more likely to be uncovered or reported? In the British context, the best selling newspaper, *The Sun*, is notable for its fierce populist agenda, combining anti-immigrant, anti-EU and anti-Establishment positions (though, despite its antipolitical stance, it remains firmly in the camp of the economic Establishment). Its editorial line is also fiercely critical of political correctness and the so-called liberal elite or metropolitan 'chattering classes'. Although the reporting styles are different, similar positions on the EU, immigration and the liberal metropolitan classes can also be found in the mid-market paper, the *Daily Mail*, and the more 'respectable' broadsheets, the *Daily Telegraph* and *The Times*. Furthermore, the focus on sleaze and corruption has been particularly notable throughout the press since the early 1990s with first the Conservative governments of John Major from 1990–1997 and then the Blair administration thereafter being subject to intense scrutiny on matters ranging from the private lives and sexual peccadilloes of ministers to financial irregularities, improper relations with certain controversial entrepreneurs and, in the latter throes of Blair's tenure, the granting of peerages to donors and lenders to party funds. Whether or not the behaviour of these governments was significantly worse than that of their predecessors is rather difficult to ascertain. Certainly, government ministers were involved in all manner of dubious practices in previous periods, but what appears to have changed is the way these are reported by the media. In this respect, the way politics is reported on television and radio is also highly significant. Reporting has become less deferential, and interviewers have become more aggressive in their questioning and more adept at exposing what they view as incompetence, hypocrisy or dishonesty when questioning politicians.

Immigration, nationality and ethnicity in 'multicultural' Britain

Although legislation by Conservative governments meant that primary immigration from the New Commonwealth was virtually ended by the early 1970s, the numbers entering the country have continued to increase, mainly due to family reunion and occasional refugee influxes. Moreover, the size of the British-born ethnic minority population (holding UK citizenship), i.e. the descendants of the first generation of immigrants, has continued to rise considerably. This has spawned debates about the social inclusion or otherwise of the British-born minorities, and the development of Britain into a multicultural society. Tensions arose in the 1970s around the emergence of the extreme right National Front (NF). It received 3.5 per cent of the vote in the seats it contested (in areas where there were immigrant populations) in the 1970 election, and 3.4 per cent in October 1974. In the late 1970s, however, the rightward shift by the Conservative party towards a more overt nationalist agenda meant the NF had some of the ground taken from under it. For example, in the run-up to the 1979 election, Thatcher referred to the dangers posed to British social and cultural values and the threat of 'Britain being swamped by alien cultures'. In 1979, the NF vote dropped to 1.4 per cent in the constituencies it stood in.

By the late 1990s, and the advent of Blair's New Labour government, and with primary immigration now severely restricted, the focus of debate and controversy switched to the issue of asylum seekers, the numbers of whom entering Britain had risen dramatically. In 1999 this figure had risen to

97,000 – the highest in Europe at the time. While claims that many of these asylum seekers were bogus (i.e. conventional migrants pretending to be fleeing persecution) were normally associated with the far Right, the right wing of the Conservative party and the populist media, it was notable that the New Labour government also gave tacit endorsement to this claim both through the asylum legislation reforms it introduced, and the language many of its ministers used to discuss the issue (often rather similar to that of its right-wing opponents). For example, Home Secretary David Blunkett referred to children of asylum-seekers 'swamping' schools (Randall, 2004: 189). One could argue that by highlighting its own tough line on this issue, the New Labour government simply encouraged a shift towards a more intolerant discourse on the subject across the political spectrum, thus giving legitimacy to the agenda and language of the far Right.

The survey of British Social Attitudes published in 2004 indicated increasing public concern about the number of immigrants living in Britain. As Lauren McLaren and Mark Johnson show, the proportion of the population who felt that there were too many immigrants increased from the already high 64 per cent in 1995 to 74 per cent in 2003 (2004: 172–173). Around 30 per cent reported themselves to have been racially prejudiced in 2003 (2004: 180–181). Public and political concern over Muslim immigration, in particular, has increased considerably since September 11. This is especially so given the presence of a minority within the Muslim population in Britain (many holding UK citizenship) who have expressed support for Al-Qaeda, and the emergence of a number of British-born Muslim suicide bombers – including those who claimed over 50 lives in the terrorist bombs on the London underground on 7 July 2005. Political discussion has increasingly focused on the extent to which British multiculturalism has failed, in the light of the apparent separation of Muslim communities from the rest of the population. The situation has been exploited by far Right activists, who openly clashed with young Muslims on the streets of the Lancashire mill towns (localities with high and generally segregated concentrations of Muslim British–Asians) in the summer of 2004.

The European question in British political debate

Britain's 'awkward' relationship with its European partners has been well documented (George, 1998). Since the 1960s, the Conservative party had been viewed as the party of Europe. However, proposals to establish a single currency and closer political integration clashed with Thatcher's economic worldview and nationalist form of Conservatism, taking the European Community beyond the barrier-free single market which she had championed. Although the opposition of many of her government colleagues to her increasingly outspoken approach to Europe led to Thatcher's removal from office, by the end of the 1990s this hostility towards the integration process had been established as the mainstream position in the Conservative party. More importantly, the bulk of public opinion had also moved in this direction. Although the Labour party has moved in the opposite direction, shedding its earlier scepticism (which peaked with a platform of withdrawal in 1983) and adopting a Europhile position by the early 1990s, its leadership has been forced to exercise caution on key policy questions such as the single currency, given public hostility. Surveys of British Social Attitudes have indicated strong public desire to reduce the EU's influence (this has hovered between 50–60 per cent since the mid-1990s) (Evans and Butt, 2005: 198–200).

Although by the end of the 1990s the Conservative party had adopted a highly Euro-sceptical platform, in some cases implying renegotiation of key tenets of membership, it has found itself outflanked by a number of new movements able to exploit the increasing public hostility to the European integration process, fuelled by the Europhobia of large swathes of the British press (including both populist tabloids and broadsheets). While political pragmatism, its relationship with the business community and the persistence of a Europhile minority within the party prevent the Conservatives from adopting a platform of withdrawal from the EU, these new Eurosceptic movements operate with no such constraints, combining a populist anti-EU discourse with promises to withdraw the UK from the EU. The most prominent of these movements is the UK Independence party (see discussion below).

Chris Gifford has argued that ideas of 'Britishness' have been asserted within the Eurosceptic movement (both within the Conservative party and beyond) that suggest that British political development (given the legacy of empire and 'global power' status) is 'exceptional and antithetical to the continent' (Gifford, 2006: 854). Gifford argues that 'in a context of imperial decline, the nation has had to be persistently regenerated and there has been a need for an "other" against which a "new" Britain can be redefined. Since the 1970s, "Europe", and more specifically the project of European integration, has played such a role' (Gifford, 2006: 856). As Gifford shows, much of the discourse used by the Eurosceptic movement has been of a populist nature, alleging that the British people have been sold out and lied to by its leaders, who can no longer be trusted on the issue. For example, the Heath government, which took Britain into the EC in 1973 stands accused of having misled parliament in claiming that Britain would retain its essential sovereignty, as did the cross-party coalition that supported continued membership in the 1975 referendum and thereafter.

Mainstream populism in Britain

Margaret Thatcher's leadership of the Conservative party and Britain in the 1980s has often been characterized as populist, reflected in an apparent identification with the 'common people' ('middle England' in British political parlance) against the elites of the British Establishment. Given her background – as the daughter of a small shopkeeper in provincial England – she identified with the suburban and provincial middle classes that made up the Conservative rank and file and its bedrock of support much better than the older generation of Conservative leaders, many from privileged backgrounds (Riddell, 1985: 9). This allowed her to appeal directly to the heartland over the heads of the old Conservative hierarchy.

More than any other post-war politician, Thatcher exploited a feeling that Britain was in decline. Indeed, many of her admirers would argue that her administrations of 1979–1990 succeeded in arresting this slide. The themes of political and economic decline, stemming from Britain's post-imperial transition from 'great power' status, had clouded political debate in Britain in the second half of the twentieth century (Gamble, 1994). Economic problems seemed to be coming to a head at the end of the 1970s – a decade of high inflation, rising unemployment and a wave of public sector strikes. Thatcher adopted a populist critique of the post-war social democratic consensus and the inadequacies of many traditional British Establishment institutions[2] (whilst simultaneously enhancing state power and the wealth and power of the economic Establishment) that was very much a departure from the traditional paternalistic 'one nation' style of previous Conservative leaders.

David Marquand summed up the Thatcher approach to politics thus: 'The Thatcherites saw themselves as a beleaguered minority, surrounded by insidious, relentless and powerful enemies. There were always new battles to fight, new obstacles to uproot, new heresies to stamp out' (Marquand, 1998: 19). This chimes with Mudde's characterization of populism as presenting 'a Manichean outlook, in which there are only friends and foes' (Mudde, 2004: 544). For Thatcher, the number one enemy was socialism: she made it her aim to ensure that all vestiges of socialism were eliminated from British politics and its institutions. She succeeded in the sense that one of the enduring legacies of her success was that it forced the Labour party to modernize and then, under Tony Blair's leadership, to reinvent itself as 'New Labour' embracing much of her legacy and distancing itself from its socialist past.

The political style and strategy of Blair has often been compared to that of Thatcher. Both appeared to operate counter to the traditions of their respective parties, appealing over their heads directly to 'the people'. Nevertheless, there were important differences, as noted by Marquand: 'Thatcherism was exclusionary; New Labour is inclusionary. Margaret Thatcher was a warrior; Tony Blair is a healer. Where she divided, he unites. Where she spoke of enemies within, he speaks of "the people".' Thus while the Thatcherites portrayed themselves as a beleaguered minority, Blairite New Labour 'speaks and acts as though it embodies a national consensus – a consensus of the well-intentioned, embracing rich and poor, young and old, suburbs and inner cities, black and white' (Marquand, 1998: 19). Though both Thatcher and Blair constituted broad coalitions, the Blairite 'catch-all' approach is perhaps closer to Margaret Canovan's definition of 'politician's populism' (1981). Thatcherism, whilst sharing this multi-class appeal, also had a more radical and exclusionary side – perhaps closer to the definition in the introduction to this volume.

The notion that New Labour is a populist phenomenon has been taken up more assertively by Peter Mair who posits a model of 'partyless democracy', operated by New Labour. According to Mair, 'the crucial actor is now government, while the crucial legitimator is now the people writ large. In this new political strategy, it is government that still proposes, but it is now the people, rather than parliament or the parties as such, that disposes. The link between the two is unmediated, and it is here that we see contemporary Britain entering the realm of populist democracy' (Mair, 2003: 94). Mair suggests that this model is characterized by an 'iron control' over party activists and parliamentarians by the senior party leadership, together with an increased reliance on plebiscitary techniques of winning support. Examples of the latter include the internal party referendums held on the 1997 election manifesto and reform of the party constitution, and – at the level of the political system – the popular referendums on the introduction of devolution to Scotland and Wales. It is argued that these strategies reflect an 'intention to eliminate the autonomous impact of party' (Mair, 2003: 94).

Moreover, Mair argues that Labour's constitutional reform programme, together with a non-partisan approach which saw Blair inviting the Liberal Democrats to take part in a key cabinet committee on constitutional reform in his first term and appointing Conservative and Liberal Democrat figures to chair various official commissions, marked a conscious move in the direction of consensus democracy. Furthermore, whereas other authors (such as Marquand) suggest that there is a contradiction between New Labour's tight party discipline and its institutional pluralism, Mair argues that the two are wholly compatible. This 'partyless democracy', according to Mair, equates to a populist democracy with populism as 'a form of governing in which party is sidelined or disappears; where the people are undifferentiated, and in which a more or less "neutral" government attempts to serve the interests of all' (Mair, 2003: 96).

While authors such as Canovan (1999) stress the difficulty populists have in reconciling themselves to the liberal or constitutional aspects of liberal democracy, Mair's model of populist democracy is regarded as compatible and indeed dependent on a robust constitutional democracy. But although Mair is correct to identify a populist style in the Blairite practice of appealing directly to the British people, his discussion of New Labour's constitutional reform programme, which is central to his description of 'partyless democracy', is rather flawed. As noted by Anthony Barnett (2000), New

Labour's constitutional reform programme lacked coherence and cogent purpose. Blair recoiled from earlier interest in electoral reform and, after the initial bold move in removing the right of most hereditary peers to vote in the House of Lords, the reform of the upper house remained stillborn with Blair appearing to favour an appointed upper house. Indeed, Blair was later mired in controversy over the appointments of his acolytes and donors to the Labour party as life peers.

Furthermore, New Labour's enthusiasm for pluralism would diminish in relation to other aspects of the reform agenda. For example, a proposed freedom of information law was severely emasculated, while senior Labour figures would later appear to regret the implications of the Human Rights Act incorporating the European Convention on Human Rights into UK law – with criticism raining down on the judiciary over its rulings in relation to the asylum and security issues against the backdrop of the war on terror.

The party's attitude to institutional pluralism leaves one to consider whether this is the true face of New Labour emerging and whether the earlier programme of constitutional reform was simply a carry-over from commitments made by Blair's predecessors as leader in Labour's earlier modernization phase. Nevertheless, a disdain for the pluralist trappings of liberal democracy might be used to support the thesis that New Labour is indeed a populist phenomenon. In fact, Blair and his colleagues have been accused of authoritarian populism for law-and-order proposals which would impinge on civil liberties and longstanding legal principles such as trial by jury (Russell, 24 April 2006) in addition to its positions on the asylum and immigration issue. There have also been New Labour outbursts of derision against 'liberal' opinion-formers who express concern about the hard line taken in these policy areas. For example, former Home Secretary Jack Straw erupted against 'BMW-driving civil liberties lawyers from the suburbs' while his successor David Blunkett dismissed 'bleeding heart liberals' (Randall, 2004: 192). As Mair illustrates, some of Blair's rhetoric also has a populist tinge. A case in point was Blair's speech to the 1999 Labour party conference in which he ventured: 'Arrayed against us: the forces of conservatism, the cynics, the elites, the establishment... On our side, the forces of modernity and justice. Those who believe in Britain for all the people...' (cited in Mair, 2003: 92).

Nevertheless, this attempt to establish himself as an anti-Establishment hero was ridiculed by Blair's opponents and criticized by his party. Indeed, there was the feeling within the party that the only 'Establishment' he was really challenging was that of the Labour movement itself. A better example of Blair's real political approach came in California in the summer of 2006, where he warned of the dangers of 'protectionism, isolationism and nativism'. In a battle between 'open or closed' responses to globalization, and between 'modern or traditional attitudes to a changing world', Blair placed himself on the side of the open, modern approach, and seemingly against the traditionalist, protectionist and closed responses proffered by populist movements (Wilby, 4 August 2006).

Barnett presents a 'corporate populism' thesis to explain New Labour under Blair, i.e. corporate in the sense that it is modelled on the behaviour of private corporations. New Labour's populism, according to Barnett, involves an inability to comprehend the strength of 'un-businesslike' or 'old-fashioned' popular sentiments, a 'dismissive yet erratic attitude towards traditional, non-market institutions such as the British constitution', an 'attachment to the media-entertainment complex as the key channel for communications strategies, and consequent by-passing of the political party as an antiquated debating machine' and their 'embrace of wealth-creators and big, especially international business' (Barnett, 2000: 88–89).

Barnett's summation of New Labour's political style and strategy seems fairly accurate. Moreover, the attachment to entrepreneurs and business management style solutions seems to have been consolidated over time, while the party's attachment to institutional pluralism continues to diminish. Indeed, while Blair has often trumpeted New Labour as bringing forward a 'whatever works' non-partisan approach, in reality this has tended to come second to favouring business management style solutions even where the evidence suggests that they have not worked. It remains open to question whether this can be described as populism. While populist rhetoric has been employed and its growing antipathy to institutional pluralism lends itself to populist interpretations, New Labour's entanglement with an economic Establishment elite which has historically favoured open and liberal global trading prevents it from presenting the protectionist anti-Establishment message favoured by most modern populists. In addition, the apparent awe Blair displays towards the rich and powerful sits rather awkwardly with the populist characterization. Furthermore, the general lack of a clearly defined 'other' in Blairite discourse makes it difficult to reconcile with the definition of populism used in this volume.

Paradoxically, New Labour's attacks on the 'civil liberties' lobby have come at the same time as the populist press and Conservative opposition have sought to make political capital out of portraying New Labour as part of an out-of-touch cosmopolitan 'politically correct' liberal Establishment – a favourite target of right-wing populists around the globe. This strategy was particularly notable during William Hague's leadership of the Conservative party from 1997 to 2001. He referred to the New Labour leadership as a 'condescending liberal elite', completely out of touch with the feelings and concerns of the English people in the country (i.e. Middle England). As Mudde notes, this had echoes of the 'classic populist distinction between the corrupt, metropolitan, urban elite and the pure, indigenous, rural people' (Mudde, 2003: 550). The struggle between New Labour and the Countryside Alliance is also worth noting in this respect. The latter (with support from the Conservatives) was mobilized initially in protest at Labour's plan to ban fox-hunting, but this broadened into a general attack on New Labour as an out-of-touch urban elite threatening the way of life of real English people (i.e. those living in the countryside) (Mudde, 2004: 550–551).

According to Daniel Collings and Anthony Seldon (2001: 628), policy under Hague seemed to be designed to appeal to populist tabloids such as *The Sun*, whose support for Blair in 1997 had been viewed as critical. New Labour was thus depicted as soft on immigration and asylum, with Hague adopting the slogan 'a safe haven, not a soft touch' in the run-up to the 2001 election. Hague also sought to make the election a referendum on membership of the Euro (with Labour alleged to be planning to betray the British people by adopting the Euro). The slogan 'last chance to save the pound' was used repeatedly with Hague assuming the role of 'defender of Britain's sacred currency'. In addition to the Countryside Alliance, support had also been given to the fuel tax protests in 2000, led by lorry drivers blocking key roads and threatening to bring the country to a halt. Celtic devolution also had the effect of feeding calls for a reassertion of English political identity, as demonstrated by Hague's proposal that new constitutional arrangements be adopted to allow English MPs to vote separately on English matters (whilst excluding Scottish and Welsh MPs). The 'English' question is a thorny one which populists might seek to exploit more fully in the future, notwithstanding the tendency of politicians of a populist persuasion in Britain, particularly on the Right, to emphasize the supremacy of *the Union* (i.e. Great Britain and Northern Ireland). Indeed while presenting itself as an English Nationalist party was a temptation for the Conservative party after the 1997 election, when it was left without a single parliamentary seat in Scotland or Wales, the historic Conservative commitment to the defence of the Union – not to mention its hopes of regaining seats in Scotland and Wales – limited this as a potential option.

While Hague's populist strategy was useful in shoring up the Conservative core vote, it was not enough for victory in Britain's FPTP system. A right-wing populist strategy would always have its limitations for a mainstream party requiring victory in a majority of FPTP constituencies, though it might be useful for smaller parties seeking a foothold in elections under a Proportional Representation system. Nevertheless, the strategies pursued by those who followed him as leader between 2001 and 2005 echoed those of Hague. His successor, Iain Duncan Smith presented himself as a 'quiet man' in tune with the 'silent majority', but very poor poll ratings led to his replacement in 2003 by the more experienced former cabinet minister, Michael Howard. The title of the Conservative manifesto for the 2005 elections: *Are you thinking what we're thinking? It's time for Action* provided a hint of Howard's strategy. As Matthew d'Ancona noted, this message could be interpreted as one of 'grubby conspiracy: whispered words, and noses tapped' about concerns such as 'uncontrolled immigration' (cited in Seldon and Snowdon, 2005: 733–734). Indeed, despite attacking the BNP and stressing his family's

Romanian Jewish refugee background, Howard focused strongly on the anti-immigration theme, placing this at the centre of his self-declared 'Battle for Britain' (ibid.). Once again, the Conservatives failed to move much beyond their core vote in 2005.

Still on the margins – radical right populism

Given the decline and splits in the NF, the BNP – formed by ex-NF members in 1982 – managed to establish itself as the dominant force on the British extreme Right by the mid-1990s. Although it initially adopted a traditional extreme Right approach, its leader since 1999, Nick Griffin, has sought to reposition the party, following the well-beaten path of radical right parties on the continent, by seeking to distance it from old style neo-fascism and by developing a more populist platform. Nevertheless, the BNP has stated that it does not regard non-white people as British, even if they have been born in the UK and are British citizens. A perhaps truer insight into Griffin's strategy can be gleaned from the speech he gave to the American Friends of the BNP in April 2001 in which he explained: 'so, what are we now doing with the British National Party? Well we tried to simplify its message in some ways and to make it a saleable message. So it's not white supremacy or racial civil war or anything like that, which is what we know in fact is going on, and we're not supremacists, we're white survivalists' (BBC Website).

The BNP's ethno-populism emerges clearly from an analysis of its recent election manifestos,[3] which illustrate its use of anti-Establishment populism (blaming the governing parties for allowing Britain to be over-run with immigrants) and ethno-pluralist frames which stress the need to maintain Britain as an ethnically homogeneous unit. Thus, its most recent general election manifesto presented immigration as a 'crisis without parallel' in which 'Britain's very existence' was threatened' (2005). Its attack on multiculturalism and the role of the political Establishment was reflected in the following excerpt:

> Abolishing multiculturalism, preserving Britain: The present regime is engaged in a profound cultural war against the British people, motivated by the desire to create a new ethnic power base to replace the working class which they have abandoned in pursuit of their enthusiasm for globalisation, justified by a quasi-Marxist ideology of the equality of all cultures. (2005: 17)

As Jens Rydgren has shown (2005) the growth of radical right populism in a number of European countries can be partly explained by the agency role of party leaders who have adopted the ethno-populist and anti-Establishment master-frames that have proved successful elsewhere, with the French *Front National* acting as a particular inspiration. Thus the radical Right populist emphasis on welfare chauvinism and the scapegoating of immigrants for taking up valuable economic resources whilst being responsible for crime and social breakdown, is also evident in recent BNP manifestos, as is its adoption of the populist critique of liberal political correctness:

> Britain is full up and the government of Britain has as its first responsibility the welfare, security and long-term preservation of the native people of Britain. (2005: 14)

> On issue after issue the views of the majority of British people have been ignored and overridden by a politically correct 'elite' who thinks it knows best. (2001:3)

Despite this populist strategy, and the significant amount of media attention given to the BNP's activities and occasional successes, the electoral returns of the party (as with the NF before it) have been rather meagre, almost negligible when compared to the performances of RRPs elsewhere in Europe. Nevertheless, the BNP vote share has increased in recent elections, and it has benefited in particular from popular concerns on the asylum issue (where, as we have seen, its positions may have been legitimized by the mainstream parties) and in relation to the position of Muslim communities in Britain. Thus in 2001, it achieved an average score of 3.7 per cent in the 34 seats it contested and 0.2 per cent of the vote as a whole. In 2005, it ran in 119 constituencies, achieving an average score of 4.2 per cent in these and 0.7 per cent of the vote across Britain as a whole. Its votes in local elections have been better: in June 2004 it scored 16.1 per cent of the vote in the council wards it fought (309 wards in total). Nevertheless, the party's total number of councillors (24) was still pretty low considering that there are 20,000 local council seats overall. A more useful pointer comes from the European elections held using PR. In 2004, the BNP won 4.9 per cent of the vote – although not enough to win any seats (Webb, 2005: 772). The BNP has also done particularly well in certain local pockets with high concentrations of ethnic minority – especially Muslim – populations, notably in East London (its best result in 2005 came in Barking where it scored 16.9 per cent), West Yorkshire and the Lancashire Mill towns, where it scored well in the wake of the 2001 riots.

In the 2006 local elections, the BNP nearly doubled its number of council seats to 46, including 11 seats on Barking and Dagenham council (making it the second biggest party there). In Barking and elsewhere, the BNP appeared to exploit a perception among white working class voters that they had been deserted by the Labour party as part of its shift to the middle ground and its courting of middle class voters. This was combined with the message that migrants and asylum seekers were being given preferential treatment. Although this strategy has given the BNP some success, it remains hampered in its attempts to become a genuine popular force by its past as an extreme

Right party which endorsed elements of Nazi ideology. As the literature on the far Right has shown, such parties usually have more success when adopting a populist platform free of linkages from old style extreme right neo-Fascism. Any such linkages are particularly disadvantageous in the British context, given the collective memory of Britain having stood alone against the Nazis in Europe in 1940.

UKIP, by contrast, has the advantage of being free from such Fascist associations. Formed in 1993, UKIP was initially overshadowed by James Goldsmith's Referendum Party,[4] but came to the fore following the 1997 election and Goldsmith's death. It has benefited in particular from the switch to PR for European elections, and the scope this contest gives it to focus its message on its core anti-EU stance. Thus in 1999 it won seven per cent of the vote and three seats, rising to 16.1 per cent and 12 MEPs in 2004.

This progress has been spectacular and rather unprecedented for a new political force in Britain. Despite the focus on the European issue, the party has also won seats in local elections and the Greater London Assembly, and received 1.5 per cent of the vote in the 2001 general election. Its call for tougher law-and-order and immigration and asylum policies, as well as withdrawal from the EU, brought it onto similar ground to the BNP, while representing a more acceptable populist alternative to the mainstream parties for disillusioned voters with right-wing inclinations. Its appeal then increased dramatically in 2004, when the popular TV personality Robert Kilroy-Silk successfully stood as one of its MEP candidates.

Kilroy-Silk was a former Labour MP who had become famous as the host of a BBC talk-show which focused on the problems and views of ordinary members of the public, but who had been sacked following the publication of a xenophobic anti-Arab newspaper article at the beginning of 2004. Kilroy (as he is popularly known) appeared to offer UKIP the essential (and missing) ingredient enjoyed by populist parties elsewhere in Europe, i.e. a charismatic leader with excellent media skills, instantly recognizable to the public and able to appeal directly to the 'common sense' (or prejudice) of the 'man in the street'. However, the problem for Kilroy and UKIP was that he was not the leader of UKIP, and his attempts to take over the leadership of the party were thwarted by its more long-standing members. This led to Kilroy's departure from UKIP in January 2004, and his formation of a new party, Veritas, that he could lead and dominate (Webb, 2005: 773).

Kilroy's anti-Establishment and ethno-populist approach can be clearly seen in the following excerpts from a speech made in September 2004, whilst still an UKIP MEP:

> Just as it has lied about Europe and Weapons of Mass Destruction, so the government has constantly misled us about immigration and asylum. It has never been honest about the numbers entering the country but, on

the evidence of the whistleblowers, has constantly sought to minimise the figures. Nor has it ever consulted the British people about the number of people from abroad that should be allowed to settle here. We have not been asked if we are prepared to have the nature of our neighbourhoods changed forever. We have not been asked if we are prepared to see our schools in some areas overwhelmed by those who cannot speak English. We were not asked if we were prepared to see our health and social services put under strain. As the polls show, people feel that they are losing their culture. (Kilroy-Silk, 2004)

Similar themes were picked up by Kilroy's new Veritas party. Indeed, the Veritas and UKIP election manifestos for the 2005 election were rather similar. However, neither did as well as hoped. Veritas won an average of just over 1.5 per cent in the 62 seats it fought, while Kilroy received only 5.8 per cent of the vote in his constituency. UKIP did slightly better, winning 2.3 per cent nationally, and 2.8 per cent on average in the seats where it stood (Webb, 2005: 773–774). Although this was an improvement on the 2001 result, it was seen as a disappointment given the expectations raised by the spectacular success of 2004. The effect of the splits created by Kilroy were a salutary reminder of what happens when new populist forces fail to unite behind one leader and the limitations to progress when the party (in the case of UKIP) does not possess an instantly recognizable and charismatic leader with considerable media skills (its existing leader Nigel Farage does not come across as a 'man of the people' and lacks a 'common touch').

Of course, in the case of Britain, the electoral system used for general elections provides a particular obstacle that would have made life difficult for Kilroy and UKIP even if they stayed together. While future European elections may tell a different story, the future impact of UKIP on the British party system will nonetheless remain contained if limited to such elections.

Conclusion

Populists on the Right have exploited the 'Britain in decline' thesis, feeding on a perceived loss of national identity and self-esteem whilst also exploiting a feeling that the Labour party has deserted the white working class. Radical right populists draw strength from public concerns over the impact of EU membership on national sovereignty, and the impact of migration and multiculturalism on the 'British way of life'. Although such issues have been exploited by populists throughout Europe, Britain's imperial past and its history as a 'great power' allow national populists to present it as an 'exceptional case'. The British tradition of liberal global free trading does however mean that the Right has not followed the example of RRPs on the continent in proposing protectionist solutions.

While the BNP and UKIP have enjoyed gains in second order elections, both suffer from the lack of a charismatic leader (although UKIP appear to have briefly found and lost one in Kilroy-Silk), staying power and party cohesion which the examples of continental Europe suggest is necessary for consistent success. Nevertheless, the continued decline in identification with the main parties combined with voter disillusionment with the lack of policy alternatives they offer (given their convergence on key policies) point to a future in which new and recycled populist movements will continue to exist as a thorn in the side of the established political mainstream, albeit possibly only as low level irritants in second order elections.

While new populist movements have been boosted by new political opportunities, the FPTP electoral system continues to restrict their ability to impact on national level politics. Thus the greatest potential for populism lies within the political mainstream, where politicians within Britain's major parties are able to harness such issues. The best example of this came with the premiership of Margaret Thatcher, who combined a combative approach on these issues with an attack on certain Establishment institutions and the pillars of the post-war social democratic consensus, a populist identification with the prejudices of middle England and a charismatic leadership which allowed her to enjoy – at least for a time – supremacy over her party. Her political heir, Tony Blair, has also benefited from some of these attributes, although when looking beyond some of his populist rhetoric, one finds an emphasis on managerialism and a desire to please powerful interests that leaves one to question whether this is really populism. Since 1997, the Conservatives have dabbled with a new nationalist populist strategy which portrays New Labour as an out-of-touch liberal metropolitan elite selling out the British people. However, its lack of electoral success again shows the limits of such a strategy under FPTP.

Notes

1. An increase possibly motivated by a perception that the contest was closer and/or a desire to protest against UK participation in the Iraq war.
2. These, according to David Marquand, were an interlocking network involving 'the elite universities, the BBC, the *noblesse oblige* Tory grandees, the bench of bishops (and) the higher ranks of the civil service' (Marquand, 1998: 22).
3. I am grateful to Dr Paul Jones of Liverpool University for allowing me to consult the analysis of the BNP manifestos he conducted as a member of the UK research team for the Xenophob project, 2002–2005 (funded by the EU 5th framework programme).
4. This party stood in a number of constituencies in 1997 and promised a referendum on continued membership of the EU.

13
The Republic of Ireland: The Dog That Hasn't Barked in the Night?

Duncan McDonnell

Introduction

The reader may be somewhat surprised to find a chapter on Ireland in a comparative study of populism in contemporary Western Europe.[1] First of all, for many years, politics in the Republic of Ireland was treated by scholars as exceptional and of little interest to the comparativist. As Peter Mair comments, Ireland was seen as a small peripheral state in which 'the patterns and structures of mass politics which are evident elsewhere in Europe have little relevance' (Mair, 1999: 128). In particular, Ireland's perceived idiosyncrasy lay in the fact that the two parties which generally accounted for over 80 per cent of the vote, Fianna Fáil (FF) and Fine Gael (FG), both seemed to be broadly of the centre/centre-right, while the main party on the Left, Labour, usually came a very distant third at elections.[2] Second, late twentieth-century Ireland has not produced a populist party akin to the likes of the Freedom Party (FPÖ) in Austria, the *Lega Nord* (LN) in Italy, or the *Lijst Pim Fortuyn* (LPF) in Holland. Thus, while politics in the Republic in the last two decades has become more similar to that on the continent due to membership of the European Union (EU), economic growth, immigration, secularization and the predominance of coalition governments, it has nonetheless escaped the rise of the type of populist challengers seen in almost every other Western European state.

However, while the new wave of (generally right-wing) European populism may not have broken yet on Irish shores, that does not mean that the conditions which have allowed populist success elsewhere are not yet present in Ireland. As Elina Kestilä's study of what she terms 'the Finnish exception' shows, the factors facilitating the success of such parties 'may exist also in cases of non-occurrences' (Kestilä, 2005: 2). They just simply may not have been politicized and/or acted upon. Indeed, if we compare Ireland with Italy – a country regularly hailed as having become 'a populist paradise' in the 1990s (see Marco Tarchi's chapter in this volume) – we find today in Ireland many of the same conditions which created the fertile terrain for such spectacular populist success in Italy: the exposure of widespread political corruption, plummeting levels of party identification, an increasingly anti-political media, unprecedented immigration, a swift decline of the Church's influence, rising Euroscepticism, etc.

The absence of a populist party of the kinds found in Italy, Denmark or Britain should not be taken to mean, however, that Irish politics is free from populism in all its guises. In fact, politics in the Republic has always been characterized by what Margaret Canovan (1981: 12–13) terms 'politicians' populism', meaning 'broad, non-ideological coalition-building that draws on the unificatory appeal of "the people"'. As Canovan (2005: 77) notes in her most recent work, 'in the USA, which escaped many of the conflicts over class and ideology from which European party systems emerged, there has long been scope for this kind of populism', and so too in Ireland, with a party system in many ways most similar to that of the United States (US), has this type of politicians' populism long flourished, especially (but not only) in the dominant party FF and its leaders.[3] However, while the US has also seen the sporadic emergence in recent decades of new right-wing populist actors similar to those found in Europe (Ross Perot being a notable example), contemporary Ireland has remained untouched by such phenomena.

To help provide answers to the questions of why that is the case and whether Ireland is likely to remain, in this sense, an exception in Western Europe, this chapter will first of all examine, in the Irish context, the same opportunity structures which have helped determine the emergence and success/failure of populist parties across the continent: political culture, cleavages, the party system, the economy, immigration, European integration and corruption. This will set the stage for the second part of the chapter, devoted to populist agency, which will look first at what populism there has been and currently is in Irish politics, before then assessing the potential in twenty-first century Ireland for the emergence and success of a populist party similar to most of those found elsewhere in Western Europe, either through the appearance of a new party or the transformation of an existing one. It will argue that, in fact, the main obstacle impeding the emergence of a new populist party is the recent success of the left-wing nationalist party Sinn Fein (SF) which, while unwilling (and unable) to embrace anti-minority or anti-pluralist positions, not only displays many of the other characteristics of populism, but has occupied much of the political and electoral space where a populist challenger (of the Right or Left) would seek to locate itself.

Opportunity structures for populism in Ireland

Political culture and cleavages

Twentieth-century Irish political culture developed in ways that would appear to hinder the rise and success of a populist challenger. First and foremost is the fact that Irish political culture has always contained a strong dose of populism. Rather than being predicated on left-right or secular/clerical cleavages, in post-independence Ireland, as Mair argues, 'there emerged a new political culture which, in its constant stress on Catholic nationalist uniformity and homogeneity...proved quite hostile to any notion of politicising internal social divisions' (Mair, 1992: 404). If, therefore, as we have said in the introductory chapter, populist appeals challenge the dominant political culture by juxtaposing 'a virtuous and homogeneous people' with an unscrupulous elite and a set of dangerous 'others', then Irish political culture was nearly unimpeachable with its twin pillars of the worthy plain Catholic people of Ireland on one side and the common enemy (and easy scapegoat for the nation's ills) of Britain and its liberal culture on the other. Within this discourse, to stir internal divisions among 'the people' was, as in US political culture with its notion of 'un-American', viewed as being 'against the national interest'. Indeed, for most of post-independence Irish history, we might say that Plato's *polis* of idealized unity has prevailed over Aristotle's, in which conflicting interests and values were instead perceived as natural. In Ireland, differences within 'the people' (the simple-living Catholic community) were discarded, swept under a carpet of rhetoric exalting a nation of pious Celts striving, together, for collective self-realization in territorial, social and economic terms. Or, to return to Plato and Aristotle, we might say that *The Republic* suppressed *The Politics*.

In this sense, Ireland had much in common with other twentieth-century postcolonial societies. In his study of the Third World in the 1960s, Peter Worsley observed that populist leaders in the newly independent states 'assert that there are no divisions in the community, or that if they are discernible, they are "non-antagonistic". Thus class divisions can then be dismissed as external ("imperialist") intrusions, alien to the society' (Worsley, 1967: 165–166). Likewise in Ireland, class politics were characterized as something that happened 'elsewhere' (in particular Britain) and not to be welcomed in a nation pursuing economic development. Of course, it could be argued that the small Irish Labour party was to some extent complicit in this (Mair, 1992). Parties are, after all, not mere passive victims of structures, but interact with them, contributing to their formation and consolidation as well as living within their boundaries (Sartori, 2005; Mair, 1987). Thus, according to Mair (1992: 403), one of the key reasons why class did not emerge as a major cleavage in Irish politics was quite simply that 'unlike in the rest of Western Europe, no party, or union, has sought sufficiently hard "to persuade" such an alignment'. Consequently, there have generally been few opportunities for a populist challenger either (a) to appeal to 'the people' beyond the right-left paradigm – which they can depict as an illusion created by professional politicians to disguise the pursuit of their own and other elite interests or (b) to appeal to 'the common working man' to rise up against a bourgeois, corrupt elite. In the first case, this was because the two main parties both already appealed to 'the people' in this way; in the second because class politics were accepted as being against the national interest. Although there are some signs that this situation may be changing – as shown by the increased vote for SF in working-class urban areas – Irish political competition still has nothing approaching even the weakened type of class cleavage found in other contemporary Western European societies.

By contrast, the secular/clerical cleavage appears more interesting for our discussion. As Jens Rydgren argues in his chapter on Sweden, opportunities for populist success are increased by changes in and greater salience of what he terms the 'sociocultural dimension' (including the secular/clerical cleavage). In this area, huge changes have occurred in Ireland since the end of the 1980s as a combination of public value shifts and serious scandals involving the clergy have led to a very considerable decline in the influence of the Church. This has been reflected in a number of ways. First of all, people have clearly voted with their feet as weekly Mass attendance amongst Catholics has fallen from 85 per cent in 1990 (European Values Survey) to just 50 per cent in 2003 (TNS mrbi Survey). Second, they have voted against the instructions of the Church hierarchy in a number of referendums over the last fifteen years. In 1995, the introduction of divorce (which had been defeated by a two-thirds majority in 1986) was narrowly approved and while abortion has not yet been fully legalized, some restrictions surrounding it have been lifted following controversial referendums. These changes within Irish society may favour a populist party in a number of (partly contrasting) ways:

(1) given the Church's promotion of tolerance towards immigrants, its decline in influence, particularly in urban areas, could make a populist party with an anti-immigrant stance more publicly acceptable;
(2) likewise, however, while many Irish have embraced secular values, there is still a large constituency amongst whom a populist appeal based on a nostalgic return to the heartland of 'clean-living old Catholic Ireland' could find favour. This is particularly so as all the current parties have now adopted positions on moral issues which conflict with the teachings of the Church.

The party system

It is to those parties that we now turn our attention. In particular, our focus here is on how has the party system transformed over the last two decades and how might this benefit/hinder a populist challenger. As with the secular/clerical cleavage, there have also been major changes in the party system since the mid-1980s, with a steady decline in the combined vote of the two main parties, FF and FG, the emergence of new parties, and the decision by FF to go into coalition, first in 1989 with a new party to the Right – the neo-liberal Progressive Democrats (PDs) – and then in 1992 with an old adversary, Labour, on the Left. Before 1989, for decades the electorate had been faced with a choice of single-party FF government versus a possible coalition of FG and Labour. Given FF's electoral strength and its refusal to countenance sharing power, FG and Labour always had to accept that, if they wanted to govern, it would have to be with one another, despite their centre-right/centre-left differences. Indeed, despite the fall in its vote since the 1970s, it remains the case that, for FF to be put into opposition, FG, Labour and at least one of the new parties would have to enter government together. If we take FF as being closer to the centre than FG (as has been the case for most of the histories of the two parties, although not always), FF fulfil Christoffer Green-Pedersen's criterion for what he terms a 'pivotal center party', by which he means one that can only be removed from power by an overarching coalition of parties from both Right and Left. (Green-Pedersen, 2004: 337). As Green-Pedersen warns, however, this can lead to an 'implosion' of the party system (as happened, for example, in Holland) in which 'all major parties become center parties capable of governing with each other' (Green-Pedersen, 2004: 324). Certainly, this would allow a populist challenger to accuse such parties of being prepared to sacrifice their principles and identities in pursuit of office and its spoils. Moreover, the inability since the 1980s of FF to secure enough seats to govern alone has now made all parties possible coalition partners of one another, with the exception of FF and FG – whose unwillingness to contemplate governing together, despite being the two parties closest to one another, remains the great Rubicon of Irish politics. The policy convergence between these two parties (especially now that they substantially agree on the Northern Ireland question) offers an obvious opportunity for those wishing to paint them as being essentially the same, with only their civil war histories dividing them (as the PDs, for example, initially did). Indeed, as Michael Gallagher and Michael Marsh (2004) found, even a large portion of FG members see little difference between the two parties in terms of policy.

Thus, although no party has polled more than FF since 1928, we can still say that if the Irish party system was one which was 'frozen *par excellence*' for many years, it has thawed significantly over the last two decades (Mair, 1997a: 15). As we can see from Table 13.1, the combined first preference vote of FF and FG has fallen from 84.4 per cent in 1982 to 64 per cent in 2002 while that of Labour has remained substantially unchanged. This slide in the vote for the main traditional parties has been accompanied by declines in party identification and turnout. In the first Irish National Election Study (INES), held in 2002, only 25 per cent of respondents said they felt 'close to' a particular party (Laver, 2005: 194). The comparison with Mair's figure (1997a: 128) of over 72 per cent in 1981 expressing a sense of identification with political parties tells its own story. Disillusionment with the parties is also reflected by the fall in turnout at general elections from 76.2 per cent

---

Table 13.1 General elections in the Republic of Ireland, 1982–2002

Party	1982 (ii)*		1987		1989		1992		1997		2002	
	%	S	%	S	%	S	%	S	%	S	%	S
FF	45.2	75	44.1	81	44.1	77	39.1	68	39.3	77	41.5	81
FG	39.2	70	27.1	51	29.3	55	24.5	45	28.0	54	22.5	31
Lab.	9.4	16	6.4	12	9.5	15	19.3	33	10.4	17	10.8	21
PD	N/A	N/A	11.8	14	5.5	6	4.7	10	4.7	4	4.0	8
Green	N/A	N/A	0.4	0	1.5	1	1.4	1	2.8	2	3.8	6
SF	N/A	N/A	1.9	0	1.2	0	1.6	0	2.6	1	6.5	5
WP/ DL**	3.1	2	3.8	4	5.0	7	2.8	4	2.5	4	N/A	N/A
Ind. + others	3.1	3	4.5	4	3.9	5	5.9	5	9.4	7	11	14

Notes: The left-hand columns for each year refer to the percentage of first preference votes obtained, the right-hand columns to the number of seats gained. * Two general elections were held in 1982. The data here refers to the second one, in November of that year. ** WP refers to the Workers' Party. All of its deputies bar one left in 1992 to form Democratic Left (DL). DL then merged with the Labour Party at the end of 1998.

Source: Elaboration of electoral data from the appendix in John Coakley and Michael Gallagher (2004), (eds), Politics in the Republic of Ireland (Fourth edition), London: Routledge.

in 1981 to 62.6 per cent in 2002 – a figure which placed Ireland at the bottom of the 'turnout league' among the fifteen members of the EU at the time (Lyons and Sinnott, 2003: 143). The potential effects of partisan dealignment are notoriously complex and diverse, but among them are the opening up of voters to new offers and the possibility that the electorate will become susceptible to demagogic appeals by charismatic populist leaders as happened, for example, in Austria and France (Dalton, McAllister, and Wattenberg, 2002: 60–61).

Certainly, an increasing section of the electorate has shown itself willing to vote for new opposition parties rather than those of the 'old opposition' (see Table 13.1). Indeed, if the decline of the FF vote has been moderate since the 1980s, that of FG has been dramatic, with the party securing just 31 seats compared to FF's 81 at the 2002 election. Furthermore, despite being the party which might have expected to benefit most from secularization, Labour has seen its vote stagnate – barring the false dawns of Mary Robinson's election as President in 1990 and the party's excellent result at the 1992 election. Furthermore, its chronic weakness in large swathes of the West, as noted by Tom Garvin (1974: 313) over thirty years ago, has remained intact and its merger in 1998 with a smaller party to its left – Democratic Left – appears to have brought no significant rise in its vote. Rather, the beneficiaries of dealignment and disillusionment with FF and FG have been a series of new entries into the *Dáil* (Irish Parliament): the PDs, the Greens, SF and various Independent *Teachtaí Dála* (TDs – deputies).

204 *Twenty-First Century Populism*

As mentioned in the introduction, the emergence and success of SF represents perhaps the most significant impediment to the rise of a new populist party as it appears to be occupying much of the space which such a challenger might seek to enter. The populism of SF will be examined in the second part of the chapter, but here three points are worth mentioning. First of all, the profile of SF voters in the Republic is similar to those of most populist parties elsewhere in Western Europe. As Michael Laver (2005: 197) notes, at the 2002 election, they were predominately young (average age 36), male (58 per cent) and more likely to be on lower incomes than voters of all other parties except FF. Moreover, as John Garry (2006) finds, they are more likely to have low levels of political knowledge, low trust in the existing parties and a low sense of their political efficacy. Put simply, they are the most alienated voters in the Republic. Second, it is important to note the financial and organizational resources of SF which, for a 'new' party, are enormous. Indeed, according to Stephen Collins, it was probably the best-funded party at the 2002 election, after FF (Collins, 2003: 34). This not only enabled the party to field candidates in almost every constituency, but also helps pay for a highly efficient administrative staff, including eight full-time press officers, covering both sides of the border (Maillot, 2005: 74). A populist party targeting the urban working-class vote would obviously find it hard to compete with such a well-oiled and well-funded party machine. Third, and most important, not only does SF already exploit discontent regarding mainstream parties, the economy, Irish sovereignty and the EU, but it explicitly puts itself forward as a 'clean', anti-Establishment party which is close to the common people in local communities. As such, while SF's support for pluralism and minority rights disqualify it from membership of the populist canon, it does articulate much of the discourse which a populist party might seek to employ.

Finally, we should also note the large (and rising) vote for Independents/others: 11 per cent in 2002. In particular, Independents have recently done increasingly well in parts of rural Ireland where former FF and FG voters have not turned to Labour or the 'new opposition', but to local-issue candidates. Their presence, while pointing to the existence of a dealigned vote in these areas, is not necessarily encouraging for a populist challenger as it also indicates the continuing strength of the local and personalized aspects of election campaigning in Ireland (requiring door-to-door canvassing, high familiarity with constituency issues and preferably prior county council experience) which would work against a quick populist breakthrough. As Gallagher (2003: 101–102) says of Green and SF candidates, so too would it apply to those of any new party that they 'cannot expect to be swept into the *Dáil* on a national tide; they need to build up a strong local support base first'. This is essential since, as the 2002 INES showed, 40 per cent of people voted entirely on the basis of the candidate rather than the party and would have supported that candidate irrespective of which party he/she represented

(Laver, 2005: 193). A populist party like the LPF or the *Lega Nord* – heavily reliant on the national image of the leader and often fielding a series of unfamiliar local names in constituencies – would therefore need a miracle (or at least a moment of severe national crisis) to emerge as a significant parliamentary force in Ireland over just one or two elections as happened in Holland and Italy (see the chapters in this volume by Paul Lucardie and Marco Tarchi).

The economy

The structural element in Ireland which has changed most radically over the last fifteen years is, of course, the economy. While the 1980s was a decade of spiralling national debt, high unemployment and large numbers of young people emigrating, the period since has seen spectacular and previously unimaginable growth in a country which had been one of the poorest in the EU. As a result, the national debt has been slashed, Irish Gross National Product has surpassed the EU 15 average (having been just two-thirds of it in the 1980s), emigrants are returning and the unemployment rate is now the lowest in the EU. On the surface, therefore, the Celtic Tiger would appear to offer few opportunities for the Celtic populist given that, elsewhere in Western Europe, populist parties have fruitfully exploited economic crises, or at least the prospect of them.

The situation is not quite so clear-cut, however. First of all, as we have seen, throughout the history of the Irish state, economic development and 'the national interest' have been put forward as the goals at whose altar all cleavages should be sacrificed. Now that very considerable economic development has indeed been achieved in Ireland, this may allow other, more divisive, issues to come to the fore of political and public debate – to the obvious advantage of the populist. Second, it is important to note that, despite the very real economic growth and improvements in living standards which have taken place, the 'rising tide' has not lifted all boats. Or, at least, it has lifted some boats far more than others. With the economic boom has come a high level of earnings inequality and the gap between rich and poor in Ireland has widened quite considerably. Indeed, the 2005 United Nations Human Development Report showed Ireland to be one of the most unequal countries in the developed world 'with the richest 10 per cent of the population having 9.7 times more wealth than the poorest 10 per cent' (Humphreys, 2005). Third, and related to the previous point, one of the keys to economic growth in Ireland has been the system of Social Partnership, the pillars of which have been wage restraint and tax cuts. As Brian Nolan, Philip J. O'Connell and Christopher T. Whelan (2000: 352) conclude, now that the goals of economic development and employment growth on which it was based have been fulfilled, 'the institutions of social partnership are likely to come under increasing pressure', especially as those on middle and lower incomes become frustrated with the very visible wealth disparities in the population. Moreover, one of the cornerstones of Social Partnership has been to 'co-opt' the trade unions, which no longer play the very vocal opposition role they once used to. While SF has secured some of this market already, there still remains a large part of the electorate, many of whom do not vote at all, which could be open to a populist party appealing to the 'common working men and women', abandoned by their representatives and exploited by the new economic elites.

Immigration

One of the side-effects of the economic boom has been the arrival in Ireland, for the first time in the nation's history and over a very short period, of large numbers of immigrants. As the preliminary results of the 2006 census show, nearly 10 per cent of the population are nationals of other states and the number of non-nationals in the country has nearly doubled in just four years, from 220,000 in 2002 to over 400,000 in 2006, in large part due to the arrivals of citizens from the new accession countries of the EU (O'Brien, 2006). While Ireland has long prided itself on being the land 'of a hundred thousand welcomes', now that those arriving are not just free-spending American tourists, but Nigerians, Poles and others in search of work, the country's attitudes to outsiders has noticeably changed. Using data from the 2003 Eurobarometer survey, Michael Breen (2006: 18) finds that 38.5 per cent of Irish respondents 'completely agreed' that there were too many immigrants in the country while a further 36.2 per cent 'tended to agree' with this. Over half of respondents also 'completely agreed' or 'tended to agree' with the statement that immigrants are responsible for crime. As in the UK, these attitudes have been shaped by parts of the media with the term 'asylum seeker' becoming synonymous with 'sponger' and used to denote all immigrants. In reality, although the number of people requesting asylum in Ireland did rise from just 39 in 1992 to over 11,000 in 2002, this still represented less than 10 per cent of all those coming to live in Ireland (Loyal, 2003: 76).

The hardening of Ireland's position towards non-nationals was highlighted by the 2004 Citizenship Referendum to remove a constitutional clause giving anyone born on the island of Ireland the automatic right to Irish citizenship. Strongly backed by the PD Minister for Justice, Michael McDowell, the referendum took place amidst talk of 'citizenship tourists' and accusations that maternity wards were being 'swamped' by African women arriving heavily pregnant in Ireland in order to give birth and thus acquire Irish (and hence EU) passports for their children. While no clear evidence was offered to support these accusations beyond anecdotal accounts, the referendum was passed with a 79 per cent vote in favour. Given that almost every populist party discussed in this volume has sought to exploit non-European immigration, it is self-evident that the sudden influx which has taken place in Ireland offers a very significant opportunity for a populist challenger.

European integration

Immigration from new member states is also one of the factors impacting on how the Irish now view the EU. While Ireland has benefited enormously from its membership of the Union, attitudes are slowly changing and Euroscepticism is likely to grow as the country becomes a net contributor to the EU budget for the first time in its history, but with less representation in the supranational institutions of an enlarged Union. As the Autumn 2005 Eurobarometer survey showed, although the number of Irish viewing the EU positively was still the highest of any member state (69 per cent), this represents a six point drop on those who thought the same a year previously (Eurobarometer 64, 2006: 6). Moreover, the authors of the report warn that 'failure to communicate with people, particularly over a period of change in Ireland's economic relationship with the EU, may alter what is currently a favourable attitudinal climate' and that support for the EU in the less-educated sectors of the population 'is built on fragile foundations' (Ibid.: 22). A very public and unexpected warning sign of this trend for the government and major parties was the 54 per cent 'no' vote (albeit from a 35 per cent turnout) in the June 2001 referendum on the Nice Treaty. While a second referendum in October 2002 (with a turnout of almost 50 per cent) was passed by a 63 per cent majority, the two campaigns and results showed that Ireland's role in Europe is becoming politicized and open to debate. Furthermore, given the Irish constitutional requirement to hold referendums on EU treaty changes, there are likely to be many further opportunities to focus public attention on Europe and mobilize this constituency. However, we should note here that the extensive use of referendums in Ireland to decide key secular/clerical issues and matters related to the EU integration process may also serve to provide an alternative outlet to elections for the expression of public discontent with party policies on these questions (Sinnott, 1995).

Thus far, only SF and the Greens have adopted clear stances against key aspects of integration, primarily those which might encroach on Irish neutrality. However, it is interesting that even among members of FG – traditionally the most pro-European party – 31 per cent believed that the integration process had already gone too far in 1999 (Gallagher and Marsh, 2004: 418). As with immigration, the vast majority of the populist parties discussed in this book have made Europe one of their main themes and an Irish populist party depicting the Union as a self-serving, unelected Brussels elite interested in spending newly enriched taxpayers' money on faraway countries and dictating how the Irish should manage their internal affairs might find itself mining a rich and growing seam. Indeed, in the future, rather than Irish neutrality being compromised, it is likely only to be when membership of the EU can be convincingly portrayed as compromising the Irish economy that the Eurosceptic genie will really emerge from the bottle in Ireland. Thus, as the country becomes a net contributor and the EU eventually tackles the very generous tax system for companies in Ireland, Europe may well become a central and contentious issue in Irish politics, with obvious opportunities for a populist party.

Corruption

A major element in Irish political life over the last fifteen years has been the uncovering of widespread political corruption through a series of Tribunals of Inquiry. However, while in countries such as France and Italy, corruption scandals have provided extremely fertile terrain for populists seeking to portray the professional political class as beholden to vested interests, in Ireland their exposure seems to have had little effect so far on the newly-prosperous electorate. Despite the fact that many of the scandals involving high-ranking FF members (including the party's former leader, Charles Haughey) broke during the late 1990s, the incumbent FF/PD government was returned with an increased majority in 2002. Put simply, the 'feel-good' factors of, first and foremost, the booming economy and, secondly, the Northern Ireland peace process, were far more important. Indeed, according to Stephen Collins, although the FG leadership contemplated making corruption a higher-profile issue in its 2002 campaign, they decided that 'the voters were just not interested and that raising the issue could be counterproductive'. This was probably a wise decision as 'Fianna Fáil focus group research had independently come to the same conclusion' (Collins, 2003: 29). Of course, FG's decision may well have been partly based on the consideration that a number of its own members (most notably, the former Minister, Michael Lowry) have also been named as recipients of cash from businessmen and property developers. Indeed, corruption is a tricky issue to deal with even for the 'new opposition' of the Greens and SF since, although putting themselves forward as cleaner and more ethical alternatives to FF, they currently (beginning of 2007) refuse to exclude the possibility of coalition with them. In that sense, a populist party, ruling out any collaboration with either FF or FG, might find an anti-corruption stance more profitable. Nonetheless, the perception that the Irish public is ambivalent about corruption would appear confirmed by the fact that in the weeks following the revelation that the FF *Taoiseach* (Prime Minister) Bertie Ahern had received cash gifts from business friends in the 1990s while he was Minister for Finance, FF's share in an October 2006 opinion poll actually rose by 8 points to 39 per cent – its highest level since the 2002 general election (*The Irish Times*/TNS mrbi poll).

Populist agency in Ireland

The only historical case of a party in Ireland which comes close to matching the definition of 'populist' used by us in the introduction has been the relatively small *Clann na Talmhan* which reached a high of 11 per cent at the 1943 general election and participated in the inter-party governments of 1948 and 1951, before eventually disappearing in the 1960s (Mair, 1987: 24–26). Appealing to the small farming communities of the west and northwest which had become disillusioned with FF, the party's programme was, according to Garvin (2005: 188), 'anti-political and anti-urban, its leaders' speeches being peppered with condemnations of politicians, civil servants, Jews, Freemasons and "money-grabbers"'. One of the reasons why *Clann na Talmhan* has remained an exception of course is the populism already in mainstream Irish political culture, as outlined earlier. The following section will therefore examine what populism there has been, and currently is, in Irish politics through a brief discussion of the politicians' populism of FF and its leaders. For reasons of space, FG will not be examined, although there are many past and present examples of politicians' populism amongst its leaders too.

Politicians' populism

As discussed in the introductory chapter, one of the charges laid at the door of the term 'populism' is that it is often employed in vague and undefined ways. We can see this in the case of Ireland where FF is often referred to in passing as being 'populist' or having 'populist' characteristics, without any explanation of the term or why it is applicable. For example, Garvin (1974: 307) refers to FF as a 'nationalist-populist' party, Gary Murphy (2003: 1) terms it 'a classically populist party', while Laver notes its 'populist appeal' (Laver, 2005: 183). Irrespective of whether we agree with these descriptions, it is striking that, in all three cases, no attempt is made to qualify or expand on this use of 'populist'. This is a pity as both Garvin and Laver touch on important questions by linking populism with FF's nationalism and its appeal to the electorate. As discussed above and in the introduction, Irish political culture has always contained a strong dose of populism and 'politician's populism' (Canovan, 1981: 12–13) has always been a feature of FF in particular. Thus, while FF does not fully match the definition of populism employed in the introduction to this book, its approach to politics does resonate with the characteristics of 'politicians' populism'.

As many scholars have found (see Garvin, 1997), it is hard to locate FF within a comparative Western European party framework. Indeed, historically, in some ways it resembles more a party like the *Partido Revolucionario Institucional* (PRI) in Mexico which, Canovan (1981: 276) observes, 'is an all-embracing, non-ideological organization that integrates many different and potentially conflicting groups and sections of the people'. Like the PRI, despite having been in office and enjoyed the trappings of power for the vast majority of the last century, FF can also hark back to its revolutionary, 'Republican' identity when required. Moreover, like populists everywhere, leaders such as its founder Eamon De Valera and Jack Lynch explicitly defined FF as a 'national movement', representative of all people, rather than as a 'political party' (Mair, 1987: 178). If De Valera's vision of FF contained much populism, so too did his vision of Ireland, which recalls Paul Taggart's concept of the populist 'heartland'. As Taggart (2000: 3) says, 'populism tends to identify itself with an idealized version of its chosen people, and to locate them in a similarly idealized landscape' and we can clearly see this type of populist heartland in De Valera's much-cited 1943 St. Patrick's Day radio broadcast:

> The Ireland we have dreamed of would be the home of a people who valued material wealth only as a basis of right living, of a people who were satisfied with frugal comfort and devoted their leisure to the things of the spirit; a land whose countryside would be bright with cosy homesteads, whose fields and villages would be joyous with the sound of industry, with the romping of sturdy children, the contest of athletic youths, the laughter of comely maidens; whose firesides would be the forums for the wisdom of old age. It would, in a word, be the home of a people living the life that God desires men should live. (Cited in Coogan, 1995: 72)

Sixty years later, FF and its leading figures still borrow regularly from the populist toolbox. For example, after the result of the first Nice Treaty referendum in 2001, Minister of State and grandson of De Valera, Éamon Ó Cuiv announced that, despite having campaigned for a 'yes' vote, he had in fact voted 'no' and condemned the attitude of 'the Establishment' to the result. The Finance Minister (and now Ireland's European Commissioner), Charlie McCreevy, welcomed the result and commented proudly to journalists: 'here we had all the political parties, all of the media, both broadcast and print, all of the organisations ... yet the plain people of Ireland in their wisdom have decided to vote no. I think that's a very healthy sign' (Staunton and Brennock, 2001). However, eclipsing his ministers in the use of populist rhetoric and communication strategies is the current FF leader and *Taoiseach*, Bertie Ahern, who, despite leading the most neo-liberal government in Irish history, has claimed to be 'one of the few socialists left in Irish politics' (Brennock, 2004). There is not the space here for a long discussion of Ahern's populism, but the extract below from a 2004 interview should suffice for our purposes. In it, we can see the same type of populist self-image as put forward by the likes of Umberto Bossi who, in similar fashion to Ahern, dresses and speaks like 'the common man', boasts that he has no interest in the trappings of office such as wealth or trips abroad and claims to have made a personal sacrifice by entering public life out of a desire to serve his people. Noting how he was offered work in the past which would have made him far wealthier than politics has, Ahern said:

> I opted not to do that. If I can go on my annual holidays to Kerry, get a few days sometimes, if I can get now and again to Old Trafford, if I can have enough money for a few pints and if I can look after Miriam and the kids, I don't care a damn, I couldn't care. And tomorrow if I hadn't got very much it wouldn't matter. I'm well paid so I can't moan. But if I hadn't got that I wouldn't moan too much either. I have no desire to have a big house, no desire to have land. I'd consider it a nuisance, actually. (Brennock, 2004)

While Ahern and his colleagues may borrow extensively from populism, however, FF is clearly more a 'catch-all', self-proclaimed 'natural party of government' than an anti-Establishment exclusionary populist one and, as such, it does not meet the criteria in the definition set out in the introduction to this book. It is, therefore, to the prospect of such a party emerging in twenty-first century Ireland that we now turn.

Prospects for populism

In an opinion piece in September 2005 entitled 'A silent, unhappy majority arrives at the tipping point', Marc Coleman of *The Irish Times* discussed the increasing disillusionment with mainstream parties in Ireland before finishing with the question: 'If none of the parties is able to recapture middle Ireland, could a new party emerge to represent it?' (Coleman, 2005). Based on our discussion in the previous section on the opportunity structures for populism, we can say that, to different degrees, secularization, the economy, immigration, European integration and corruption all offer potential for populist mobilization and many of the conditions which have facilitated the rise of populist parties elsewhere also exist in Ireland. While these conditions may exist, however, another matter is whether the space in the party system does. From that perspective, the existence, resources, voter profile and recent success of SF would appear to make it very difficult for a populist party targeting the urban working-class constituency, especially as SF itself already exploits the opportunities provided by the inequalities of the Celtic Tiger, the European integration process, the exposure of corruption and the declining influence of the Church.

Indeed, at this point we should perhaps tackle the question of whether we might consider *Sinn Féin* as a populist party itself. Certainly, it has many populist traits. For example, in its Members Training Programme, as Agnès Maillot notes, it differentiates between 'ideology' and 'principles'. While the latter constitute immutable 'fundamental truths' such as the sovereignty of a thirty-two county united Irish Republic, the former can be 'a flexible and constantly evolving concept', thus recalling the populist tendency to pick and choose from different ideologies according to the needs of the moment (Maillot, 2005: 4). Furthermore, consistent with its targeting of working-class and alienated voters, it has constructed an image of itself as an 'ethical' party which is close to 'the people' and particularly 'local communities', in contrast to the corrupt and detached elites of the traditional parties. As its leader, Gerry Adams, was keen to emphasize in the 2002 election campaign, unlike other parties, SF is not bothered with 'the trappings of office or politics of self-interest' (SF Press Release 23/3/02, cited in Maillot, 2005: 105). *Sinn Féin* thus presents a discourse which conceives of the common and virtuous people as being exploited by the untrustworthy political and economic elites of the Celtic Tiger. In contrast to this, it evokes an image of an undivided, peaceful and sovereign Irish heartland, free from the dangerous external influences of Britain, the EU and globalization.

Nonetheless, for the moment SF falls short of full populist membership for a series of reasons. First of all, although Adams clearly commands great respect within the party (which he has led for over twenty years), and is a media-savvy and personable leader, he does not correspond to the charismatic-leader type embodied by Jean-Marie Le Pen, Pim Fortuyn or Silvio Berlusconi. Unlike these figures, Adams does not dominate coverage of the party and other SF senior figures are allowed to gain media visibility and establish significant public profiles. Nor does Adams break the linguistic codes of normal political discourse or make recourse to 'common man' rhetoric as the likes of Bossi and Jorg Haider have done. Rather, like Gianfranco Fini of *Alleanza Nazionale* in Italy who also leads a party with a dubious extra-parliamentary past, he seems keen to present an articulate, 'statesman-like' and cultured demeanour, perhaps in order to show voters that, despite his long association with paramilitary activities, he now 'belongs' in representative politics.

Second, SF rejects the anti-pluralism and intolerance found in many other populist discourses in Western Europe. Similarly, it does not promote a vision of a 'homogeneous' people or subscribe to the idea that the rights and values of the majority should be enforced at the expense of others. For example, the party has been particularly strong in its defence of the rights of immigrants, Travellers, homosexuals and other minority groups. By way of example, it is worth looking here at the 2001 SF policy review 'Many Voices One Country'. Although we find populist tones in its condemnation of the 'cynical' political class, the document stands out for its promotion of tolerance and the principle that heterogeneity within Irish society is a good thing. We are told that 'the challenge is to embrace our growing diversity as a source of strength and opportunity. To do this we must begin by opposing racism, discrimination and intolerance of any kind wherever it occurs' (SF, 2001: 1). Indeed 'as Socialist Republicans [the party] must be to the fore in combating racism' (Ibid.: 9), unlike those 'unscrupulous people in politics and other spheres of society [who] have nurtured it for their own cynical interests' (Ibid.: 1). Unsurprisingly, given SF's nationalist identity, racism is explicitly linked to the legacy of imperialism 'as practised by a handful of countries' (first and foremost, Britain) and it is argued that the Irish experience of colonialism and human rights abuses should lead to greater empathy with those now in similar situations (Ibid.: 6). That this has not necessarily happened in part arises 'from large numbers of asylum seekers being "dumped" in particular areas, often the poorest and least-resourced working-class areas of Dublin' (Ibid.: 7). What is needed therefore is spending on education and integration programmes although, again in contrast to populists on the continent (and many within mainstream Irish parties), the form of integration advocated by SF is one in which immigrants do not have to 'trade off their native culture and traditions in return for equal participation in Irish society' (Ibid.: 6).

In an interview with Agnès Maillot (2005: 127), Mitchell McLaughlin (a leading figure within SF) acknowledged that there is a disparity between the policies promoted by the party leadership and the views of some members on issues like immigration. It could thus happen of course that when the current party leadership is gone, its successors will be less inclined to insist on the same principles of tolerance and could seek to exploit immigration, particularly if the economy is in decline. Nonetheless, it is still difficult to see how SF could embrace the populist intolerance of minority rights and/or re-cast immigrants as 'dangerous others', particularly as a move in that direction in the Republic would surely weaken its position as the defender of Catholic minority rights in the North, not to mention its attempts to establish its international democratic credentials as a respectable and responsible party of government after decades of involvement in violence.

Another possibility is that one of the parties on the Right could take a populist turn as happened with the FPÖ in Austria and the Swiss People's Party when they came under new leadership. The most likely candidates for such a change would appear to be the strongly neo-liberal PDs. Certainly, some of their leading figures have not been averse to populist tactics and rhetoric, particularly on topics such as immigration or law-and-order, and the party has positioned itself very clearly on the side of the hard-working, 'silent majority' of taxpayers and business people who just want to be left alone by the state to get on with things. Echoing the type of 'hyperglobalist Euroscepticism' patented by the Conservatives in the UK, its former leader, Mary Harney has spoken out against the creation of a 'centralized' or 'federal Europe' and asserted that American investors in Ireland 'find a country that believes in essential regulation but not over-regulation. On looking further afield in Europe they find also that not every European country believes in all of these things' (Harney, 2000). However, the PDs have perhaps been too long in coalition with FF to be able to rebrand themselves as being against the political elite, and the urban middle-classes which represent its core vote might be uneasy with a more overtly populist party. Similarly, while FG under its new leader Enda Kenny has adopted more populist communication strategies, full of 'tough' rhetoric on crime, negative campaigning and comments on the risks posed by immigration to 'Celtic and Christian' Ireland (Molony, 2007), the party is far too closely identified with the Establishment to be able to adopt a fully populist discourse.

In fact, the greatest market for a populist party might not be in the cities of Ireland, but in rural areas, particularly those of the West where *Clann na Talmhan* was successful in the 1940s. In these parts of the country, Labour, SF and the Greens have made little headway (apart from those areas bordering with Northern Ireland in the case of SF) and disgruntled voters have instead turned to local, often single-issue, Independent candidates. One of the many reasons for this is that Mass attendance is significantly higher in rural Ireland than in urban areas and the policies of SF, Labour and the Greens – more so than those of FF and FG – conflict with the teachings of the Church. It is important to remember, amidst all the talk of 'the new Ireland', that while the passing of divorce in 1995 was a milestone for secularization, 49 per cent of the electorate, and more outside Dublin, voted against it. Nor should we overlook the growing marginalization of the farming community within the Irish economy and society in general at a time when this sector faces competition from the new countries of the EU and the loss of the lucrative subsidies of the Common Agricultural Policy. Given all this, there may well be space for a new conservative populist party offering a nostalgic vision of 'old clean-living Catholic Ireland', juxtaposed with the materialistic and immoral new multicultural one foisted upon the country by a self-interested, Dublin-based liberal economic and political elite, its media and the European Union. Thus, while the victory in the 1999 European Parliament election of the Catholic conservative candidate Dana Rosemary Scallon in the Connacht-Ulster constituency may have seemed like a blip, all kinds of everything could yet happen across the western half of the country if a new, well-organized populist party with a charismatic leader were to mobilize on a similar platform.

Conclusion

In his chapter in this volume, Gianfranco Pasquino concludes that, ultimately, the most important condition for the rise of populism is 'the presence of a leader willing and able to exploit existing social conditions of *anxiety* and *availability*'. While Pasquino's comment may seem, at first sight, somewhat tautological, the situation is in fact that simple. If the structural conditions do not exist, populist agency cannot be successful. However, those conditions can also exist in the absence of a populist party. Thus, while no populist party akin to those on the continent has emerged in twenty-first century Ireland, this does not mean that it will not do so in the future and, if it does, it will find many of the same opportunities around which populist parties elsewhere in Western Europe have successfully mobilized over the last two decades. Of course, the climate for populism in Ireland could be better. For example, greater politicization of immigration and European integration over the coming years would clearly favour a populist breakthrough. Indeed, given the numbers of immigrants who have arrived in Ireland over the last decade and the fact that the country will have to get used to an EU in which it has obligations and duties rather than privileges and handouts, this is quite likely. Public anxiety about a downturn in the economy and an increase in salience of the secular/clerical cleavage would also facilitate the rise of populism and, again, both of those are liable to happen at some point over the next decade. Most importantly, perhaps, a decline in the fortunes of *Sinn Féin* would open up a significant space in the electoral market for a new populist party, whether of the Left or the Right.

Along with the existence of a capable, charismatic leader, however, a *sine qua non* for populist success is what has been termed as an 'antipolitical climate' or a widespread sense of 'political malaise' (Mastropaolo, 2000; 2005), that is the loss of trust in, and development of cynicism about, political institutions and actors. From this perspective it is interesting to consider, as John Coakley notes, that while a 1990 survey showed the Irish were more likely than others in Europe to have confidence in their institutions, 'by 1997 this position had changed...trust in parliament was low, comparable with the position elsewhere in Europe, and trust in political parties was lower still: 72 per cent distrusted them' (Coakley, 1999: 56–57). Likewise, it is worth noting that, in his study of newspaper coverage of the 2002 general election campaign, Heinz Brandenburg (2005: 297) finds that the most significant aspect was 'the predominantly negative attitude of all Irish print media towards political actors...in Ireland we seem to be faced with a rather homogeneous anti-politics bias'. Finally, as a May 2006 opinion poll published in *The Irish Times* reported, 42 per cent of Irish voters believed that the next general election would make no difference to how the country is run and 36 per cent felt it would make only a minor difference. 57 per cent said it would make no difference to their lives personally (Brennock, 2006). If, as Canovan (1999) argues, therefore, populists exploit the decline of the 'redemptive' and the rise of the 'pragmatic' face of democracy, then the prospects for a populist party in Ireland seem rather good indeed. Whenever the dog decides to bark, of course.

Notes

1. I would like to thank Michael Gallagher, Peter Mair, Alfio Mastropaolo and Eoin O'Malley for their comments on an earlier version of this chapter. Thanks also to David Connolly for proofreading the final draft and to Daragh O'Connell both

for his help in gathering materials and for, along with Ian Curtin, playing devil's advocate on a number of points.

2. Both FF and FG can trace their roots to the pre-independence *Sinn Féin* (SF) party. Following the end of the War of Independence in 1921, the party split into two factions: those who accepted the Treaty with the British and partition, and those who did not. A civil war between the two sides in 1922–23 was won by the pro-Treaty forces, which governed as *Cumann na nGaedhael* from 1923 until 1932, before merging with the Centre Party and the quasi-fascistic National Guard (better known as 'the Blueshirts') of Eoin O'Duffy to form FG in 1933. FF resulted from a split in SF in 1926 when De Valera and his supporters decided to recognize the Irish Free State and enter the *Dáil* (Irish Parliament). For detailed accounts of the development of the Irish party system and nationalist politics in Ireland, see Mair (1987) and Garvin (2005).

3. As Mair (1997b: 66) points out: 'Both party systems were born in civil wars; both more or less sustained that original opposition for some decades afterwards despite otherwise limited ideological differences; and both might be seen to have fostered personalistic representational linkages while devaluing programmatic appeals'.

14
Conclusion: Populism and Twenty-First Century Western European Democracy
Daniele Albertazzi and Duncan McDonnell

Whose democracy is it anyway?

Gerry Stoker concludes his recent book *Why Politics Matters* by affirming: 'Achieving mass democracy was the great triumph of the twentieth century. Learning to live with it will be the great achievement of the twenty-first' (Stoker, 2006: 206). Like Stoker, a whole series of scholars at the beginning of the new millennium have argued that the pillars of representative liberal democracy – in particular, parties and popular participation – are creaking (Pharr and Putnam, 2000; Diamond and Gunther, 2001; Dalton and Wattenberg, 2002; Crouch, 2004). In fact, apart from the euphoric period surrounding the fall of the Berlin Wall and the seemingly inexorable move towards a united, peaceful, harmonious and liberal democratic Europe, there has long been a tendency to focus on the negative aspects of how Western European democracies function. Indeed, as we can see from even a brief glance at *The Crisis of Democracy* (Crozier, Huntington and Watanuki, 1975), in the past the portents have been worse and the prophecies far gloomier. For example, in the opening paragraphs of that landmark volume, under the heading 'The Current Pessimism about Democracy', we find the comment by the former West German Chancellor Willy Brandt before leaving office that 'Western Europe has only 20 or 30 more years of democracy left in it' (ibid.: 2).

With the end of the Cold War, the broad acceptance by all parties of the basic merits of democracy and the decline of political terrorism in Western Europe, such apocalyptic scenarios are no longer being put forward. Nonetheless, as Robert Putnam, Susan Pharr and Russell Dalton (2000: 6) write in their introduction to *Disaffected Democracies*, while support for democracy *per se* appears to be greater then ever, faith in its agents (i.e. politicians and parties) and its institutions has declined. As they point out, the percentage of the public 'expressing a partisan attachment has declined in 17 out of 19' established democracies examined (ibid.: 17) and in 11 out of 14, 'confidence in parliament has declined' (ibid.: 19). Moreover, as Frank Furedi (2004: 47) says, with the decline of ideologies and polarization in much of the political sphere 'passion appears to be conspicuously absent'. In this picture of passionless politics, we can see the contours of the type of 'post-democracy' described by Colin Crouch where 'boredom, frustration and disillusion have settled in after a democratic moment; when powerful minority interests have become far more active than the mass of ordinary people in making the political system work for them; where political elites have learned to manage and manipulate popular demands; where people have to be persuaded to vote by top-down publicity campaigns' (Crouch, 2004: 19–20).

Eric Hobsbawm wrote in the last decade of the twentieth century about 'the dilemma of the role of the common people' as 'the century of the common man' came to an end. It was, he said, 'the dilemma of an age when government could – some would say: must – be "of the people" and "for the people", but could not in any operational sense be "by the people", or even by representative assemblies elected among those who competed for its vote' (Hobsbawm, 1995: 579). As Gianfranco Pasquino's chapter in this volume discusses, democracy is inevitably characterized by 'the constitutive tension between its ideology (the power of the people) and its functioning (the power of the elites chosen by the people)' (Mény and Surel, 2002: 8). And it is in this gap between what democracy is and the promises that it inevitably has to make to achieve legitimization that populism flourishes (Canovan, 1999). Of course, as John Lukacs (2005: 5) contends, democracy is in reality 'neither the rule *of* the people or *by* the people'. Rather, it is rule *'in the name of* the people' (our emphasis). However, within the complex systems of governance in the twenty-first century globalized world, can 'the people' still be credibly sovereign, even in name? As Robert Dahl argued in 1999,

> although international organizations have become the locus of important decisions and will doubtless be even more so in the future, they are not now and probably will not be governed democratically. Instead they will continue to be governed mainly by bargaining among bureaucratic and political elites, operating within extremely wide limits set by treaties and international agreements. (Dahl, 1999: 16)

We have thus moved, it would appear, into a form of democracy where 'the people' of twenty-first century Western Europe may enjoy more enshrined rights than ever before, but in exchange for less real (or at least less perceptible) voice and sovereignty than in the past (Mair, 2006). Citizens are thus steered away from direct participation in politics (other than voting) and instead encouraged to adopt a 'consumerist' concept of politics whereby the only thing that is said to 'count' (as the rhetoric of the Labour party in contemporary Britain shows) is resolving the practical, immediate and usually local problems of the 'man in the street' such as schools, jobs and crime. Politics is characterized, even by many politicians themselves, as something which most ordinary people naturally prefer to be involved in as little as possible. It is held that they have better things to do, such as attending to their personal and professional lives, and that politics should facilitate them to do this with minimal interference.

All the above is of course fuel to the fire for the populist. And, as the evidence in this volume clearly demonstrates, the twenty-first century provides ample and ever-increasing opportunities for populist actors in Western Europe seeking to portray the homogeneous and virtuous people's rights, values, prosperity, identity, voice and sovereignty as being under threat from a series of elites and dangerous 'others'. National political elites can easily be depicted as having 'sold the people out' to an unelected (and uncontrollable) supranational oligarchy in Brussels and to the rapacious financial elites of multinational corporations. The same elites and immigrants can be blamed for the scaling down of the Welfare State, as a result of which the people are now 'less protected' and the state and political parties can thus be accused of having 'abandoned' the people. Moreover, the community, the safe place where the people once lived in harmony, can be characterized as under attack from all sides – from above by the elites and from below by a series of 'others'. Indeed, in this way, 'the community', like Taggart's 'heartland', becomes, as Zygmunt Bauman (2001: 3) says, 'another name for paradise lost' – a place that we long to return to because 'we miss security, a quality crucial to a happy life, but one which the world we inhabit is ever less able to offer and ever more reluctant to promise' (Bauman, 2001: 145). Populists, by contrast, are not reluctant to promise. They promise security. They promise prosperity. They promise identity. They promise to return the sceptre of democracy to its rightful owner. They promise to make the people, once more, masters in their own homes, in the widest sense of the term.

Western Europe: a fertile terrain for populism

We believe that the analyses offered in this book point to the importance, in particular, of four structural factors in explaining the rise and success of populism: the features of specific party systems (and the detachment between voters and parties which has developed in contemporary Western Europe within such systems); the changing logic and work practices of Western media; the politicization of the socio-cultural dimension (especially immigration); and, finally, economic changes (especially due to globalization).

Party systems

Reflecting on the 'short twentieth century' as it came to a close, Eric Hobsbawm wrote that:

> By the century's end large numbers of citizens were withdrawing from politics, leaving the affairs of state to the 'political class' ... who read each other speeches and editorials, a special-interest group of professional politicians, journalists, lobbyists and others whose occupations ranked at the bottom of the scale of trustworthiness in sociological enquires. (1995: 581)

As we have reiterated, what is referred to in German as *parteienverdrossenheit* – the crisis of party legitimacy – has affected the whole of Western Europe, including those countries where populism has not yet flourished. Mainstream parties have moved closer together and further away from the people, who participate in ever-decreasing numbers in elections across the continent. As Peter Mair (2006: 15) says, all the evidence points towards a withdrawal from the 'zones of engagement' between parties and the public, a mutual disengagement which occurs 'in each of the cases for which data is available'. Reflecting this, 'the election of 2001 in the UK was marked by the lowest level of turnout since the advent of mass democracy, for example, while historic lows were also recorded in Spain in 2000, in Italy and Norway in 2001, in France, Ireland and Portugal in 2002, and in Finland and Switzerland in 2003' (Ibid: 15). As Alfio Mastropaolo notes in this volume, this detachment from the political process has much to do with the transformation of parties from agencies of socialization into slimmed-down electoral machines and party leaders increasingly act as if they were accountable to their members only following an election, thus basically treating them as mere 'shareholders'. It is not surprising, therefore, that membership of political parties has dramatically decreased everywhere in Europe, in some cases by as much as half (Mair and Van Biezen, 2001). Nonetheless, as we see in the chapter on Switzerland (and as the BNP's success in mobilizing support at recent local elections in Britain indicates), when people feel able to affect the course of events, when they perceive the electoral choice to be a real one, more of them take part and turn out to vote. The success of populists is thus predicated on their ability to convince voters that, unlike all the other parties, they represent something different and that they can achieve change.

The media

The contribution of the media to the establishment of a 'populist *Zeitgeist*' in the twenty-first century appears to be threefold. First, as Mastropaolo argues in his chapter, the function of politically educating the citizenry (once played by mass parties) is now largely delegated to the national media, which in turn favours those telegenic politicians who speak in slogans and soundbites. The relevance of the media, and particularly television, as the main mode of communication between a party (through its leader) and the public, has increased across Western Europe in a context where the party press has either disappeared or has become, at best, residual. This strategy of relying almost entirely on national media is particularly evident in Britain where political parties only invest in direct communication with voters (through canvassing, sending brochures etc.) when there is a realistic chance of gaining a constituency or if it is under threat. If this is not the case, they simply do not bother. Hence, voters who live in a 'safe' seat may happily go through life without ever being contacted by a party, other than through the medium of national media. Second, the media now play a growing role in setting the political agenda. For a party to win back at least some of its control over this agenda and make sure that its priorities gain visibility, it needs to manage the media and create 'media events'. This clearly benefits populists, who tend to be the most adept of all when it comes to spectacular politics (as the cases of the *Lega Nord* in Italy and the *Lijst Pim Fortuyn* in the Netherlands clearly demonstrate). Third, the values and practices of what in Britain is called 'the popular press' have affected all western media, leading to the ever-increasing personalization of politics (see Gianpietro Mazzoleni in this volume). Moreover, the tendency of the media to present complex problems in black-and-white terms, sensational-ize events, focus on scandals, reduce political competition to personality contests and dramatize questions such as immigration mirrors, comple-ments and, in turn, presents a welcoming environment for the communica-tion style of populist leaders across the whole continent. Thus, as Mauro Calise (2004: 28–29) says, 'having been thrown out the front door by the great historical tragedies of the first half of the century, the charismatic leader has come back in through the window of the television screen in the second half'.

The politicization of the socio-cultural dimension: immigration

In the twenty-first century, immigration into Western Europe will continue and this will inevitably offer greater opportunities for populist mobiliza-tion. In particular, in the current climate of 'clash of civilizations' rhetoric, populists in different countries will continue to exploit both the Christian v. Muslim cleavage (e.g. the *Front National*) and the secular/liberal v. Muslim one (e.g. the *Lijst Pim Fortuyn*). Indeed, rather than witnessing the collapse of old boundaries within Europe, Bauman detects a 'zeal for boundary draw-ing and for the erection of closely guarded boundary checkpoints' (2001: 76) and warns that the logic of the 'recognition wars', exacerbated by the post-September 11 insistence on 'identity issues', prompts adversaries to exaggerate and highlight their differences. Or, as Francis Fukuyama (2006: 5) puts it, 'angry, unassimilated cultural minorities produce backlash on the part of the majority community, which then retreats into its own cultural and religious identity'. The fact that, in countries such as France, Switzerland and Britain, the logic and language of populists on immigration has now been adopted by mainstream parties on both sides of the political divide indicates that more, and not less, politicization of this issue is likely to occur. In this respect Sweden, where, as Jens Rydgren shows in this book, issues of identity have not yet been politicized to a great extent (despite the 'natives' being increasingly suspicious of foreigners), may have become the exception that confirms a Europe-wide rule.

Economic change and the shrinking of the welfare state

If the twentieth century was the century of the Welfare State, by the turn of the millennium, notes Jürgen Habermas, 'benefits have been reduced, while at the same time access to social security has been tightened and the pressure on the unemployed has increased' (2001: 50). He warns that: 'In the long run, a loss of solidarity such as this will inevitably destroy a liberal political culture whose universalistic self-understanding democratic societies depend on' (ibid.). Processes of globalization, especially when presented as unstoppable, inevitable and impossible to manage, provide excellent opportunities for the rhetoric of those (from the SVP/UDC to UKIP) who would rather retrench into the reassuring confines of the 'heartland' and the 'community'. The more the powers of the state and its traditional functions (i.e. defence, setting taxation levels, etc.) are taken over (or made redundant) by multinational corporations and international organizations, the stronger becomes populist rhetoric, offering protection and security *vis-à-vis* new enemies and new competitors and promising the 'rediscovery' of allegedly forgotten traditional cultures.

The future

Paul Taggart (2004: 282) observes that 'the idea of living at a turning point in history is an important one for populist ideas' and, as we have seen in this volume, populists in Western Europe play on the sense that we are at a historical juncture in which, if the people do not act, they will 'lose everything'. Twenty-first century Western Europe democracy offers them a fertile terrain for this message. In fact, although the first classic comparative study on populism (Ionescu and Gellner, 1969) ignored Western Europe, we can see that the symptoms for what is happening now were already present then. Robert Dahl (1965: 21–22) wrote four years before the publication of Ionescu and Gellner's volume that 'among the possible sources of alienation in Western democracies that may generate new forms of structural opposition is the new democratic Leviathan itself' and noted that even 'in high-consensus European systems', many young people, intellectuals and academics found it 'too remote and bureaucratized, too addicted to bargaining and compromise, too much an instrument of political elites and technicians with whom they feel slight identification'. If that then translated into support for the Left movements of the late 1960s, in the ensuing decades, popular discontent with the democratic Leviathan has been channelled into support for populist movements of both the Right and Left. As we have seen in this volume, this phenomenon has reached new heights in the latter years of the twentieth century and the first decade of the twenty-first.

In terms of the prospects for research, the events of the last fifteen years offer us a number of new and interesting opportunities in the study of populism. For example, for the first time, at different levels of government and in different Western European states, we have gained important empirical information about how populists behave both when in power and when in coalition with conventional parties. As noted in the introduction, the experiences of the FPÖ in Austria, the LPF in Holland and the *Lega Nord* in Italy have provided some answers to the question of how populists fare when in government. Similarly, in the case of the FPÖ, and soon in that of the *Front National*, we can test the conditions under which charismatic populist leadership can be successfully passed on or seized. There are also numerous contexts where we are now seeing what the long-term effects of the *cordon sanitaire* on populist parties might be. Moreover, we are witnessing a wide range of mainstream political leaders borrowing from the populist repertoire and the impact this is having both on parties and public perceptions of politics. It remains to be seen what the effects of 'the populist *Zeitgeist*' will be on Western European democracy, however the evidence of this book is that in the twenty-first century, there exist better conditions for the emergence and success of populism than ever before.

Bibliography

Akkerman, T. Anti-immigration Parties and the Defense of Liberal Values: the Exceptional Case of the List Pim Fortuyn, *Journal of Political Ideologies*, 10(3), 2005, 337–354.

Albertazzi, D. The Lega dei Ticinesi: The Embodiment of Populism, *Politics* 26(2), 2006, 133–139.

Albertazzi, D. and McDonnell, D. The Lega Nord in the Second Berlusconi Government: In a League of Its Own, *West European Politics*, 28(5), 2005, 952–972.

Andeweg, R. B. (1999) Parties, Pillars and the Politics of Accommodation: Weak or Weakening Linkages? The Case of Dutch Consociationalism, in Kurt, R. L. and Deschouwer, K. (eds), *Party Elites in Divided Societies: Political Parties in Consociational Democracy*, London and New York: Routledge.

Andeweg, R. B. Beyond Representativeness? Trends in Political Representation, *European Review*, 11(2), 2003, 147–161.

Andeweg, R. B. and Irwin, G. A. (2005) *Governance and Politics of the Netherlands*, Basingstoke: Palgrave.

Arditi, B. Populism as a Spectre of Democracy: A Response to Canovan, *Political Studies*, 52(1), 2004, 135–143.

Arnauts, L. Belgique. Souper avec le diable? *Courrier International*, 10 December, 2003.

Arzheimer, K. and Carter, E. Political Opportunity Structures and Right-Wing Extremist Party Success, *European Journal of Political Research*, 45(3), 2006, 419–443.

Austen, J., Butler, D. and Ranney, A. Referendums, 1978–1986, *Electoral Studies*, 6(2), 1987, 139–147.

Bailer-Galanda, B. and Neugebauer, W. (1997) *Haider und die Freiheitlichen in Österreich*, Berlin: Elefanten Press.

Bakker, P. and Scholten, O. (2003) *Communicatiekaart van Nederland. Overzicht van Media en Communicatie*, Alphen aan den Rijn: Kluwer.

Balme, R. (2002) The pluralist and divisible Republic: French public opinion and representative democracy in the turmoil, paper presented at the conference *Transforming the Democratic Balance among State, Market and Society: Comparative Perspectives on France and the Developed Countries*, Minda de Gunzburg Center for European Studies, Harvard University, 17–18 May 2002.

Bank, D. E. (1973) *Politics in Venezuela*, Boston: Little, Brown and Company.

Banning, C. Niet uit eerbetoon stemmen op LPF, *NRC Handelsblad* (48) 11 May 2002.

Bara, J. and Budge, I. (2001) Party Policy and Ideology: Still New Labour? in Norris, P. (ed.), *Britain Votes 2001*, Oxford: Oxford University Press.

Bardi, L. Anti-party Sentiment and Party System Change in Italy, *European Journal of Political Research*, 29(3), 1996, 345–363.

Barnett, A. Corporate Populism and Partyless Democracy, *New Left Review*, 3, 2000, 80–90.

Bauman, Z. (2001) *Community – Seeking Safety in an Insecure World*, Cambridge: Polity.

BBC Website, *BNP:Under the Skin*, http://news.bbc.co.uk/hi/english/static/in_depth/programmes/2001/bnp_special (seen 30 January 2007).

Bélanger, E. and Aarts, K. Explaining the Rise of the LPF: Issues, Discontent, and the 2002 Dutch Election, *Acta Politica*, 41(1), 2006, 4–20.

Bell, D. C. and Criddle, B. (1994) *The French Communist Party in the Fifth Republic*, Oxford: Clarendon.

Bennett, W. L. (1988) *News: The Politics of Illusion*, New York: Longman.

Bennett, W. L. and Manheim, J. B. (2001) The Big Spin: Strategic Communication and the Transformation of Pluralist Democracy, in Bennett, W. L. and. Entman, R. M. (eds) *Mediated Politics: Communication in the Future of Democracy*, Cambridge: Cambridge University Press.

Berlusconi, S. (2000) *L'Italia che ho in mente*, Milano: Mondadori.

Berlusconi, S. (2001) *Discorsi per la democrazia*, Milano: Mondadori.

Betz, H. G. The New Politics of Resentment: Radical Right-Wing Populism in Western Europe, *Comparative Politics*, 25(4), 1993, 413–27.

Betz, H. G. (1994) *Radical Right Wing Populism in Western Europe*, Basingstoke: Palgrave.

Betz, H. G. Exclusionary Populism in Austria, Italy and Switzerland, *International Journal*, 56(3), 2001, 393–419.

Betz, H. G. Rechtspopulismus in Westeuropa: Aktuelle Entwicklungen und politische Bedeutung, *Österreichische Zeitschrift für Politikwissenschaft*, 3, 2002, 251–264.

Betz, H. G. and Johnson, C. Against the Current – Stemming the Tide: the Nostalgic Ideology of the Contemporary Radical Populist Right, *Journal of Political Ideologies* 9(3), 2004, 311–27.

Betz, H. G. (2005) Mobilising Resentment in the Alps. The Swiss SVP, the Italian Lega Nord and the Austrian FPÖ, in Caramani, D. and Mény, Y. (eds) *Challenges to Consensual Politics – Democracy, Identity and Populist Protest in the Alpine Region*, Brussels: P.I.E.-Peter Lang.

BfWuS – Beirat fuer Wirtschafts und Sozial Fragen (1992) *Ostöffnung*, Vienna: Ueberreuther.

Biorcio, R. (1997) *La Padania promessa*, Milano: Il Saggiatore.

Biorcio, R. (2003a) Italian populism: from protest to governing party, paper presented at the Conference of the *European Consortium for Political Research*, Marburg 18–21 September.

Biorcio, R. (2003b) The Lega Nord and the Italian Media System, in Mazzoleni, G., Stewart, J. and Horsfield, B. (eds) *The Media and Neo-Populism: A Contemporary Comparative Analysis*, Westport, CT: Praeger.

Bischof, G. and Pelinka, A. (1997) *Austrian Historical Memory and National Identity*, New Brunswick: Transaction Publisher.

Blocher, C. (2006) Per un Svizzera Libera, Sicura e Indipendente, Dipartimento Federale di Giustizia e Polizia, http://www.ejpd.admin.ch/ejpd/it/home/dokumentation/ red/2006/2006-07-31.html (seen 28 July 2006).

Bluhm, W. T. (1973) *Building an Austrian Nation: The Political Integration of the Western State*, New Haven: Yale University Press.

Blumler, J. G. and Gurevitch, M. (1987) Journalists' Orientations towards Social Institutions: The Case of Parliamentary Broadcasting, in Golding, P., Murdock, G. and Schlesinger, P. (eds) *Communicating Politics*, Leicester: University of Leicester Press.

Blumler, J. G. and Kavanagh, D. The Third Age of Political Communication: Influences and Features, *Political Communication*, 16(3), 1999, 209–230.

BNP (2001) *People Just like You Striving for a Better Britain*. General Election Manifesto 2001.

BNP (2005) *Rebuilding British Democracy.* General Election Manifesto 2005.

Bodei, R. La sottile arte di trascinare le folle, *La Repubblica*, 12 November, 2003.

Boréus, K. (1994) *Högervåg: nyliberalismen och kampen om språket i svensk debatt 1969–1989*, Stockholm: Tiden.

Boréus, K. The Shift to the Right: Neo-Liberalism in Argumentation and Language in the Swedish Public Debate since 1969, *European Journal of Political Research*, 31(3), 1997, 257–286.

Brants, K. (2002) Naar een mediacratie? in van Holsteyn, J. and Mudde, C. (eds) *Democratie in verval?* Amsterdam: Boom.

Brandenburg, H. Political Bias in the Irish Media: A Quantatitive Study of Campaign Coverage during the 2002 General Election, *Irish Political Studies*, 20(3), 2005, 297–322.

Bréchon, P. and Mitra, S. K. The National Front in France. The Emergence of an Extreme Right Protest Movement, *Comparative Politics*, 25(1), 1992, 63–82.

Breen, M.J. (2006) Enough Already: Empirical Data on Irish Public Attitudes to Immigrants, Minorities, Refugees and Asylum Seekers, *Media and Migration, The Dialogue Series 6*, Antwerp: University of Antwerp.

Brennock, M. All things to all people, *The Irish Times*, 13 November 2004.

Brennock, M. Alternative government the preference by margin of 4%, *The Irish Times*, 20 May 2006.

Brennock, M. Prospect of alternative government has suddenly become credible, *The Irish Times*, 19 May 2006.

Bromley, C. and Curtice, J. (2002) Where have all the voters gone? in Bromley, C. *et al.* (eds) *British Social Attitudes – The 19th Report*, National Centre for Social Research, London: Sage.

Brubaker, R. (1992) *Citizenship and Nationhood in France and Germany*, Cambridge, Mass.: Harvard University Press.

Budge, I. and Farlie, D. (1983) Party Competition – Selective Emphasis or Direct Confrontation? An Alternative View with Data, in Daalder, H. and Mair, P. (eds) *West European Party Systems: Continuity and Change*, London: Sage.

Burger R. Romantisches Österreich, *Leviatan*, 28(1), 2000, 3–13.

Caciagli, M. and Corbetta, P. (2002) *Le Ragioni dell'Elettore. Perché Ha Vinto il Centro-Destra nelle Elezioni Italiane del 2001*, Bologna: Il Mulino.

Calise, M. (2000) *Il Partito Personale*, Rome: Laterza.

Campbell, A., Converse, P. H., Miller, W. E. and Stokes, D. E. (1960) *The American Voter*, New York: John Wiley and Sons.

Canovan, M. (1981) *Populism*, New York and London: Harcourt Brace Jovanovich.

Canovan, M. Trust the People! Populism and the Two Faces of Democracy, *Political Studies*, 47(1), 1999, 2–16.

Canovan, M. (2002) Taking Politics to the People: Populism as the Ideology of Democracy, in Mény, Y. and Surel, Y. (eds) *Democracies and the Populist Challenge*, Basingstoke: Palgrave.

Canovan, M. (2005) *The People*, Cambridge: Polity Press.

Carter, E. Proportional Representation and the Fortunes of Right-Wing Extremist Parties, *West European Politics*, 25(3), 2002, 125–46.

Carter, E. (2005) *The Extreme Right in Western Europe: Success or Failure?*, Manchester: Manchester University Press.

CBS (2002) *De Nederlandse economie 2001*, Voorburg/Heerlen: Centraal Bureau voor de Statistiek.

CBS (2003) *De Nederlandse economie 2002*, Voorburg/Heerlen: Centraal Bureau voor de Statistiek.

CBS (2006) Islamieten en hindoes in Nederland, 1 januari, http://statline.cbs.nl/ StatWeb/table.asp? (seen 16 January 2006).

Cento Bull, A. The Politics of Industrial Districts in Lombardy: Replacing Christian Democracy with the Northern League, *The Italianist*, 13, 1993, 209–229.

Cento Bull, A. (1996) Ethnicity, Racism and the Northern League, in Lévy, C. (ed.) *Italian Regionalism: History, Identity and Politics*, Oxford-Washington: Berg.

Cento Bull, A. and Gilbert, M. (2001) *The Lega Nord and the Northern Question in Italian Politics*, London: Palgrave.

Chebel d'Appollonia, A. (1996) *L'Extrême-droit en France. De Maurras à Le Pen*, Brussels: Éditions Complexe.

Cherribi, O. Olanda (s)velata: intolleranza, populismo e media, *Comunicazione Politica*, 4(2), 2003, 141–165.

Chorus, J. Wij zijn keurige, nette meiden, *NCR Handelsblad*, 2, 23 April 2002.

Chorus, J. and de Galan, M. (2002) *In de ban van Fortuyn. Reconstructie van een politieke aardschok*, Amsterdam: Mets and Schilt.

Church, C. H. (2003) The Contexts of Swiss Opposition to Europe, SEI Working Paper No. 64, the Sussex European Institute.

Church, C. H. (2004a) Swiss Euroscepticism: Local Variations on Wider Themes, in Harmsen, R. and Spiering, M. *Euroscepticism, Party Politics, National Identity and European Integration*, Amsterdam and New York: Rodopi (*European studies*, 20), 269–290.

Church, C. H. (2004b) *The Politics and Government of Switzerland*, Basingstoke: Palgrave.

Coakley, J. (1999) Society and Political Culture, in Coakley, J. and Gallagher, M. (eds), *Politics in the Republic of Ireland*, London: Routledge.

Codding, G. A. (1961) *The Federal Government of Switzerland*, London: George Allen and Unwin.

Coleman, M. A. Silent, unhappy majority arrives at the tipping point, *The Irish Times*, 16 September 2005.

Collier, D. and Levitsky, S. Research Note: Democracy with Adjectives: Conceptual Innovation in Comparative Research, *World Politics*, 49(3), 1997, 430–451.

Collings D. and Seldon A. Conservatives in Opposition, *Parliamentary Affairs*, 54(4), 2001, 624–637.

Collins, S. (2003) Campaign Strategies, in Gallagher, M., Marsh, M. and Mitchell, P. (eds), *How Ireland Voted 2002*, Basingstoke: Palgrave Macmillan.

Collovald, A. (2004) *Le 'populisme du Fn': un dangereux contresens*, Bellecombe-en-Bauges: Éditions du Croquant.

Coogan, T. P. (1995) *De Valera: Long Fellow. Long Shadow*, London: Arrow Books.

Crick, B. Populism, Politics and Democracy, *Democratization*, 12(5), 2005, 625–632.

Crosti, M. 2004 Per una definizione del populismo come antipolitica, *Ricerche di Storia Politica*, 3, 2004, 425–443.

Crouch, C. (2004) *Post-Democracy*, Cambridge: Polity.

Crozier, M., Huntington, S. P. and Watanuki, J. (1975) *The Crisis of Democracy: Report on the Governability of Democracies to the Trilateral Commission*, New York: New York University Press.

Curtice, J. Turnout: Electors Stay Home – Again, *Parliamentary Affairs*, 58(4), 2005, 776–785.

Dahl, R. A. (1956) *A Preface to Democratic Theory*, Chicago: The University of Chicago Press.

Dahl, R. A. Reflections on Opposition in Western Democracies, *Government and Opposition*, 1(1), 1965, 7–24.

Dahl, R. A. (1999) The Past and the Future of Democracy, Occasional Paper No. 5/1999, Centre for the Study of Political Change, University of Siena.

Dalton, R. J. (1999) Political Support in Advanced Industrial Societies, in Norris, P. (ed.) *Critical Citizens: Global Support for Democratic Government*, Oxford: Oxford University Press.

Dalton, R. J., McAllister, I. and Wattenberg, M. P. The Consequences of Partisan Dealignment, in Dalton, R. J. and Wattenberg, M. P. (eds) *Parties without Partisans: Political Change in Advanced Industrial Democracies*, New York: Oxford University Press.

Davies, P. (1999) *The National Front in France: Ideology, Discourse and Power*, London: Routledge.

Decker, F. (2004) *Der Neue Rechtspopulismus*, Opladen: Leske und Budrich.

Decker, F. (2006) Die populistische Herausforderung. Theoretische und länderver-gleichende Perspektiven, in Decker, F. (ed.) *Populismus*, Wiesbaden, VS-Verlag.

Demker, M. (2003) Trendbrott i flyktingfrågan – och polariseringen har ökat, in Holmberg, S. and Weibull, L. (eds) *Fåfängans marknad: SOM-undersökningen 2002*, Gothenburg: SOM-Institutet.

Deutsch, K. W. Social Mobilisation and Political Development, *American Political Science Review*, 55(3), 1961, 493–514.

Diamanti, I. (1996) *Il male del Nord. Lega, localismo, secessione*, Rome: Donzelli.

Diamanti, I. (2004) Anti-politique, télévision et séparatisme: le populisme à l'italienne, in Taguieff, P. A. (ed.) *Le retour du populisme: un défi pour les démocraties européennes*, Paris: Universalis.

Diamond, L. and Gunther, R. (eds) (2001) *Political Parties and Democracy*, Baltimore and London: The John Hopkins University Press.

Duraffour, A. and Guittonneau, C. (1991) Des mythes aux problèmes: l'argumentation xénophobe prise au mot, in Taguieff, P. A. (ed.) *Face au Racisme. Tome 1. Les Moyens d'Agir*. Paris: Éditions la Découverte.

Dutch Government (2002) *Het kabinet Balkenende*, The Hague: Sdu.

Duverger, M. (1954) *Political Parties*, London: Methuen.

Eatwell, R. The Rebirth of the 'Extreme Right' in Western Europe?, *Parliamentary Affairs* 53(3), 2000, 407–425.

Eatwell, R. (2003) Ten Theories of the Extreme Right, in Merkl, P. H. and Weinberg, L. (eds) *Right-wing Extremism in the Twenty-First Century*, London: Frank Cass.

Eatwell, R. (2005) Charisma and the Revival of the European Extreme Right, in Rydgren, J. (ed.) *Movements of Exclusion: Radical Right-wing Populism in the Western World*, New York: Nova Science.

Eatwell, R. (2006) Towards a New Model of Right-Wing Charismatic Leadership, http://staff.bath.ac.uk/mlsre/Charisma-Simon2.htm University of Bath (seen 1 October 2006).

Entman, R. M. (1989) *Democracy Without Citizens: Media and the Decay of American Politics*, Oxford and New York: Oxford University Press.

EUMC (2001) *Attitudes towards Minority Groups in the European Union: A Special Analysis of the Eurobarometer 2000 Survey*, Vienna: SORA.

Eurobarometer 64, Autumn 2005 (2006), National Report: Ireland, Brussels: The European Commission, http://ec.europa.eu/public_opinion/archives/eb/eb64/eb64_ie_nat.pdf (seen 15 January 2007).

Evans, G. and Butt, S. (2005) Leaders or Followers? Parties and Public Opinion on the European Union in Bromley, C. (ed.), *British Social Attitudes, The 22nd Report-Two terms of New Labour: The Public's Reaction* (National Centre for Social Research) London: Sage.

Faas, T. and Wüst, A. The Schill Factor in the Hamburg State Election 2001, *German Politics*, 11(2), 2002, 1–20.

Fallend, F. Are Right-Wing Populism and Government Participation Incompatible? The Case of the Freedom Party of Austria, *Representation*, 40(2), 2004, 115–130.

Fortuyn, P. Op weg naar een geatomiseerde samenleving? *Namens*, 6(5), 1991, 7–11.

Fortuyn, P. (1993) *Aan het volk van Nederland. De contractmaatschappij, een politiek-economische zedenschets*, Amsterdam and Antwerp: Contact.

Fortuyn, P. (1995) *Uw baan staat op de tocht! De overlegeconomie voorbij*, Utrecht: Bruna.

Fortuyn, P. (1997) *Zielloos Europa. Tegen een Europa van technocraten, bureaucratie, subsidies en onvermijdelijke fraude*, Utrecht: Bruna.

Fortuyn, P. (1998) *Babyboomers: autobiografie van een generatie*, Utrecht: Bruna.

Fortuyn, P. (2001) *De islamisering van onze cultuur: Nederlandse identiteit als fundament*, Uithoorn- Rotterdam: Karakter Uitgevers-Speakers Academy.

Fortuyn, P. (2002a) *De puinhopen van acht jaar paars. Een genadeloze analyse van de collectieve sector en aanbevelingen voor een krachtig herstelprogramma*, Uithoorn-Rotterdam: Karakter Uitgevers-Speakers Academy.

Fortuyn, P. (2002b) *De verweesde samenleving: een religieus-sociologisch traktaat*, Uithoorn-Rotterdam: Karakter Uitgevers-Speakers Academy.

Front National (1985) *Pour la France*, Paris: Editions Albatros.

Fryklund, B. and Peterson, T. (1981) *Populism och missnöjespartier i Norden. Studier i småborgerlig klassaktivitet*, Lund: Arkiv Förlag.

Fukuyama, F. (2006) After the 'end of history', http://www.opendemocracy.net (seen 9 March 2007).

Furedi, F. (2004) *Therapy Culture: Cultivating Vulnerability in an Uncertain Age*, London: Routledge.

Gallagher, M. (2003) Stability and Turmoil: Analysis of the Results, in Gallagher, M., Marsh, M. and Mitchell, P. (eds) *How Ireland Voted 2002*, Basingstoke: Palgrave Macmillan.

Gallagher, M. and Marsh, M. Party Membership in Ireland: The Members of Fine Gael, *Party Politics*, 10(4), 2004, 407–425.

Gamble, A. (1994) *Britain in Decline: Economic Policy, Political Strategy and the British State*, Basingstoke: Palgrave.

Gapper, S. The Rise and Fall of Germany's Party of Democratic Socialism, *German Politics*, 12(2), 2003, 65–85.

Garry, J. (2006) Political Alienation, in Garry, J., Hardiman, N. and Payne, D. (eds) *Irish Social and Political Attitudes*, Liverpool: Liverpool University Press.

Garvin, T. Political Cleavages, Party Politics and Urbanisation in Ireland: The Case of the Periphery-Dominated Centre, *European Journal of Political Research*, 2(4), 1974, 307–327.

Garvin, T. (2005) *The Evolution of Irish Nationalist Politics*, Dublin: Gill & Macmillan.

Garvin, T. and Mair, P. Reflections: The periphery-dominated centre, *European Journal of Political Research*, 31(1 and 2), 1997, 66–71.

Gaxie, D. (1978) *Le cens caché. Inégalités culturelles et ségrégation politique*, Paris: Seuil.

Gellner, E. and Ionescu, G. (eds) (1969) *Populism. Its Meanings and National Characteristics*, London: Weidenfeld and Nicolson.

George, S. (1998) *An Awkward Partner -Britain in the European Community*, Oxford: Oxford University Press.

Germani, G. (1975) *Autoritarismo, fascismo e classi sociali*, Bologna: Il Mulino.

Germani, G. (1978) *Authoritarianism, Fascism, and National Populism*, New Brunswick: Transaction Books.

Gifford, C. The Rise of Post-Imperial Populism: The Case of Right-Wing Euroscepticism in Britain, *European Journal of Political Research*, 45(5), 2006, 851–869.

Gijsberts, M. (2005) Opvattingen van autochtonen en allochtonen over de multi-etnische samenleving, in *Jaarrapport Integratie 2005*, The Hague: Centraal Bureau voor de Statistiek.

Gilljam, M. and Holmberg, S. (1993) *Väljarna inför 90-talet*, Stockholm: Norstedts Juridik.

Girardet, R. (1966) *Le nationalisme Français 1871–1914*, Paris: Armand Colin.

Gitlin, T. (1980) *The Whole World is Watching – Mass Media in the Making and Unmaking of the New Left*, Berkeley: University of California Press.

Gnoli, A. Populismo. Un nuovo spettro si aggira per il mondo, *La Repubblica*, 12 November 2003.

Gold, T. (2003) *The Lega Nord and Contemporary Politics in Italy*, New York: Palgrave.

Golder, M. Explaining Variation in the Success of the Extreme Right Parties in Western Europe, *Comparative Studies* 36(4), 2003, 432–466.

Goul Andersen, J. and Bjørklund, T. Structural Changes and New Cleavages: The Progress Parties in Denmark and Norway, *Acta Sociologica*, 33(3), 1990, 195–217.

Green-Pedersen, C. Center Parties, Party Competition, and the Implosion of Party Systems: A study of Centripetal Tendencies in Multiparty Systems, *Political Studies*, 52(2), 2004, 324–341.

Gruner, E. (1984) 'Parteien', in Klöti, U. (ed.) *Handbuch Politisches System der Schweiz*, Bern: Haupt.

Habermas, J. (2001) Learning from Catastrophe? A Look Back at the Short Twentieth Century, in Habermas, J. *The Postnational Constellation – Political Essays*, Cambridge: Polity.

Hainsworth, P. (1992) The Extreme Right in Post-war France: The Emergence and Success of the Front National, in Hainsworth, P. (ed.) *The Extreme Right in Europe and the USA*, London: Pinter.

Hainsworth, P. (2000) The Front National: From Ascendancy to Fragmentation on the French Extreme Right, in Hainsworth, P. (ed.) *The Politics of the Extreme Right: From the Margins to the Mainstream*, London: Pinter.

Hargreaves, A. G. (1995) *Immigration, 'Race' and Ethnicity in Contemporary France*, London: Routledge.

Harney, M. (2000) Remarks by Tánaiste, Mary Harney at a Meeting of the American Bar Association in the Law Society of Ireland, Blackhall Place, Dublin on Friday 21 July 2000, http://www.entemp.ie/press/2000/210700.htm (seen 15 October 2006).

Harrison, L. Maximising Small Party Potential: The Effects of Electoral System Rules on the Far Right in German Sub-National Elections, *German Politics*, 6(3), 1997, 132–151.

Hartleb, F. (2004) Auf- und Abstieg der Hamburger Schill-Partei, in Zehetmair, H. (ed.), *Das deutsche Parteiensystem*, Wiesbaden: VS-Verlag.

Hay, C. (1995) 'Structure and Agency', in Marsh, D. and Stoker, G. (eds) *Theory and Methods in Political Science*, Basingstoke: MacMillan.

Heinisch, R. (2002) *Populism, Proporz and Pariah – Austria Turns Right: Austrian Political Change, Its Causes and Repercussions*, Huntington NY: Nova Science Publishing.

Heinisch, R. Success in Opposition – Failure in Government: Exploring the Performance of the Austrian Freedom Party and other European Right-wing Populist Parties in Public Office, *West European Politics*, 26(3), 2003, 91–130.

Heinisch, R. Die FPÖ – Ein Phänomen im Internationalen Vergleich Erfolg und Misserfolg des Identitären Rechtspopulismus, *Österreichische Zeitschrift für Politikwissenschaft*, 33(3), 2004, 247–60.

Hermet, G. (2001) *Les populismes dans le monde. Une histoire sociologique, XIXe-XXe siècle*, Paris: Fayard.

Hine, D. (1993) *Governing Italy. The Politics of Bargained Pluralism*. Oxford: Clarendon Press.

Hipfl, B. (2005) Politics of Media Celebrities: The Case of Jörg Haider, in Ociepka, B. (ed.), *Populism and Media Democracy*, Wroclaw: Wroclaw University Press.

Hobsbawm, E. (1995) *Age of Extremes: The Short Twentieth Century 1914–1991*, London: Abacus.

Holmberg, S. (2000) *Välja parti*, Stockholm: Norstedts Juridik.

Holmberg, S. and Oscarsson, H. (2002) *Svenskt väljarbeteende*, Stockholm: Statistics Sweden.

Holmberg, S. and Weibull, L. (1997) Förtroendets fall, in Holmberg, S. and Weibul, L. (eds) *Ett missnöjt folk? SOM-undersökningen 1996*, Gothenburg: SOM-Institutet.

Holmberg, S. and Weibull, L. (2003a) 'Fåfängans marknad', in Holmberg, S. and Weibull, L. (eds) *Fåfängans marknad: SOM-undersökningen 2002*, Gothenburg: SOM-Institutet.

Holmberg, S. and Weibull, L. (2003b) Förgängligt förtroende, in Holmberg, S. and Weibull, L. (eds) *Fåfängans marknad: SOM-undersökningen 2002*, Gothenburg: SOM-Institutet.

Hopkin, J. (2004) New Parties in Government in Italy: Comparing Lega Nord and Forza Italia, paper presented to 2004 ECPR Joint Sessions, Uppsala, 13–18 April 2004.

Horner, F. (1997) Programme-Ideologiesn: Dissens oder Konsens, in Dachs, H. *et al.* (eds), *Handbuch des Politischen Systems Österreichs – Die Zweite Pepublik*, Vienna: Manz.

Horsfield, B. and Stewart, J. (2003) One Nation and the Australian Media, in Mazzoleni, G., Stewart, J. and Horsfield, B. (eds) *The Media and Neo-Populism. A Contemporary Comparative Analysis*, Westport, CT: Praeger.

Hout, M., Brooks, C. and Manza, J. (1996) The Persistence of Classes in Post-industrial Societies, in Lee, D. J. and Turner, B. S. (eds) *Conflicts about Class – Debating Inequality in Late Industrialism*, London: Longman.

Humphreys, J. Ireland ranked as second wealthiest country, *The Irish Times*, 8 September 2005.

Huysseune, M. (2006) *Modernity and Secession. The Social Sciences and the Political Discourse of the Lega Nord in Italy*, Oxford and New York: Berghan.

Ignazi, P. (1994) *L'estrema destra in Europa*, Bologna: Il Mulino.

Ignazi, P. (1996) Un nouvel acteur politique, in Mayer, N. and Perrineau, P. (eds) *Le Front National à découvert*, Paris: Presses de la Fondation Nationale des Sciences Politiques.

Ignazi, P. (2003) *Extreme Right Parties in Western Europe*, Oxford: Oxford University Press.

Inglehart, R. (1977) *The Silent Revolution: Changing Values and Political Styles among Western Publics*, Princeton: Princeton University Press.

Irwin, G. and van Holsteyn, J. (2002) De kloof tussen burger en bestuur, in van Holsteyn, J. and Mudde, C. (eds) *Democratie in verval?* Amsterdam: Boom.

Ivaldi, G. Le Front national à l'assaut du système, *Revue Politique et Parlamentaire*, 100(995), 1998, 5–22.

Jackman, R. W. and Volpert, K. Conditions Favouring Parties on the Extreme Right in Western Europe, *British Journal of Political Science*, 26(4), 1996, 501–521.

Jagers, J. and Walgrave, S. *Populism as a Political Communication Style*, paper presented at the ICA Conference, San Diego, May 2003.

Jenkins, B. and Copsey, N. (1996) Nation, Nationalism and National Identity in France, in Jenkins, B. and Sofos, S. A. (eds) *Nation and Identity in Contemporary Europe*, London: Routledge.

Johansson, G. Partiledaren, *SD-Kuriren*, 48, 2002.

Karapin, R. Radical-Right and Neo-Fascist Political Parties in Western Europe, *Comparative Politics*, 30(2), 1998a, 213–234.

Karapin, R. Explaining Far-Right Electoral Successes in Germany. The Politicization of Immigration-Related Issues, *German Politics and Society*, 16(1), 1998b, 24–61.

Katz, R., Mair P. *et al.* The Membership of Political Parties in European Democracies, 1960–90, *European Journal of Political Research*, 22(3), 1992, 329–345.

Katz, R. and Mair, P. (eds) (1994) *How Parties Organize: Change and Adaptation in Party Organization in Western Democracies*, London: Sage.

Katz, R. and Mair, P. Changing Models of Party Organization and Party Democracy, *Party Politics*, 1(1), 1995, 5–28.

Katzenstein, P. J. (1984) *Corporatism and Change: Austria, Switzerland and the Politics of Industry*, Ithaca: Cornell University Press.

Kavanagh, D. (1980) Political Culture in Great Britain: The Decline of the Civic Culture, in Almond, G. A. and Verba, S. (eds) *The Civic Culture Revisited*, Boston and Toronto: Little, Brown and Company.

Kazin, M. (1995) *The Populist Persuasion*, New York: Basic Books.

Kellner, D. (1990) *Television and the Crisis of Democracy*, Boulder, Colo.: Westview Press.

Kelsen, H. (1929) *Vom Wesen und Wert der Demokratie*, Tübingen: J. C. B. Mohr.

Kestilä, E. (2005) The Finnish Exception: Is the Party Competition in Finland Inaccessible to Radical Right Populist Parties? unpublished paper, Workshop: Participation in Established Frameworks: Party System and Voting.

Kilroy-Silk R. (2004) Limit immigration to 100,000 a year and withdraw from the Geneva Convention on Refugees, speech at the London UKIP Annual Dinner, 11 September 2004.

Kirchheimer, O. (1966) The Transformation of the Western European Party Systems, in LaPalombara, J. and Weiner, M. (eds) *Political Parties and Political Development*, Princeton: Princeton University Press.

Kitschelt, H. Political Opportunity Structures and Political Protest: Anti-Nuclear Movements in Four Democracies, *British Journal of Political Science*, 16(1), 1986, 57–85.

Kitschelt, H. (with McGann, A.) (1995) *The Radical Right in Western Europe. A Comparative Analysis*, Ann Arbor, Mich.: University of Michigan Press.

Kjellberg, A. (2000) Sweden, in Ebbinghaus, B. and Visser, J. (eds) *The Societies of Europe. Trade Unions in Western Europe since 1945*, London: MacMillan.

Kleinnijenhuis, J. and Scholten, O. (1989) Veranderende verhoudingen tussen dagbladen en politieke partije, *Acta Politica*, 24(4), 1989, 433–460.

Kleinnijenhuis, J. *et al.* (1995) *Democratie op drift*, Amsterdam: VU Uitgeverij.

Kleinnijenhuis, J. *et al.* (2003) *De puinhopen in het nieuws. De rol van de media bij de Tweede-Kamerverkiezingen van 2002*, Alphen aan den Rijn-Malines: Kluwer.

Klingemann, H. D. (1999) Mapping Political Support in the 1990s: A Global Analysis, in Norris, P. (ed.) *Critical Citizens: Global Support for Democratic Government*, Oxford: Oxford University Press.

Klöti, U. Consensual Government in a Heterogeneous Polity, *West European Politics*, (24)2, 2001, 19–34.

Kobach, K. W. (1993) *The Referendum: Direct Democracy in Switzerland*, Darmouth: Aldershot.

Koole, R. and Daalder, H. (2002) The Consociational Democracy Model and the Netherlands: Ambivalent Allies? in Steiner, J. and Ertman, T. (eds) *Consociationalism and Corporatism in Western Europe: Still the Politics of Accomodation?* Amsterdam: Boom – Special issue of *Acta Politica*, 37(1/2).

Koopmanns, R. and Statham, P. (2000) Migration and Ethnic Relations as a Field of Political Contention: An Opportunity Structure Approach, in Koopmanns, R. and Statham, P. (eds) *Challenging Immigration and Ethnic Relations Politics: Comparative European Perspectives*, Oxford: Oxford University Press.

Koopmans, R. Movement and the Media: Selection Processes and Evolutionary Dynamics in the Public Sphere, *Theory and Society*, 33(3), 2004, 367–91.

Koopmans, R. *et al.* (2005) *Contested Citizenship. Immigration and Cultural Diversity in Europe*, Minneapolis: University of Minnesota Press.

Kornhauser, W. (1959) *The Politics of Mass Society*, New York: The Free Press of Glencoe.

Kranenburg, M. De stille revolutie, *NCR Handelsblad*, (11)24 October 2003.

Kriesi, H. (1999) Movements of the Left, Movements of the Right: Putting the Mobilisation of Two New Types of Social Movements into Political Context in Kitschelt, H. *et al.* (eds) *Continuity and Change in Contemporary Capitalism*, Cambridge: CUP.

Kriesi, H. (2005) *Direct Democratic Choice. The Swiss Experience*, Oxford: Lexington.

Kriesi, H. Role of the Political Elite in Swiss Direct-Democratic Votes, *Party Politics*, 12(5), 2006, 599–622.

Kriesi, H. *et al.* (1995) *New Social Movements in Western Europe: A Comparative Analysis*, Minneapolis: University of Minnesota Press.

Kriesi, H. *et al.* (eds) (2005) *Der Aufstieg der SVP. Acht Kantone im Vergleich*, Zurich: NZZ.

Kruse, I., Orren, H. E. and Angenendt, S. The Failure of Immigration Reform in Germany, *German Politics*, 12(3), 2003, 129–145.

Laclau, E. (2005) *On Populist Reason*, London: Verso.

Ladner, A. Swiss Political Parties: Between Persistence and Change, *West European Politics*, 24(2), 2001, 123–144.

Ladner, A. (2003) The Political Parties and the Party System, in Klöti, U. *et al.* (eds) *Handbook of Swiss Politics*, Zurich: Neue Zürcher Zeitung.

Landman, N. (1992) *Van mat tot minaret: de institutionalisering van de islam in Nederland*, Amsterdam: VU Uitgeverij.

Lane, J. E. The Political Economy of Switzerland: A Monetarist Success? *West European Politics*, 24(2), 2001, 191–210.

Larsson, S. and Ekman, M. (2001) *Sverigedemokraterna. Den nationella rörelsen*, Stockholm: Ordfront – Expo.

Lash, S. and Urry, J. (1988) *The End of Organized Capitalism*, Cambridge: Polity.

Laver, M. (2005) Voting Behaviour, in Coakley, J. and Gallagher, M. (eds) *Politics in the Republic of Ireland*, London: Routledge.

Le Pen, J. M. (1985) *La France est de retour*, Paris: Editions Carrere – Michel Lafon.

Lehingue, P. (2003) L'objectivation statistique des électorats: que savons-nous des électeurs du Front national? in Lagroye, J. (ed.), *La politisation*, Paris: Belin.

Lehmbruch, G. (1967) *Proporzdemokratie. Politisches System und politische Kultur in der Schweiz und in Österreich*, Tübingen: Mohn – Siebeck.

Lerner, D. (1958) *The Passing of Traditional Society: Modernising the Middle East*, New York: The Free Press.

Lijphart, A. (1968) *The Politics of Accommodation. Pluralism and Democracy in the Netherlands*, Berkeley: University of California Press.

Lijphart, A. (1984) *Democracies. Patterns of Majoritarian and Consensus Government in Twenty-One Countries*, London: Tale University Press.

Lindahl, R. (1994) Inför avgörandet – åsikter om EU, in Holmberg, S. and Weibull, L. (eds) *Vägval. SOM-undersökningen 1993*, Gothenburg: SOM-Institutet.

Linder, W. (1998) *Swiss Democracy: Possible Solutions to Conflict in Multicultural Societies*, London: Macmillan.

Linder, W. (2003a) Political Culture, in Klöti, U. *et al.* (eds) *Handbook of Swiss Politics*, Zurich: Neue Zürcher Zeitung.

Linder, W. (2003b) Direct Democracy, in Klöti, U. *et al.* (eds) *Handbook of Swiss Politics*, Zurich: Neue Zürcher Zeitung.

Linz, J. J. (2000) *Totalitarian and Authoritarian Regimes*, Boulder and London: Lynne Rienner Publishers.

Lipset, S. M. and Rokkan, S. (1967) Cleavage Structures, Party Systems, and Voter Alignments: An Introduction, in Lipset, S. M. and Rokkan, S. (eds) *Party Systems and Voter Alignments: Cross-National Perspectives*, New York: The Free Press.

Lloyd, J. A European Media Manifesto, *Axess*, 4, 2005.

Lösche, P. The German Party System after the 2002 Bundestag Elections – Continuity or Discontinuity, *German Politics*, 12(3), 2003, 66–81.

Loyal, S. (2003) Welcome to the Celtic Tiger: Racism, Immigration and the State, in Coulter, C. and Coleman, S. (eds), *The End of Irish History? Critical Reflections on the Celtic Tiger*, Manchester: Manchester University Press.

Lucardie, P. (1998) The Netherlands: The Extremist Center Parties, in Betz, H.G. and Immerfall, S. (eds) *The New Politics of the Right: Neo-Populist Parties and Movements in Established Democracies*, New York: St. Martin's Press, 1998.

Lucardie, P. Prophets, Purifiers and Prolocutors. Towards a Theory on the Emergence of New Parties, *Party Politics*, 6(2), 2000, 175–185.

Lucardie, P. (2003) Populismus im Polder: Von der Bauernpartei bis zur Liste Pim Fortuyn, in Werz, N. (ed.), *Populismus: Populisten in Übersee und Europa*, Opladen: Leske and Budrich.

Lucardie, P. and Voerman, G. Liberaal Patriot of Nationaal Populist? Het gedachtegoed van Pim Fortuyn, *Socialisme en Democratie*, 59(4), 2002, 32–42.

Luhmann, N. (1990) *Political Theory in the Welfare State*, New York: Walter de Gruyter.

Lukacs, J. (2005) *Democracy and Populism: Fear and Hatred*, New Haven: Yale University Press.

Luther, K. R. (1997) Die Freiheitlichen, in Dachs, H. *et al.* (eds), *Handbuch des Politischen Systems Österreichs – Die Zweite Pepublik*, Vienna: Manz.

Luther, K. R. (2006) Die Freiheitliche Partei Österreichs und das Bündnis Zukunft Österreich, in Dachs, H. *et al.* (eds) *Politik in Österreich: Das Handbuch*, Vienna: Manz.

Lyons, P. and Sinnott, R. (2003) Voter Turnout in 2002 and Beyond, in Gallagher, M., Marsh, M. and Mitchell, P. (eds) *How Ireland Voted 2002*, Basingstoke: Palgrave Macmillan.

Mach, A. (2003) Interest Groups, in Klöti, U. *et al.* (eds) *Handbook of Swiss Politics*, Zurich: Neue Zürcher Zeitung.

Macrae, K. (1964) *Switzerland: Example of Cultural Coexistence*, Canadian Institute of International Affairs: Toronto.

Madsen, D. and Snow, P. G. (1991) *The Charismatic Bond: Political Behavior in Time of Crisis*, Cambridge, Mass.: Harvard University Press.

Maillot, A. (2005) *New Sinn Féin: Irish Republicanism in the Twenty-First Century*, Oxford: Routledge.

Mair, P. (1987) *The Changing Irish Party System: Organisation, Ideology and Electoral Competition*, London: Frances Pinter.

Mair, P. (1992) Explaining the Absence of Class Politics in Ireland, in Goldthorpe, J. H. and Whelan, C. T. (eds) *The Development of Industrial Society in Ireland*, Oxford: Oxford University Press.

Mair, P. (1997a) *Party System Change: Approaches and Interpretations*, Oxford: The Clarendon Press.

Mair, P. Nomination: The Periphery-Dominated Centre, *European Journal of Political Research*, 31, 1997b, 63–66.

Mair, P. (1999) Party Competition and the Changing Party System, in Coakley, J. and Gallagher, M. (eds) *Politics in the Republic of Ireland*, London: Routledge.

Mair, P. Partyless Democracy – Solving the Paradox of New Labour, *New Left Review* 2, March–April 2000.

Mair, P. and van Biezen, I. Party Membership in Twenty European Democracies. 1980–2000, *Party Politics*, 7(1), 2001, 5–21.

Mair, P. (2002) Populist Democracy vs Party Democracy, in Mény, Y. and Surel, Y. (eds) *Democracies and the Populist Challenge*, Houndmills: Palgrave.

Mair, P. Polity-Scepticism, Party Failings, and the Challenge to European Democracy, Uhlenbeck Lecture 24, delivered at Wassenaar 9 June 2006, NIAS, www.nias.knaw.nl/en/new_3/new_1/peter_mair/ (seen 10 October 2006).

Manin, B. (1997) *The Principles of Representative Government*, Cambridge: Cambridge University Press.

Mannheimer, R. (1992) The Electorate of the Lega Nord, in Pasquino, G. and McCarthy, P. (eds) *The End of Post-War Politics in Italy: The Landmark 1992 Elections*, Boulder: Westview Press.

Marcus, J. (1995) *The National Front and French Politics: The Resistible Rise of Jean-Marie Le Pen*, London: MacMillan.

Marquand, D. The Blair Paradox, *Prospect*, May 1998.

Mastropaolo, A. (2000) *Antipolitica. Alle Origini della Crisi Italiana*, Napoli: L'Ancora del Mediterraneo.

Mastropaolo, A. (2005) *La Mucca Pazza della Democrazia*, Torino: Bollati Boringhieri.

Mathis, F. (1997) 1,000 Years of Austria and Austrian Identity: Founding Myths, in Bischof, G. and Pelinka, A. (eds) *Austrian Historical Memory and National Identity*, New Brunswick NJ: Transaction Publisher.

Mayer, N. (1998) The French Front National, in Betz, H. G.and Immerfall, S. (eds) *The New Politics of the Right: Neo-Populist Parties and Movements in Established Democracies*, New York: St. Martin's Press.

Mayer, N. (1999) *Ces Français qui votent FN*, Paris: Flammarion.

Mayer, N. (2002) *Ces Français qui votent Le Pen*, Paris: Flammarion.

Mazzoleni, G. Quando la pubblicità elettorale non serve, *Polis*, 6(2), 1992, 291–304.

Mazzoleni, G. (2003) The Media and the Growth of Neo-Populism in Contemporary Democracies, in Mazzoleni, G., Stewart, J. and Horsfield, B. (eds) *The Media and Neo-Populism: A Contemporary Comparative Analysis*, Westport, CT: Praeger.

Mazzoleni, G. and Schulz, W. Mediatization of Politics: A Challenge for Democracy? *Political Communication*, 16(3), 1999, 247–261.

Mazzoleni, G., Stewart, J. and Horsfield, B. (eds) (2003) *The Media and Neo-Populism: A Contemporary Comparative Analysis*, Westport, CT: Praeger.

Mazzoleni, O. (1995) Identità e modernizzazione: una Lega nella Svizzera italiana, in Bonomi, A. and Poggio, P. (eds) *Ethnos e Demos: dal Leghismo al Neopopulismo*, Milano: Mimesis.

Mazzoleni, O. La Lega dei Ticinesi: Vers l'intégration? *Swiss Political Science Review*, 5(3), 1999, 79–95.

Mazzoleni, O. (2003a) Unité et diversité des 'national-populismes' suisses: L'Union Démocratique du Centre et la Lega dei Ticinesi, in Ihl, O. *et al.* (eds) *La Tentation Populiste au Coeur de l'Europe*, Paris: La Découverte.

Mazzoleni, O. (2003b) *Nationalisme et Populisme en Suisse: La radicalisation de la 'nouvelle' UDC*, Lousanne: Presses Polytechniques et Universitaires Romandes.

Mazzoleni, O. (2005) Multi-Level Populism and Centre-Periphery Cleavage in Switzerland – The Case of the Lega dei Ticinesi, in Caramani, D. and Mény, Y. (eds) *Challenges to Consensual Politics – Democracy, Identity and Populist Protest in the Alpine Region*, Brussels: P.I.E.-Peter Lang.

McDonnell, D. A Weekend in Padania: Regionalist Populism and the Lega Nord, *Politics*, 26(2), 2006, 126–132.

McLaren, L. and Mark, J. (2004) Understanding the Rising Tide of Anti-immigrant Sentiment, in Bromley, C. *et al.* (eds) *British Social Attitudes – The 21st Report* (National Centre for Social Research) London: Sage.

Mény, Y. and Surel, Y. (2000) *Par le peuple, pour le peuple*, Paris: Librairie Arthème Fayard.

Mény, Y. and Surel, Y. (2002) The Constitutive Ambiguity of Populism, in Mény, Y. and Surel, Y. (eds) *Democracies and the Populist Challenge*, London: Macmillan.

Mény, Y. and Surel, Y. (2004) *Populismo e Democrazia*, Bologna: il Mulino.

Mete, V. Cittadini contro i partiti. Antipartitismo e antipartitici in Italia, *Polena*, 2(3), 2005, 9–36.

Möller, T. (2000) *Politikens meningslöshet. Om misstro, cynism och utanförskap*, Malmö: Liber.

Molony, S. Kenny Warns of Risk to 'Christian' Ireland, *Irish Independent*, 24 January 2007.

Morlino, L. and Tarchi, M. The Dissatisfied Society. The Roots of Political Change in Italy, *European Journal of Political Research*, 30(1), 1996, 41–63.

Mudde, C. (2000) *The Ideology of the Extreme Right*, Manchester: Manchester University Press.

Mudde, C. The Populist Zeitgeist, *Government and Opposition*, 39(4), 2004, 541–563.

Murphy, G. (2003) The Background to the Election, in Gallagher, M., Marsh, M. and Mitchell, P. (eds) *How Ireland Voted 2002*, Basingstoke: Palgrave Macmillan.

Neidhart, L. (1970) *Plebiszit und pluralitäre Demokratie: Eine Analyse der Funktion des schweizerischen Gesetzesreferendums*, Berne: Franke.

Neumann, S. (1956) Towards a Comparative Study of Political Parties, in Neumann, S. (ed.), *Modern Political Parties*, Chicago: University of Chicago Press.

Neustadt, R. E. (1991) *Presidential Power and the Modern Presidents: The Politics of Leadership from Roosevelt to Reagan*, New York: The Free Press.

Nilsson, L. (1992) Den offentliga sektorn under åtstramning och omprövning, in Holmberg, S. and Weibull, L. (eds) *Trendbrott? SOM-undersökningen 1991*, Gothenburg: SOM-Institutet.

Nolan, B., O'Connell, P. J. and Whelan, C. T. (2000) *Bust to Boom? The Experience of Growth and Inequality*, Dublin: IPA.

Norris, P. (ed.) (1999) *Critical Citizens: Global Support for Democratic Governance*, Oxford: Oxford University Press.

Norris, P. (2005) *Radical Right: Voters and Parties in the Electoral Market*, Cambridge: Cambridge University Press.

O'Brien, C. 400,000 Foreign Nationals Living in the State, *The Irish Times*, 20 July 2006.

Obbema, F. and Van Praag, P. Moord op Fortuyn vesterkte trends onder kiezers, *De Volkskrant*, (3), 16 May 2002.

Ociepka, B. (2005) Populism as 'Good Communication with People'. The Polish Case during the Referendum Campaign, in Ociepka, B. (ed.) *Populism and Media Democracy*, Wroclaw: Wroclaw University Press.

Ociepka, B. (ed.) (2005) *Populism and Media Democracy*, Wroclaw: Wroclaw University Press.

OECD (Organisation for Economic Co-operation and Development) (1999) OECD Economic Surveys. Switzerland 1999. Special Issue: Tax Reform., www.oecd.org (seen 3 November 2006).

OECD (Organisation for Economic Co-operation and development) (2006) Economic Survey of Switzerland 2006: Executive Summary, www.oecd.org (seen 13 February 2007).

Orfali, B. (1996) Le droit chemin ou les mécanismes de l'adhésion politique, in Mayer, N. and Perrineau, P. (eds) *Le Front National à découvert*, Paris: Presses de la Fondation Nationale des Sciences Politiques.

Oscarsson, H. (1998) *Den svenska partirymden. Väljarnas uppfattning av konfliksstrukturen i partisystemet*, Gothenburg Studies in Politics 54, Gothenburg: Gothenburg University.

Panebianco, A. (1988) *Political Parties: Organization and Power*, Cambridge: Cambridge University Press.

Panizza, F. (ed.) (2005) *Populism and the Mirror of Democracy*, London: Verso.

Papadopoulos, Y. Quel rôle pour les petits partis dans la démocratie directe?, *Annuaire Suisse de Science Politique*, 31, 1991, 131–150.

Papadopoulos, Y. How Does Direct Democracy Matter? The Impact of Referendum Votes on Politics and Policy-Making, *West European Politics*, 24(2), 2001, 35–58.

Papadopoulos, Y. (2005) Populism as the Other Side of Consociational Multi-Level Democracies, in Caramani, D. and Mény, Y. (eds) *Challenges to Consensual Politics – Democracy, Identity and Populist Protest in the Alpine Region*, Brussels: P.I.E.-Peter Lang.

Parnreiter, C. Migrationspolitik im Wandel. Bestimmungsfaktoren österreichischer Wanderungspolitik im Lichte des Umbruchs der Weltwirtschaft, *Österreichische Zeitschrift für Politikwissenschaft*, 23(3), 1994, 283–298.

Pasquino, G. (1979) Populismo, in Carmagnani, M. (ed.) *Storia dell'America Latina*, Firenze: La Nuova Italia Editrice.

Pelinka, A. (1981) *Modellfall Österreich? Möglichkeiten und Grenzen der Sozialpartnerschaft*. Vienna: Braumüller.

Pelinka, A. (1996) Kammern und Sozialpartnerschaft in Österreich in Pelinka, A. and Smekal, C. (eds.), *Kammern auf dem Prüfstand: Vergleichende Analysen institutioneller Funktionsbedingungen*, Vienna: Signum.

238 *Bibliography*

Pelinka, A. (2005) Right Wing Populism Plus 'X': The Austrian Freedom Party (FPÖ) in Caramani, D. and Mény, Y. (eds) *Challenges to Consensual Politics – Democracy, Identity and Populist Protest in the Alpine Region,* Brussels: P.I.E.-Peter Lang.

Pels, D. (2003) *De geest van Pim. Het gedachtegoed van een politieke dandy,* Amsterdam: Anthos.

Pennings, P. The Evolution of Dutch Consociationalism, 1917–1997, *The Netherlands Journal of Social Sciences,* 33(1), 1997, 9–26.

Perrineau, P. (1996) Les étapes d'une implantation électorale (1972–1988), in Mayer, N. and Perrineau, P. (eds) *Le Front National à découvert,* Paris: Presses de la Fondation Nationale des Sciences Politiques.

Perrineau, P. (1997) *Le Symptôme Le Pen. Radiographie des électeurs du Front National,* Paris: Fayard.

Pharr, S. J. and Putnam, R. D. (eds) (2000) *Disaffected Democracies: What's Troubling the Trilateral Countries?* Princeton: Princeton University Press.

Plasser, F. and Ulram, P. A. (1996) Akzeptanz und Unterstützung sozialpartnerschaftlicher Interessenvertretung in Österreich, in Pelinka, A. and Smekal, C. (eds) *Kammern auf dem Prüfstand: Vergleichende Analysen institutioneller Funktionsbedingungen,* Vienna: Signum.

Plasser, F. and Ulram, P. A. (2000) Rechtspopulistische Resonanzen – Die Wählerschaft der FPÖ, in Plasser, F., Ulram, P. A. and Sommer, F. (eds) *Das Österreichische Wahlverhalten,* Vienna: Signum.

Plasser, F. and Ulram, P. A. (2003) Striking a Responsive Chord: Media and Right-Wing Populism in Austria, in Mazzoleni, G., Stewart, J. and Horsfield, B. (eds) *The Media and Neo-Populism: A Contemporary Comparative Analysis,* Westport, CT: Praeger.

Plasser, F., Seeber, G. and Ulram, P. A. (2000) Breaking the Mold: Politische Wettbewerbsräume und Wahlverhalten Ende der neunziger Jahre, in Plasser, F., Ulram, P. A. and Sommer, F. (eds) *Das Österreichische Wahlverhalten,*Vienna: Signum.

Poggi, G. (1990) *The State: Its Nature, Development and Prospect,* Cambridge: Polity.

Poguntke, T. Anti-Party Sentiment. Conceptual Thoughts and Empirical Evidence: Explorations into a Minefield, *European Journal of Political Research,* 29(3), 1996, 319–344.

Poguntke, T. and Webb, P. (2005) *The Presidentialization of Politics: A Comparative Study of Modern Democracies,* Oxford: Oxford University Press.

Poli, E. (2001). *Forza Italia. Strutture, Leadership e Radicamento Territoriale,* Bologna: Il Mulino.

Programm/FPÖ (1999) Das Programm der Freiheitlichen Partei Österreichs, in Kotanko, C. (ed.), *Die Qual der Wahl – Die Programme der Parteien im Vergleich,* Vienna: Czernin.

Przeworski, A., Stokes, S. C. and Manin, B. (1999) *Democracy, Accountability, and Representation,* Cambridge: Cambridge University Press.

Pujas, V. and Rhodes, M. Party Finance and Political Scandals in Italy, Spain and France, *West European Politics,* 22(3), 1999, 41–63.

Putnam, R. (1993) *Making Democracy Work: Civic Traditions in Modern Italy,* Princeton: Princeton University Press.

Putnam, R. D., Pharr, S. J. and Dalton, R. J. (2000) Introduction: What's Troubling the Trilateral Democracies? in Pharr, S. J. and Putnam, R. D. (eds) *Disaffected Democracies: What's Troubling the Trilateral Countries?* Princeton: Princeton University Press.

Randall, N. (2004) Three Faces of New Labour: Principle, Pragmatism and Populism in New Labour's Home Office, in Ludlam, S. and Smith, M. J. *Governing as New Labour – Policy and Politics under Blair*, London: Palgrave.

Riddell, P. (1985) *The Thatcher Government*, Oxford: Basil Blackwell.

Riedlsperger, M. (1998) The Freedom Party of Austria: From Protest to Radical Right Populism, in Betz, H. G. and Immerfall, S. (eds) *The New Politics of the Right: Neo-Populist Parties and Movements in Established Democracies*, New York: St. Martins Press.

Riesman, D. (1989) *The Lonely Crowd*, New Haven and London: Yale University Press.

Riker, W. E. (1982) *Liberalism Against Populism: A Confrontation Between the Theory of Democracy and the Theory of Social Choice*, San Francisco: W. H. Freeman and Company.

Russell, J. Tony Blair's authoritarian populism is indefensible and dangerous, *The Guardian*, 24 April 2006.

Rydgren, J. Radical Right Populism in Sweden: Still a Failure, but for How Long? *Scandinavian Political Studies*, 26(1), 2002, 26–57.

Rydgren, J. Mesolevel Reasons for Racism and Xenophobia: Some Converging and Diverging Effects of Radical Right Populism in France and Sweden, *European Journal of Social Theory*, 6(1), 2003a, 45–68.

Rydgren, J. (2003b) *The Populist Challenge: Political Protest and Ethno-Nationalist Mobilisation in France*, New York: Berghahn Books.

Rydgren, J. Explaining the Emergence of Radical Right-Wing Populist Parties: The Case of Denmark, *West European Politics*, 27(3), 2004, 474–502.

Rydgren, J. Is Extreme Right-Wing Populism Contagious? Explaining the Emergence of a New Party Family, *European Journal of Political Research*, 44(3), 2005, 413–437.

Rydgren, J. (2006) *From Tax Populism to Ethnic Nationalism: Radical Right-wing Populism in Sweden*, New York: Berghahn Books.

Rydgren, J. The Sociology of the Radical Right, *Annual Review of Sociology*, 33, 2007, 241–262.

Sartori, G. (1976) *Parties and Party Systems: A Framework for Analysis*. Cambridge: Cambridge University Press.

Sartori, G. (1987) *The Theory of Democracy Revisited*, Chatham, N.J.: Chatham House Publishers.

Sartori, G. (2005) *Parties and Party Systems: A Framework for Analysis*, Colchester: ECPR Press.

Sassen, S. (1996) *Losing Control? Sovereignty in an Age of Globalization*, New York: Columbia University Press.

Scarrow, S. E. Party Competition and Institutional Change: The Expansion of Direct Democracy in Germany, *Party Politics*, 3(4), 1997, 451–472.

Scarrow, S. E. (2000) Parties without Members? Party Organization in a Changing Electoral Environment, in Dalton, R. J. and Wattenberg, M. P. (eds) *Parties without Partisans: Political Change in Advanced Industrial Democracies*, New York: Oxford University Press.

Schain, M. A. Immigration and Changes in the French Party System, *European Journal of Political Research*, 16, 1988, 597–621.

Schattschneider, E. E. (1975) *The Semisovereign People: A Realist's View of Democracy in America*, London: Wadsworth.

Schedler, A. Zur (nichtlinearen) Entwicklung des Parteienwettbewerbes (1945 bis 1994), *Österreichische Zeitschrift für Politikwissenschaft*, 24(1), 1995, 17–34.

Schedler, A. Anti-political-establishment Parties, *Party Politics*, 2(3), 1996, 291–312.
Schedler, A. (1997) Introduction: Antipolitics – Closing or Colonizing the Public Sphere, in Schedler, A. (ed.) *The End of Politics? Explorations into Modern Antipolitics*, New York: St. Martin's Press.
Schmidtke, O. (1996) *Politics of Identity: Ethnicity, Territories, and the Political Opportunity Structure in Modern Italian Society*, Sinzheim: Pro Universitate Verlag.
Schmitt, C. (1928) *Verfassungslehre*, Berlin: Duncker & Humblot.
Schmitt, C. (1931) *Der Hüter der Verfassung*, Berlin: Duncker & Humblot.
Schmitt, C. (1976) *The Concept of the Political*, New Brunswick: Rutgers University Press.
Schmitt, C. (1985) *The Crisis of Parliamentary Democracy*, Cambridge MA: MIT Press.
Schoen, H. and Falter, J. W. Die Linkspartei und ihre Wähler, *Aus Politik und Zeitgeschichte*, (51–52), 2005, 33–40.
Schumpeter, A. J. (1942) *Capitalism, Socialism and Democracy*, New York: Harper & Row.
Schweitzer, A. (1984) *The Age of Charisma*, Chicago: Nelson Hall.
Selb, P. and Lachat, R. (2004) *Elezioni 2003. L'Evoluzione del Comportamento Elettorale*, Zurich: Institut für Politikwissenschaft.
Seldon, A. and Snowdon, P. The Conservative Campaign, *Parliamentary Affairs*, 58(4), 2005, 725–742.
Setta, S. (2005) *L'Uomo Qualunque (1944–1948)*, Bari: Laterza.
Shadid, W. A. R. and van Koningsveld P. S. (1997) *Moslims in Nederland: minderheden en religie in een multiculturele samenleving*, Houten-Diegem: Bohn Stafleu Van Loghum.
Shils, E. A. (1956) *The Torment of Secrecy*, London: William Heinemann.
Simmons, H. G. (1996) *The French National Front: The Extremist Challenge to Democracy*, San Francisco: Westview.
Sinn Féin (2001) Many Voices One Country: Cherishing all the children of the nation equally, Policy review, http://www.sinnfein.ie/pdg/Policies_Racism.pdf (seen 12 February 2007).
Sinnott, R. (1995) *Irish Voters Decide: Voting Behaviour in Elections and Referendums since 1918*, Manchester: Manchester University Press.
Skenderovic, D. The Swiss Radical Right in Perspective – A Reevaluation of Success Conditions in Switzerland, ECPR Joint sessions of Workshops, Grenoble, 6–11 April 2001.
Socialistische Partij (1999) Heel de mens. Kernvisie van de SP, zoals vastgesteld door het congres op 18 december 1999, www.sp.nl/partij/theorie/kernvisie/heel_de_mens.pdf (seen 22 April 2005).
Södergran, L. (1998) *Återvandringsproblematiken och svensk integrationspolitik. Senare decenniers intresse-och värderingsförskjutning*, Umeå: MERGE.
Sohlberg, P. and Leiulfsrud, H. (2000) Social ojämlikhet, sociala klasser och strukturperspektiv, in Goldberg, T. (ed.) *Samhällsproblem*, Lund: Studentlitteratur.
Solomos, J. and Wrench, J. (1993) Race and Racism in Contemporary Europe, in Wrench, J. and Solomos, J. (eds) *Racism and Migration in Western Europe*, Oxford: Berg.
Souchard, M. *et al.* (1997) *Le Pen – Les Mots. Analyse d'un discours d'extrême-droite*, Paris: Le Monde Éditions.
Staunton, D. and Brennock, M. Rejection of Nice a healthy sign, says McCreevy, *The Irish Times*, 16 June 2001.

Stewart, J., Mazzoleni, G. and Horsfield, B. (2003) Conclusion: Power to the Media Managers, in Mazzoleni, G., Stewart, J. and Horsfield, B. (eds) *The Media and Neo-Populism: A Contemporary Comparative Analysis*, Westport, CT: Praeger.

Stoker, G. (2006) *Why Politics Matters: Making Democracy Work*, Basingstoke: Palgrave Macmillan.

Sverigedemokraterna (2002) Partiprogram 1999 med justeringar 2002, www.sverige demokraterna.se (seen 30 January 2004).

Sverigedemokraterna (2003) Sverigedemokraternas principprogram. www.sverige demokraterna.se (seen 30 January 2004).

SVP/UDC (2003) Piattaforma Elettorale 2003–2007, http://www.svp.ch (seen 1 July 2006).

SVP/UDC (2006) Nos règles sont valables pour tous – Document stratégique sur la politique d'asile et des étrangers, http://www.svp.ch (seen 1 July 2006).

SVP/UDC (2007) Piattaforma Elettorale 2007–2011. La Mia Casa – La Nostra Svizzera, http://www.svp.ch (seen 6 January 2007).

Swank, D. and Betz, H. G. Globalization, the Welfare State and Right-wing Populism in Western Europe, *Socio-Econonic Review*, 1(2), 2003, 215–45.

Swissinfo, Non sono un demagogo, interview with Cristoph Blocher, 9 November 2003, www.blocher.ch/it/artikel/031109demagogo.htm (seen 1 July 2006).

Taggart, P. (1996) *The New Populism and New Politics: New Protest Parties in Sweden in a Comparative Perspective*, London: Macmillan.

Taggart, P. (2000) *Populism*, Buckingham: Open University Press.

Taggart, P. (2002) Populism and the Pathology of Representative Politics, in Mény, Y. and Surel, Y. (eds) *Democracies and the Populist Challenge*, London: Palgrave.

Taggart, P. Populism and Representative Politics in Contemporary Europe, *Journal of Political Ideologies*, 9(3), 2004, 269–288.

Tagle Salas, A. Il populismo in America Latina: l'esperienza dei caudillos di formazione militare Perón, Velasco Alvarado e Chávez, in *Trasgressioni*, 38, January–April, 2004, 61–97.

Taguieff, P. A. (2002) *L'illusion populiste. De l'archaïque au médiatique*, Paris: Berg International.

Talos, E. Sozialpartnerschaft: Entwicklung und Entwicklungsdynamik, in Gehrlich, P., Grande, E. and Müller, W. C. (eds) (1985) *Sozialpartnerschaft in der Krise; Leistungen und Grenzen des Neokorporatismus in Österreich*, Vienna: Böhlau.

Tarchi, M. (1998) The Lega Nord, in De Winter, L. and Huri T. (eds), *Regionalist Parties in Western Europe*, London and New York: Routledge.

Tarchi, M. (2002) Populism Italian Style, in Mény, Y. and Surel, Y. (eds), *Democracies and the Populist Challenge*, Houndmills: Palgrave.

Tarchi, M. (2003) *L'Italia populista. Dal Qualunquismo ai Girotondi*, Bologna: Il Mulino.

Tarchi, M. Il Populismo e la Scienza Politica. Come Liberarsi del 'Complesso di Cenerentola', *Filosofia politica*, 18(3), 2004, 411–429.

Tarrow, S. (1998) *Power in Movement: Social Movements and Contentious Politics*, Cambridge: Cambridge University Press.

Te Velde, H. Passie, theater en narcisme, *Pluche*, 1(1), 2003, 63–69.

Thomassen, J. (2000) Politieke veranderingen en het functioneren van de parlementaire democratie in Nederland, in Thomassen, J., Aarts, K. and van der Kolk, H. (eds) *Politieke veranderingen in Nederland, 1971–1998. Kiezers en de smalle marges van de politiek*, The Hague: Sdu.

Tourret, P. Il caso Blocher divide gli svizzeri, *Limes*, 3, 2000, 49–60.

Trechsel, A. H. (2003) Popular Votes, in Klöti, U. *et al.* (eds) *Handbook of Swiss Politics*, Zurich: Neue Zürcher Zeitung.

Trechsel, A. H. and Sciarini, P. Direct Democracy in Switzerland: Do Elites Matter? *European Journal of Political Research*, 33(1), 1998, 99–123.

Ulram, P. (1994) Political Culture and the Party System in the Kreisky Era, in Bischof, G. and Pelinka, A. (eds) *The Kreisky Era in Austria*, New Brunswick NJ: Transaction Publishers.

Van Biezen, I. Political Parties as Public Utilities, *Party Politics*, 10(6), 2004, 701–722.

Van der Brug, W. How the LPF Fuelled Discontent: Empirical Tests of Explanations of LPF-support, *Acta Politica*, 38, 2003, 89–106.

Van der Brug, W., Fennema, M. and Tillie, J. 'Why Some Anti-immigrant Parties Fail and Others Succeed', *Comparative Political Studies*, 38(5), 2005, 537–573.

Van der Horst, E. Untitled, *Trouw*, (2) 16 May, 2002.

Van der Steen, P. (1995) De doorbraak van de 'gewone mensen'-partij: de SP en de Tweede-Kamerverkiezingen van 1994, *Jaarboek 1994 DNPP* Groningen: Documentatiecentrum Nederlandse Politieke Partijen.

Van Herwaarden, C. (2005) *Fortuyn, chaos en charisma*, Amsterdam: Bert Bakker.

Van Holsteyn, J. and Den Ridder, J. (2005) *Alles blijft anders. Nederlandse kiezers en verkiezingen in het begin van de 21e eeuw*, Amsterdam: Aksant.

Van Holsteyn, J., Irwin, G. and den Ridder, J. In the Eye of the Beholder: The Perception of the List Pim Fortuyn and the Parliamentary Elections of May 2002, *Acta Politica*, 38(1), 2003, 69–87.

Van Praag, P. (2003) De LPF-kiezer: rechts, cynisch of modaal? *Jaarboek 2001 DNPP*, Groningen: Documentatiecentrum Nederlandse Politieke Partijen.

Van Zoonen, L. (2005) *Entertaining the Citizen: When Politics and Popular Culture Converge*, Lanham, MD: Rowman & Littlefield.

Veugelers, J. and Magnan, A. Conditions of Far-right Strength in Contemporary Western Europe: An Application of Kitschelt's Theory, *European Journal of Political Research*, 44(6), 2005, 837–860.

Voerman, G. (1987) De 'Rode Jehova's'. Een geschiedenis van de Socialistiese Partij, *Jaarboek 1986 DNPP*, Groningen: Documentatiecentrum Nederlandse Politieke Partijen, 1987.

Voerman, G. (1996) De ledentallen van politieke partijen, 1945–1995, *Jaarboek 1995 DNPP*, Groningen: Documentatiecentrum Nederlandse Politieke Partijen.

Volkens, A. and Klingemann, H. D. (2002) Parties, Ideologies and Issues: Stability and Change in Fifteen European Party Systems 1945–1998, in Luther, K. R. and Müller-Rommel, F. (eds) *Political Parties in the New Europe: Political and Analytical Challenges*, Oxford: Oxford University Press.

Walgrave, S. and De Swert, K. The Making of the (Issues of the) Vlaams Blok, *Political Communication*, 21(4), 2004, 479–500.

Ware, A. (2002) The United States: Populism as Political Strategy, in Mény, Y. and Surel, Y. (eds) *Democracies and the Populist Challenge*, Houndmills: Palgrave.

Webb, P. The Continuing Advance of the Minor Parties, *Parliamentary Affairs*, 58(4), 2005, 757–775.

Weber, M. (1978) *Economy and Society: An Outline of Interpretive Sociology*, Los Angeles: University of California Press.

Weber, M. (1980) Parliament und Regierung im neugeordneten Deutschland, in Weber, M. *Gesammelte Politische Schriften*, 4th ed., Tübingen: JCB Mohr.

Weil, P. (1991) *La France et ses étrangers: l'aventure d'une politique de l'immigration, 1938–1991*, Paris: Calmann-Lévy.

Wiesli, R. (2003) Switzerland: The Militia Myth and Incomplete Professionalization, in Borchert, J. and Zeiss, J. (eds) *The Political Class in Advanced Democracies*, Oxford: Oxford University press.

Wilby P. Tony Blair means only one thing when he talks about his values, *The Guardian*, 4 August 2006.

Wiles, P. (1969) A Syndrome, not a Doctrine: Some Elementary Theses on Populism, in Ionescu, G. and Gellner, E. (eds) *Populism: Its Meaning and National Characteristics*, London: Weidenfeld and Nicolson.

Williams, R. (1973) *The Country and the City*, Oxford: Oxford University Press.

Williams, R. (1977) *Marxism and Literature*, Oxford: Oxford University Press.

Wils, B.A. and Fassmann, H. Stocks and Flows: Bestand der Veränderung der österreichischen Wohnbevölkerung in Österreich, *Österreichische Zeitschrift für Politikwissenschaft*, 23(3), 1994, 341–50.

Windeskog, J. (1999) Politik är *inte* att vilja, *SD-Kuriren*, 35/1999.

Winkler, J. R. and Schumann, S. (1998) Radical Right-Wing Parties in Contemporary Germany, in Betz, H. G. and Immerfall, S. (eds), *The New Politics of the Right*, New York: St. Martin's Press.

Winock, M. (1998) *Nationalism, Anti-Semitism, and Fascism in France*, Stanford: Stanford University Press.

Wischenbart, R. National Identity and Immigration in Austria, *West European Politics*, 17(2), 1994, 73–92.

Wodak, R. and Matouschek, B. We Are Dealing with People Whose Origins One Can Clearly Tell Just by Looking: Critical Discourse Analysis and The Study of Neo-Racism in Contemporary Austria, *Discourse and Society*, 4(2), 1993, 225–48.

Worsley, P. (1967) *The Third World*, London: Weidenfeld and Nicholson.

Zanatta, L. *Il Populismo. Sul Nucleo Forte di un'Ideologia Debole, Polis*, 16(2), 2002, 263–292.

Zöchling, C. (1999) *Haider; Licht und Schatten einer Karriere*, Vienna: Molden.

Index

250 *Index*

Plato 200
Poland 62, 120
political correctness 59, 72, 148, 184,
 191, 194
political culture 125–6
political parties 21, 38–43, 124–5,
 201–5, 219–20
 convergence of 144–5
 identification with 141, 174, 182,
 199
 legitimization of 145–6, 178
 membership of 155, 220
 reasons for change in 42–6
politicization 143–4, 219, 222
politics and politicians
 mediatization of 52–3, 57
 rejection of 21; *see also* anti-politics
populism
 characteristics of 84, 176
 definitions of 2–6, 16, 19, 32, 121–2,
 158, 181–2, 189, 209
 'hard' and 'soft' 58, 63
 left-wing 123, 134
 organisational and political
 failures of 128–31
 as perjorative term 2–3, 34
 political conditions for success
 of 26–7
 and popular culture 21
 principles of 6–7
 reasons for success of 36–8
 right-wing 121–5, 128, 133–4
 and social conditions 23–6
 ubiquity of 46–8
Portugal 220
Poujadist movement 122, 167
power-sharing 101, 115, 134
privatization 73
Prodi, Romano 98
Pröll, Erwin 75–6
propaganda 45
protectionism 190–1
protest voting 124, 127, 174
Putnam, Robert 87, 217

racism 212–13
Reagan, Ronald 137
referendums 107–10, 189, 206–7
religion 9, 23, 39, 97, 99, 102, 152–3,
 156–7, 173, 183, 222

Republican Party, German 129–30,
 146
Riedlsperger, Max 71
right, the
 extreme 4, 31, 36, 60, 90, 177, 181,
 185, 193, 195
 radical 3–4, 31–3, 83, 135–6, 140,
 143, 166, 178, 181, 183, 195–6
Riker, William H. 18–19
Robinson, Mary 203
Roosevelt, Franklin 158
Russia 24

sans culottes 16
Sarkozy, Nicolas 58, 179
Sartori, Giovanni 9, 17–18, 33, 152
Scallon, Dana Rosemary 214
Schain, Martin 172
Schill, Ronald (and Schill Party) 120,
 130–1
Schlesinger, Arthur 19
Schlierer, Rolf 139
Schmid, Heide 79
Schmitt, Carl 35, 38
Schönhuber, Franz 129–30, 146
Schumpeter, Joseph 17–18
Schüssel, Wolfgang 81, 83
*Schweizerische Volkspartei / Union
 Democratique du Centre* (SVP/
 UDC) 4, 9, 31, 52, 100–17, 213,
 222
Scotland 182, 189, 192
secularization 87, 152–3, 198, 201,
 203, 211, 214
Selb, Peter 107
Seldon, Anthony 192
September 11th 2001 attacks 91
Sheridan, Tommy 182
'silent majority' 22, 213
Sinn Féin (SF) 199, 204–7, 211–15
Skenderovic, D. 108, 111
Slovakia 120
socialism 188
Söderberg, Björn 148–9
Spain 220
Springer, Axel 130
Statt-Partei 130–1
Steger, Norbert 77
Stewart, Julianne 59
Stoiber, Edmund 133

Breinigsville, PA USA
29 December 2010
252402BV00003B/20/P